EMERGING INDIAN SOCIETIES:
Present Status

EMERGING INDIAN SOCIETIES: Present Status

By

P.K. Arora

2008

CYBER TECH PUBLICATIONS
4264/3, Ansari Road, Daryaganj, New Delhi-110002 (India)
Ph.: 011-23244078. Fax: 011-23280028
E-Mail: cyberpublicationsdelhi@yahoo.com

EMERGING INDIAN SOCIETIES: PRESENT STATUS

P.K. Arora

First Edition 2008

Published by :

G.S. Rawat for **Cyber Tech Publications**
4264/3, Ansari Road, Daryaganj, New Delhi-110002 (India)
Ph.: 011-23244078. Fax: 011-23280028
E-Mail: cyberpublicationsdelhi@yahoo.com

Printed at : **Amit Enterprises**, Maujpur, Delhi, (9810878184)

Preface

In conformity with her democratic ideals, India has decided to expand her educational facilities so that all her citizens may enjoy equality of opportunity. Simultaneously, she has undertaken a vast reconstruction of her educational system to make it a more suitable instrument for her growing needs and aspirations.

After a rapid survey of the situation as it existed on the eve of independence and the progress achieved since then, these studies are devoted mainly to a discussion of the experiments India has undertaken or is undertaking in various fields of education. At the elementary level, she is evolving a pattern in Basic Education, which is full of exciting possibilities and is likely to interest educationists throughout the world. Similarly, her essays in a new type of adult education may be of significance to other countries as well. In the field of technical education, on the other hand, she is in the main repeating what other countries have already achieved. In spite of an almost phenomenal expansion in technical education I have therefore included no separate study in this field.

The book attempts to analyse the role of education in bringing about a peaceful and silent revolution for ushering in an era of harmony, peace, progress and prosperity in India. Various emerging problems of education in India are discussed in their philosophical, sociological and global perspectives. The special focus of this publication is on the realization of the aspirations, ideals and values as enshrined in the constitution of India and the vital role of education in this task.

I have drawn extensively upon articles I have written from time to time on different aspects of Indian education for journals and other publications in India. In every case I have revised and in some cases largely rewritten them. I shall consider my labour rewarded if these studies can give the reader—and more particularly to the scholars—some idea of the vigour, vitality and variety of India's educational effort.

—Author

Contents

1

The 21st Century Education

We are reaching the end of the 20th century and it is time we take stock of what we have achieved in the field of education, what have been our failures and whether we need to continue in the same direction into the 21st century or do things differently.

In considering this question I would like to explore the situation globally and not with reference to any particular nation; also I would like to give a wide meaning to that word education, to cover the entire process of bringing up the next generation of children into adulthood and not limit it to only what transpires in a classroom in the school.

A child is educated by the entire environment in which it grows and that environment is determined equally by the parents, the teachers and the society around him/her. All this and more determines the kind of individual we produce, which in turn determines the kind of society we live in. It is important to bear in mind the relationship of the individual to society.

If we produce individuals who are self-centred, aggressive, ambitious, greedy and competitive, one cannot organize them into a society that is non-violent, peaceful, cooperative and harmonious. If we organize them into a communist society we shall have the violence and domination that we have seen in communist societies. If we organise them into a capitalistic, so-called free society, we will have the violence and the divisions that we see in such societies.

It is not possible to bring a fundamental transformation in society unless the individual is transformed. Education is therefore the main engine of social transformation, since it determines the kind of individual we are producing. Governments, legislatures and the law enforcement agencies are only organizations to control the individual, they do not transform him. Therefore, true social change is the major responsibility of education, not merely the production of trained personnel. The test of right education today is whether it is producing good planetary citizens.

The way we live has changed drastically over the last century and that change can be traced to what we have achieved in the field of education. At the beginning of the 20th century human society, all over the world, was beset with tremendous problems of natural disasters, famines, epidemics, primitive transportation, inefficient communication, lack of health care and poor agriculture. Our system of education has helped us to change all that, to develop all the knowledge and the power that was necessary to make the transition to the modern society in which we live today. There may still be some parts of the world that are struggling to make those changes, but at least we know how to do it. The great strides that we have made in this century in the field of engineering, medicine, agriculture, transport, telecommunications and power are all a direct consequence of our achievements in education and we have reason to feel proud of what we have achieved. However, the problems that human society is facing now are totally different and the question that we need to ask is whether the present problems can also be solved the way we have solved the other problems, through greater knowledge, better organization, more efficiency and more power. If so, then we should continue in the same direction. If not, then we must seriously consider whether we need an altogether different vision of education for the 21st century. To examine that, let me list what to my mind are the major challenges facing mankind today.

MAJOR CHALLENGES OF TODAY'S WORLD

Groupism/division: Perhaps the greatest problem we are facing today is the fact that human beings are divided into groups—racial groups, national groups, religious groups, linguistic groups, economic groups, political groups, professional groups—and each individual identifies with his or her own group, feels rivalry with other groups and cares only for the security and progress of a particular group. These groups are in turn willing to exploit each other, cheat each other and even destroy each other in wars. This has become the greatest single cause of insecurity in the world today. It is responsible for most of the violence that we see in the form of wars, terrorism, rioting and militancy. This is a malady that afflicts the most progressive and highly educated people as well as the most backward and illiterate people in the world today. The reason for this is not difficult to see. The individual identifies with a particular family, country, religion and culture in which he/she is born. He/she is taught to feel proud of it and defend its ways. The mind of the individual then works like that of a lawyer defending the me and the mine and attacking the 'other'. He/she feels secure in identifying with his or her group but this identification is in actual fact creating the greatest insecurity in the world today.

The Power Unleashed by Science and Technology: Human beings have lived with wars and rivalry for thousands of years but we cannot afford it any more due to the tremendous power that science and technology have placed in our hands. Our hatred of each other could only manifest in the killing of a few individuals when we lived with bows and arrows, spears and knives. Today, with our atomic and nuclear bombs we can decimate a whole nation in a matter of minutes and no war is a local war any more. This has greatly enhanced the urgency of the problem since mankind is in danger of annihilating itself in a nuclear war. We cannot therefore afford to postpone the solution to this problem. Human history has been a history of wars and if we do not learn now, we shall soon be fighting our last war.

The Environmental Catastrophes: Another major problem we are facing today are the environmental catastrophes about which we are constantly reading in our newspapers and magazines: depletion of the ozone layer, global warming industrial pollution, deforestation, soil-erosion, nuclear fall-outs and over-population. The root cause of most of these is the attitude we have developed towards nature in the course of this century, treating it as a resource meant to be exploited for our benefit. With the development of science and technology and the consequent industrialization there is a race between different nations of the world to be the first to capture the profits in the international market and achieve the economic progress of their nation at any cost. Animals are not looked upon as fellow living beings but merely as raw materials for the meat industry. Rivers and mountains are looked upon as objects to be exploited for producing electricity or promoting tourism.

Even children are regarded as the 'wealth' of the family. Nature is regarded as something meant for our use, we being the masters of the world. But are we really masters of the world? Was the world created for us? Or, we are a part of the world, as is every thing else and we need to live in harmony with all the other parts, regarding them as friends and not as resources? That is the way mankind related to nature for thousands of years but in the last one century our attitude has changed surreptitiously and unless this paradigm shift is undone we are going to face more and more environmental catastrophes. We may have better computers and faster planes but we will not have fresh air to breathe and new diseases caused by the disequilibrium will make life not worth living.

Dictatorships: Another great problem facing mankind is the fact that most of the governments in the world, especially in the third world countries, are still dictatorships — military dictatorships, communist dictatorships, religious dictatorships and dictatorships in the garb of democracy. There are very few countries where there is real democracy and freedom of expression, political freedom, freedom to grow, freedom to question, to think, to write what you believe in. Dictatorships stifle dissent, they tell people what to think, what to do and what not to do. The greatest crimes of this century have been perpetrated under dictatorships.

The very basis of dictatorship is the exploitation of the weak by the powerful. So long as we believe that power is meant for exploiting the weak, we still accept that might is right, which is the law of the jungle. Both between nations and within a nation one can see this uncivilized use of power as a means of exploiting others. It has been said that power corrupts and absolute power corrupts absolutely; but the evil does not lie in power itself. Power is just the ability to do things. What dictates that it should be used to exploit and dominate the weak and not help or protect them? Unless mankind can change its relationship with power, power will continue to be used for destruction and domination. So education must concern itself with bringing about the right use of power, which is the true spirit of democracy.

We object to dictatorship when it is at the level of the government but all dictatorship is evil, whether it is in an organization, a business or in the family. Therefore the spirit of democracy needs to be inculcated in every individual if the problems of dictatorship are to disappear.

The Breakdown of the Family: The institution of marriage and family was set up partly to regulate sexual behaviour but more importantly, to ensure that we are able to discharge our responsibilities towards the next generation. The human child needs to be looked after, protected and helped to learn not for a few days or a few months, as is the case with other mammals, but for a period of 20 years, since there is a whole new dimension of mental, emotional and spiritual growth involved.

No one has yet found a better way to ensure this than through raising a child within a family with two parents. That is a responsibility a man and a woman share when they produce a child. Today, this cooperation between man and woman is breaking down in modern society and the incidence of divorce is now as high as 60% in some affluent societies. The worst sufferers of this breakdown in cooperation are the children and consequently juvenile crime is on the rise. Obviously, we are not approaching life rightly and we need to rethink where we have gone wrong.

The Inertia in Society: Last but not the least, is the great problem that society tends to replicate itself. Prejudices and illusions tend to continue from one generation to the next and so do the problems associated with them. If the Jews teach their children that the Arabs are their enemies and the Arabs teach their children that the Jews are their enemies, the younger generation grows up with the feeling of animosity already ingrained in their mind. So the prejudices of the elders continue in the young and so does the problem of animosity. So, how is it to end? It is the same with the Catholics and the Protestants or the Hindus and the Muslims.

This animosity will never end so long as we educate the children to obey and conform to what their elders are saying. We must therefore create an inquiring mind, which questions what it is told, is aware that it has many prejudices that need to be examined and dropped and is willing to undertake this task of discovering for itself what is true. This process of doubting one's own opinions, of discriminating between what is true and what is false is the awakening of intelligence. It is inconvenient for the elders to awaken the intelligence of the child because it may begin to question them, question their values and their way of living.

But it is essential to encourage and respect dissent if we are not to create a static society that is inflexibly caught in a fossilized groove. There is too much inertia in society today and the only way to change it is to create a mind that is inquiring not only into scientific questions, but also into social, moral and religious questions. In other words a mind that is intelligent about the whole of life and not merely one aspect of it.

ROLE OF EDUCATION

If we are facing so many problems at the end of this century of stupendous progress, then we must stop and ask ourselves what it is that we have done wrong? Why are we facing so many serious problems though we have amassed so much knowledge, created so much power/ability and become so 'intelligent'. Do we need better controls or do we need to change direction? Will more of the same kind of education as we have been imparting solve these problems? Do we need still better computers, still faster airplanes, still more goods, yet more knowledge and efficiency and will that solve the problems we have discussed above? If not, then should we not re-examine our priorities in education and question the very vision with which we have been working so far?

The Present Vision of Education

What is our vision of education today? What kind of human being are we aiming to produce? The aims may vary a little from country to country but essentially, all over the world, education is aiming to produce a human being who is intelligent, knowledgeable, hard-working, efficient disciplined, smart, successful and hopefully a leader in his field of endeavour. If one may most humbly point out, Adolf Hitler had all these qualities and yet most people regard him as the most evil person of this century. The only thing he lacked was love and compassion. So what is there in our present day education to prevent the creation of a Hitler or of little Hitlers for that matter?

The holocaust, perhaps the greatest crime of this century, was perpetrated in a country that had the best of science, art, music and culture of the kind we are aiming to inculcate through education today. So what is there in present-day education to prevent the recurrence of the holocaust? Indeed, we are perhaps at the brink of a still larger holocaust in which the whole of mankind may be eliminated from the face of the earth in a nuclear war. Present day education is basically developing greater and greater power; but both God and the Devil (as conceived by us) are infinitely powerful. Are we ensuring that the power we produce will be used in godly ways and not in devilish ways? If not, then it is irresponsible to generate power.

The major challenges facing mankind today are not due to a lack of education. They are not created by the illiterate villagers in Asia or Africa, they are created by highly educated and professional minds——lawyers, business administrators, scientists, economists, military commanders, diplomats and the like —— who plan and run governments, organizations and businesses. So we need to look at the kind of education we are imparting and not the quantity. When you do that it becomes clear that we are producing lopsided human beings: very advanced, very clever, very capable in their intellect but almost primitive in other aspects of life; top scientists and engineers who can send human beings to the moon but who may be brutal with their spouses or their neighbours; human beings who have a vast understanding of the way the universe operates but little understanding of themselves or their life.

It is this lop-sided development of the individual that is responsible for all the problems we are facing today. As an educationalist we must accept that when we impart knowledge it is also our responsibility to impart or awaken the wisdom to employ it rightly. Our present day education has not paid serious attention to that responsibility.

A Different Vision of Education

Keeping in mind what we have said so far, how should we modify our vision of education for the 21st Century? that kind of mind should we aim at producing? What values should we try to inculcate? The prescription would not be identical for all countries and different cultures may go about it in their own unique way, but the broad outlines can be stated as follows:

Create a Global Mind, not a Nationalistic One: We are all citizens of one world and we share the earth as our common habitat. What affects one part of the world today is of concern to all of us. So we need to have a mind that feels for the whole world and not just for one country. We are part of one world, one humanity and if we can settle issues within a country through democratic means and adjudication, is it not right to do that also between nations? If we have a global mind that really did not believe in "might is right" there would be no armies and no wars. That is the future we must realize for the 21st century. We may work for local problems but it is important to do so with a global understanding.

Emphasise Human Development, not only Economic: Education must not regard children as raw material for achieving the economic progress of the nation. It must concern itself primarily with the development of all aspects of a human being—physical, intellectual, emotional and spiritual—so that he or she lives creatively and happily as a part of the whole. Human beings may differ in their abilities but they are not unequal, neither superior or inferior. They must be respected irrespective of their abilities. Goodness must be valued above efficiency.

Encourage Inquiry, not Conformity: It may be inconvenient for the adults but it is important that children grow up with questions, rather than answers. At each age the questions will naturally be different but the ability to inquire and to learn for oneself is more important than to obey and follow unquestioningly what one is told to do. It follows that there must be no fear in our relationship with the child since fear kills inquiry and initiative. The child must be free to make mistakes and learn for itself without the constant fear of being rebuked by an adult. Such a mind is rational, flexible and not dogmatic, open to change and not irrationally attached to an opinion or belief. This implies the absence of all propaganda for any belief, including nationalism. "Our country is the best country, our culture is the best culture" is not true — it is propaganda, which divides people.

Cultivate Cooperation, not Competition: The present emphasis in the world on individual achievement for name and fame is irrational and egotistic. We are all inter-related and inter-dependent and little that is really meaningful can be achieved alone and in isolation. Team work and the ability to work harmoniously with others is more important than individual achievement. Cooperation is the essence of democracy. One works not for personal gain or reward but for the welfare of the whole community, with love instead of arrogance. It is important that each individual does his or her best but it is not important that should be better than another. We are friends, brothers and sisters, not rivals. If something good happens to my brother I rejoice with him, there is nothing to feel unhappy. The sense of competition that we are encouraging in children today leads to envy, jealousy and rivalry. It sows the seeds of division between human beings and destroys love and friendship. Therefore, it is evil. The importance we have given to winning gold medals in world-cup matches and Olympics is based on propaganda and illusion. Does it really matter which human being can jump one millimetre higher than all the others? We are not asking the right question when we ask, "Who won?" The more important question is, "Did they enjoy the game?".

Create a Learning Mind Instead of an Acquisitive Mind: The awakening of intelligence is more important than the cultivation of memory, both in life and in academics. If we give information to the child we add to his knowledge but intelligence is the ability to learn for oneself. What can be taught is limited but learning is endless. The greatest things in life are those that cannot be taught but they can be learnt. The feeling of love, respect, beauty and friendship, cannot be taught but like sensitivity, it can be awakened and this is an essential part of intelligence. The ability to discern for oneself what is true and what is false is also intelligence. It is important to create a mind that neither accepts nor rejects an opinion or a view too readily, but stays with the question, "Is it true?"

Create a Mind that is Both Scientific and Religious in the True Sense: Unfortunately we have divided the scientific quest from the religious quest of mankind and concentrated only on the former in the educational process. In fact they are two complimentary quests, one for the discovery of the order that manifests itself in the outer world of matter, energy, space and time and the other for discovering order (peace, harmony, virtue) in the inner world of our consciousness. By mistakenly equating religion with belief we have created an antagonism between science and religion. Actually they are both quests for truth into two complimentary aspects of a single reality which is composed of both matter and consciousness.

A mind that is purely rational, scientific, intellectual, can be extremely cruel and devoid of love and compassion. One that is only religious (in the narrow sense) can be overlay emotional, sentimental, superstitious and therefore neurotic. We must therefore aim at creating a mind that is both scientific and religious at the same time — one that is inquiring, precise, rational and skeptical but at the same time has a sense of beauty, wonder, aesthetics, sensitivity, humility and an awareness of the limitations of the intellect. Without this undeniable balance between emotion and the intellect, a mind is not truly educated. Understanding oneself (self-knowledge) is as important as understanding the world. Without a deep understanding of our relationship with nature, with ideas, with fellow human beings, with society and a deep respect for all life one is not really educated.

The Art of Living: Education must concern itself with the art of living creatively, which is much vaster than the specific arts of painting, music or dance which we teach at present. We have equated the quality of life with the standard of living and we measure this in terms of the Gross National Product or the per-capita income of people. But is the quality of our life determined only by the quality of the house we live in, the car we drive, the food we eat or the clothes we wear? Doesn't the quality of our mind affect the quality of our life far more? A mind that is constantly worried, bored, envious or frustrated cannot possibly lead a life of high quality. When we educate not for economic development but for human development we must concern ourselves with the happiness of the individual as whole, in which physical well-being and comfort are a small but necessary part. Far more important is the ability to work with joy, without comparing oneself with others. If one is insensitive, there is constant boredom and to escape from it a constant pursuit of pleasure. The entire entertainment industry has come up to capitalize on human boredom. When we teach children to work for a reward and not for the joy of working, we teach them to separate work from pleasure. Such a mind is energized only when there is a reward, otherwise it lives in a state of boredom. The art of living consists in enjoying every thing one does, irrespective of the results it offers. One then works creatively, with sensitivity and not for personal ambition. This and much more, is involved in the art of living. It cannot be learnt like a formula. It is a by-product of one's understanding of life and of oneself. Therefore we must help students to come upon such understanding. Virtue, which is the flowering of goodness in human consciousness, is a by-product of self-knowledge. It is not something that can be practised mechanically like a skill.

A Holistic Development of All Faculties: At present education is geared to producing specialists. Some amount of specialization in skills may be inevitable but we are human beings first and engineers, doctors, lawyers, artists and agriculturists afterwards. Therefore specialization must not be at the cost of understanding what it means to live fully as a human being.

The human consciousness has several faculties (capacities) and I have tried to group together words that we commonly use to describe them, into four categories. Many of these overlap with each other but those within a category seem to me to have a common basis and differ in a fundamental way from those in another category.

Faculties of human consciousness:

(a) *Intrinsic:* Perception, awareness, observation, attention.

(b) *Thought-based:* Knowledge, memory, imagination, reason, analysis, criticism, science, mathematics, language, concentration, intelligence (of thought), will.

(c) *Feeling-based:* Joy, beauty, wonder, aesthetics, humour, art, music, poetry, literature, sympathy love, affection, compassion, friendship. Attachment, desire, fear, hatred, jealousy, anger, violence.

(d) *Beyond thought and feeling:* Intuition, insight, vision, wisdom, silence, meditation, peace, harmony, understanding, intelligence (not of thought).

The above list is not exhaustive and one can add several other words to it. Nor are the categories exclusive since thinking, feeling and observation all go on simultaneously in our consciousness and also interact with each other. So this classification is only for the convenience of discussion. Education, at present, greatly emphasises the thought-based faculties and to some extent cultivates those based on feeling.

For a holistic development of the individual it is important that there is a deep understanding of all the above faculties and they are developed in a balanced way. It implies that in order to cultivate one faculty we must not impair or damage another. This means one cannot use fear and punishment to make students work harder since that destroys inquiry, intelligence and initiative. One must not use comparison and competition as an incentive either since that destroys love and promotes aggression. One must not offer rewards since that cultivates greed and insensitivity.

What incentive then should we teachers use to make our students learn? It makes our task much harder. The challenge before us is to reveal the beauty of the subject to the child so that education becomes a joyous process and not a dreary task to be achieved somehow. If we accept that challenge then we must find ways to make education lively and interesting for the child. A good school is one where the children are happy, not the one which achieves the best measurable results in academics.

The real responsibility of education is to reveal to the child all the beauty of life and there is great beauty in art, in literature, in science, in mathematics, in music, in games and sports, in nature and in relationship—indeed in every aspect of life. We have a reasonably good idea of what it means for a tree to be in full bloom. But have we seriously inquired what it means for the human consciousness to be in full bloom? Must not education help us to discover that for ourselves?

DIFFICULTIES OF IMPARTING SUCH EDUCATION

There are several difficulties in actually imparting such an education. The greatest difficulty is that we have ourselves not received the right kind of education. Therefore we must not mechanically repeat what we know. We need to question our methods and not merely repeat what our teachers and parents did. It requires us to be original, intelligent, creative and not merely asserting ourselves. Our minds are conditioned into the old system, the old vision, therefore we are ourselves obstacles in the way of the new ! One has to be acutely aware of this fact and therefore not just teach but also learn to break from the past.

In the new vision of education we are not only taking the responsibility to impart information and skills but also to awaken sensitivity and creativity in the child. There is no set method for doing this. These are things that cannot be decided, practised and achieved. Yet, they get awakened in the child if there is the right atmosphere in the school and the home. It is our responsibility to create that atmosphere— an atmosphere of working cooperatively, with joy and friendship, working hard but without personal ambition or any sense of rivalry, an atmosphere of openness, of questioning, of inquiry and the joy of learning together.

Which means we ourselves must live and work that way. Sermonising does not work. A child learns from what he sees actually happening around him or her, not from what we speak in the classroom. If it finds that we say one thing and do another, it will also learn to do precisely that. Which means we end up teaching hypocrisy ! A teacher who punishes a child because he gets his sums wrong is not only conveying to the child that it does not know how to do the sum, he/she is also conveying that the strong can dominate and penalise the weak ! So one has to be very careful. There are no short-cuts for imparting the education that we have described above. The child imbibes the values he/she sees, not those that are talked about.

Intellectually we adults may know more than the child but in the larger issues of life we face the same problems, the same difficulties as the child—problems of boredom, worry, fear, habit, conflict, desire, frustration and violence. Therefore we need to learn along with the child, not merely teach. It demands great honesty, humility, sensitivity and patience. That is our difficulty—to be an educator who is willing to accept that challenge and not seek an easy way out. There isn't one. The deeper truths come to a reflective mind as insights that cannot be taught by another. One cannot do anything to create insights but one must not block them with an ambitious and overlay active mind which has no time to stand and stare.

Conclusion : Mankind is caught in a great illusion. It thinks it can solve its problems through legislation, through political and social reform, through scientific and technological progress, through greater knowledge, greater wealth, greater power and greater control. It may solve some problems with all this, but those are all trivial problems and temporary cures. By these methods we shall go on creating new problems on the one hand and trying to solve them on the other to maintain the illusion of progress.

The famous humourist Ogden Nash wrote, "Progress was all right once, but it went on too long" ! We need to consider that remark seriously. If we human beings do no transform inwardly, we shall soon join the list of those unfortunate creatures that lived a million years or so and then became extinct for they could not adapt themselves. It is not certain yet if evolution of man from the ape was really a step in the direction of survival. Only time will tell. Survival requires not the intelligence of 'progress' but the ability to cooperate and love each other and to live in harmony with nature. The ant has survived longer than man. What we need now is not more ability and more efficiency, but greater cohesion, greater compassion, greater capacity to share and work together.

Education in the 21st Century must therefore concern itself not with greater 'progress' but with the inner transformation of the human consciousness. It is not that this has not been pointed out before. The Buddha, Socrates, Christ and innumerable other sages in all cultures have pointed this out long ago. Till now we have ignored what they have said but still managed to survive somehow. We cannot afford to do that any more, for we are inexorably heading towards a nuclear holocaust which will make survival not worth it, if not impossible. Therefore the issue has acquired an urgency for mankind which was not there before.

In presenting the vision of right education for the 21st Century I have drawn heavily from the life and work of Madam Montessori (1) and of J. Krishnamurti (2), both of whom have emphasised the need for educating the whole human being and not merely the intellect. Out of this vision, Madam Montessori developed certain methods and techniques for use with small children since she took upon herself that task. But the techniques and materials she developed have meaning only when the teacher shares her vision of life; otherwise the teacher may use those very materials to inculcate a sense of competition and achievement among the children ! A school is not a Montessori school just because it adopts the use of those techniques and materials. The technique does not create the vision; it is the vision that creates the technique. It is important to come upon that vision of life and to actually live that way throughout life. Unless education helps the student to do that it has very little significance. It means we must be students all our life, living with deep and fundamental questions. One such question is, what does it mean for a human being to live in harmony with the cosmic order?

The twenty-first century demands a total change in our outlook on life and our vision of education.

2

Higher Education Status in India

India is rushing headlong toward economic success and modernization, counting on high-tech industries such as information technology and biotechnology to propel the nation to prosperity. India's recent announcement that it would no longer produce unlicensed inexpensive generic pharmaceuticals bowed to the realities of the World Trade Organization while at the same time challenging the domestic drug industry to compete with the multinational firms.

Unfortunately, India's weak higher education sector constitutes the Achilles' heel of this strategy. India's systematic disinvestment in higher education in recent years has yielded an academic characterized by mediocrity, producing neither world-class research nor very many highly trained scholars, scientists, or managers to sustain high-tech development. India's main competitors—especially China but also including Singapore, Taiwan and South Korea—are investing in large and differentiated higher education systems. They are providing access to large numbers of students at the bottom of the academic system while at the same time building some research-based universities are able compete with the world's best institutions.

The recent London Times Higher Education Supplement ranking of the world's top 200 universities included 3 in China, 3 in Hong Kong, 3 in South Korea and 1 in Taiwan and 1 (an Indian Institute of Technology at number 41—the specific campus was not specified) in India. These countries are positioning themselves for leadership in the knowledge-based economies of the coming era. There was a time when countries could achieve economic success with cheap labour and low-tech manufacturing.

Low wages still help, but contemporary large-scale development requires a sophisticated and at least partly knowledge-based economy. India has chosen that path, but will find a major stumbling block in its generally poor university system.

Higher Education Realities: India has significant advantages in the 21st century knowledge race. It has a large higher education sector—the third largest in the world in student numbers, after China and the United States. It uses English as a primary language of higher education and research. It has a long academic tradition. Academic freedom is respected. There are a small number of high quality institutions, departments and centres that can form the basis of quality sector in higher education. The fact that the states, rather than the central government, exercise major responsibility for higher education creates a rather cumbersome structure, but the system allows for a variety of policies and approaches.

Yet, the weaknesses far outweigh the strengths. India educates approximately 10 percent of its young people in higher education, still a rather low number by international standards—compared to more than half in the major industrialized countries and 15 percent in China. India's academic system has an unusually small high quality sector at the top—most of the academic system is of modest quality at best. Almost all of the world's academic systems resemble a pyramid, with a small top tier and a massive sector at the bottom. India has a tiny top tier. None of its universities occupy a solid position at the top. A few of the best universities have some excellent departments and centres and there are a small number of outstanding undergraduate colleges.

The University Grants Commission's recent major support of five universities to build on their recognized strength is a step toward recognizing a differentiated academic system—and fostering excellence. At present, the world-class institutions are mainly limited to the Indian Institutes of Technology (IITs), the Indian Institutes of Management (IIMs) and perhaps a few others such as the All India Institute of Medical Sciences and the Tata Institute of Fundamental Research. These institutions, combined, enrol well under 1 percent of the student population.

India's colleges and universities, with just a few exceptions, have become large, underfunded, ungovernable institutions. At many of them, politics has intruded into campus life, influencing academic appointments and decisions at all levels. Underinvestment in libraries, information technology, laboratories and classrooms makes it very difficult to provide top-quality instruction or engage in cutting-edge research. The rise in the number of part-time teachers and the freeze on new full-time appointments in many places have contributed to a decline in the commitment and morale of the academic profession. The lack of accountability at any level means that teaching and research performance is seldom measured. The system provides few incentives to perform to the highest standards. Bureaucratic inertia hampers change. Student unrest and occasional faculty agitation sometimes disrupts normal operations, delays examinations and foments tensions. Nevertheless, with a semblance of normalcy, faculty administrators are able to provide teaching, coordinate examinations and award degrees.

Even the small top tier of higher education faces serious problems. Political pressures on the IITs to alter admissions and other policies have jeopardized the generally effective meritocracy that has characterized those institutions. Many IIT graduates, well trained in technology, have chosen not to contribute their skills to the burgeoning technology sector in India. Perhaps half leave the country immediately upon graduation to pursue advanced study abroad—and most do not return. A stunning 86 percent of students in science and technology fields from India who obtain degrees in the United States do not return home immediately following their study. Another significant group, some estimate as many as 30 percent, decide to earn MBAs in India because local salaries are higher—and are lost to science and technology. A corps of dedicated and able teachers work at the IITs and IIMs, but the lure of jobs abroad and in the private sector makes it increasingly difficult to lure the best and brightest to the academic profession.

Few in India are thinking creatively about higher education. There is no field of higher education research. Other countries with vibrant academic systems collect data and focus analytic attention on their universities. No independent research or policy centres focusing on higher education exist. Those in government as well as academic leaders seem content to do the "same old thing." Academic institutions and systems have become large and complex. They need good data, careful analysis and creative ideas. In China, more than two-dozen higher education research centres and several government agencies are involved in higher education policy.

Why Does This Matter?: India has survived with an increasingly mediocre higher education system for decades. Now, as India strives to compete in a globalized economy in areas that require highly trained professionals, the quality of higher education becomes increasingly important. So far, India's large educated population base and its reservoir of at least moderately well-trained university graduates have permitted the country to move ahead. But the competition is fierce, with other countries rapidly upgrading their universities and research facilities.

China in particular is heavily investing in improving its best universities with the aim of making a small group of them world class in the coming decade and making a larger number internationally competitive research universities. Other Asian countries are also upgrading higher education with the aim of building world class-universities. Taiwan, which is a major designer and producer of IT hardware, is considering merging several of its top technological universities to create an "Asian MIT."

To compete successfully in the knowledge-based economy of the 21st century, India needs enough universities that not only produce bright graduates for export but can also support sophisticated research in a number of scientific and scholarly fields and produce at least some of the knowledge and technology needed for an expanding economy. India's recent decision to stop producing generic pharmaceuticals to conform with WTO rules underscores the need for the country to have an independent research capacity to develop, manufacture and market scientific products, including medicines.

Paths to Success: How can India build a higher education system that will permit it to join developed economies? The newly emerging private sector in higher education cannot spearhead academic growth. Several of the well-endowed and effectively managed private institutions maintain reasonably high standards, although it is not clear that these institutions will be able to sustain themselves in the long run. They can help produce well-qualified graduates in such fields as management, but they cannot form the basis for comprehensive research universities. This sector lacks the resources to build the facilities required for quality instruction and research in the sciences, nor can enough money be earned by providing instruction in the mainstream arts and sciences disciplines. Most of the private institutions do not focus on advanced training in the sciences.

Only public universities have the potential to be truly world-class institutions. Institutions and programmes of national prominence have already been identified by the government. But these institutions have not been adequately or consistently supported. The top institutions require sustained funding from public sources. Academic salaries must be high enough to attract excellent scientists and scholars. Fellowships and other grants should be available for bright students. An academic culture that is based on meritocratic norms and competition for advancement and research funds is a necessary component, as is a judicious mix of autonomy to do creative research and accountability to ensure productivity. World-class universities require world-class professors and students—and a culture to sustain and stimulate them.

A clearly differentiated academic system has not been created in India—a system where there are some clearly identified elite institutions that receive significantly greater resources than other universities. One of the main reasons that the University of California at Berkeley is so good is that other California universities receive much less support. India's elite universities require sustained state support—they require the recognition that they are indeed top institutions and deserve commensurate support. But they also require effective management and an ethos of an academic meritocracy. Funding institutions that are incapable of managing resources is a wasteful investment. At present, the structures are not in place to permit building and sustaining top-quality programmes even if resources are provided.

A combination of specific conditions and resources are needed to create outstanding universities.

- Sustained financial support, with an appropriate mix of accountability and autonomy.
- The development of a clearly differentiated academic system—including private institutions—in which academic institutions have different missions, resources and purposes.
- Managerial reforms and the introduction of effective administration.
- Truly meritocratic hiring and promotion policies for the academic profession and similarly rigorous and honest recruitment, selection and instruction of students.

India cannot build internationally recognized research-oriented universities overnight, but the country has the key elements in place to begin and sustain the process. India will need to create a dozen or more universities that can compete internationally to fully participate in the new world economy. Without these universities, India is destined to remain a scientific backwater.

EDUCATIONAL PROGRAMMES, FAMILY AND DEVELOPMENT

Accelerating Girls' Education—A Priority for Governments: The Population Council and the Rockefeller Foundation have compiled the attached information sheet on girls' education to give a global overview and a more in-depth understanding of not only why girls' education is an important priority, but also the challenges faced in implementing a plan to attract more girls to school and keep them there longer.

The universal right to primary education has been affirmed by the world's governments for more than 50 years. However, more than 130 million children who should be attending primary school are not. Two-thirds of these children are girls. Without education, it is difficult for women to exercise their other rights and meet their aspirations: adequate livelihoods, negotiating power in marriage, participation in political decision-making and a fair chance in the modern economy for their children. Education is an investment that stays with a woman throughout her life, is hers to use as she wishes and cannot be taken away. In addition to helping girls and women fulfil their aspirations as individuals, educating girls also has well documented benefits for the broader society. These include increased economic productivity, improvements in health, delayed age at marriage, lower fertility, increased political participation and generally more effective investments in the next generation. While there are many other possible interventions to achieve these social goods, girls' education is the only one which impacts all of them simultaneously.

Government investment in schooling for girls, especially at the primary school level, is particularly justified in that it brings so many benefits for the broader society. Most governments already have policies affirming primary education and some apparatus for delivering education exists in virtually all countries. Even in settings with low enrolment for both boys and girls, the argument for governments to focus resources on girls is compelling given the positive effect of girls' education on development. With relatively modest modifications in the content and quality of schooling, teachers and materials, a far higher percentage of girls could enrol in and complete primary school, or remain there long enough to acquire basic literacy and numeracy skills.

Governments exhibit a wide range of commitment to financing education. In Pakistan, for example, only 2.6 percent of the national budget was invested in education in 1987, while nearby Bangladesh spent 10.6 percent of its national budget on education. Some countries, including Costa Rica and Bolivia, have invested as much as 20 percent of their budgets in education.

ADVANTAGES OF GIRLS' EDUCATION

Educating girls is associated with numerous social benefits across a variety of sectors

Increased Economic Productivity: Women with some education are more likely to work in the wage economy and more likely to earn higher wages.

- Women's wages rise by 10 to 20 percent for each year of schooling.

Education enhances women's productivity in both farm and non-farm sectors.

- Four years of school boosts farmers' annual productivity by an average of 9 percent.
- In the urban informal sector, there is a positive association between education and earnings.

Evidence from some Asian countries links investment in primary education directly to rapid economic growth and resultant poverty alleviation.

Increased Political Participation: Educated women are better informed about their rights, more likely to exercise them and more likely to participate in the formal political system.

Improved Health: At the national level, women's education is associated with longer life expectancy, lower infant and maternal mortality and lower fertility. At the family level, women's education has a major impact on health by increasing access to and use of information, improving use of health services and increasing the proportion of family income earned by and allocated by women.

Women's education can also mitigate the negative health effects of low income. This has been demonstrated in China, Costa Rica, Sri Lanka and Kerala, India, where female education is a clear priority of government and health achievements are high, despite family income remaining quite low. Even modest levels of maternal education result in higher child survival independent of family income.

- This is especially striking in the poorest countries where each year of maternal education is associated with a 5 to 10 percent decline in child mortality.
- Even one to three years of maternal schooling decreases child mortality by approximately 15 percent; the same level of paternal education results in a 6 percent decrease.
- A study conducted in 13 African countries shows that a 10 percent increase in female literacy leads to a 10 percent decline in child mortality. Male literacy has little influence.
- In Peru, seven or more years of maternal education reduces mortality risks by 75 percent.

Delayed Marriage: Educated women tend to marry later, with implications for their economic opportunities and choices and for fertility.

- In Africa, women with seven or more years of schooling marry five years later than women with no education. While the effect on age at first birth is not uniform across Africa, it has increasing importance in some countries, including Kenya and Ghana.

Lower Fertility: Educated women have lower desired and actual family size. They are also much more likely to use contraception and have longer intervals between births. Among married couples, the wife's education has a much stronger effect on fertility than husband's.

- In Asia, Africa and Latin America, women with seven or more years of schooling have two to three children less than women with up to three years of schooling.
- In Latin America and Asia, well-educated women are increasingly having the number of children they want.
- In Peru and Brazil, women with no education have approximately six children while women with a secondary education have about three children.

More Effective Investments in the Next Generation: Children of educated mothers, especially daughters, are more likely to receive education.

- Mothers' education has a greater effect on children's education than fathers', even though fathers' education implies a greater effect on income.
- In Pakistan, mothers' education is the single strongest determinant of schooling for their children, especially for girls.
- In Peru, mothers' education increases girls' school enrolment as much as 40 percent more than fathers' education.

Education improves women's opportunities to participate in the wage economy. Increasing women's access to income can be especially beneficial to children's health.

- In Guatemala, it takes 15 times as much spending to achieve improvement in child nutrition when income is earned by the father rather than the mother.

While there are many other possible interventions to achieve these social goods, girls' education is the only one which impacts all of them simultaneously.

Girls Get Less Schooling Than Boys: Globally, two-thirds of the children who are not enrolled in primary school are girls. In the world's 40 poorest countries, the gap in primary school enrolment between girls and boys averages 20 percent. In almost all developing countries, gender gaps exist in enrolment and completion.

Enrolment: For all developing countries, approximately 10 percent of boys and 40 percent of girls ages 6 to 11 never enrol in school.

- This is especially pronounced in rural areas where other factors such as employment prospects and mothers' education are lower and where girls are more likely to have other responsibilities like housework and child care.
- In South Asia, the gap in school enrolment for boys and girls has widened because policies to increase enrolment benefit boys more than girls.
- In Peru, the proportion of school-age children enrolled in secondary school is 9 percent higher for boys than for girls. In rural areas, this figure rises to 17 percent.

Completion: On average, 9.6 percent of girls in low income countries leave primary school before finishing, compared to 8.2 percent of boys.

- In Africa, 8.6 percent of girls who start school drop-out before completing primary school.
- In India, no more than one-third of girls complete a primary education.
- In Pakistan, only 17 percent of girls in rural areas complete primary school.

Getting Girls to School: There are many reasons why girls are kept out of school, resulting from a combination of community and national priorities and family factors. A number of recent studies have demonstrated policy alternatives to address some of these issues.

Reducing Direct Costs: Many families, especially those who are poor, cannot afford the costs of school fees, transportation, materials, or clothing for their children to attend school. In most cases where resources are scarce, poor parents prioritize educating their sons over their daughters.

- Fee waivers, subsidies, scholarships and free books and uniforms can be made available for girls to decrease the direct costs to their parents.

Reducing Opportunity Costs: Young girls tend to have numerous other responsibilities in the family and household, such as caring for younger siblings, housework, farming, or trade which prevent them from attending school.

- Flexible school times can help girls meet their other family responsibilities without missing or dropping out of school.
- Programmes for pre-school or sibling child care during school hours enable girls to attend school and to focus on learning rather than caring for their brothers and sisters.
- In Bangladesh, these measures have been shown to increase girls' enrolment and retention in school without increasing cost.

Addressing Safety and Modesty Concerns: Community and cultural standards of modesty may preclude girls from attending school, especially if they must travel outside their communities, after they reach puberty and where other students or teachers are male.

- In Pakistan, when school is available in a girl's village, girls are as likely to attend school as boys. When a school is nearby, but not in the village, girls are 10 percent less likely to go to school than boys.
- Several programmes have demonstrated that modifications in the delivery system can significantly increase girls' enrolment and retention. These steps include locating schools or satellite schools close to girls' homes, initiating single sex schools or classrooms and using female teachers, especially those who come from the community. These need not entail significant extra cost.

Changing Family Perceptions of Investment: Decisions about sending children to school are made by parents, often based on their perceptions of the likely return on their investment. Parents sometimes perceive that the economic return for educating daughters is lower than for educating sons. In fact, there is little evidence to show that wage rates are lower for females than males in the labour force, although in most settings female labour force participation is lower because of bias.

A related problem is parents' perception of the quality and relevance of education. There is growing evidence that as curriculum builds more on "hard skills" like math and science, parents are more willing to send their daughters to school. In fact, in some settings, improving educational quality seems to increase girls' school enrolment more than boys'. Some relatively simple steps can be taken to begin to address these concerns:

- Help girls gain access to science and math education.
- Depict girls and women as income earners in textbooks and broader media.
- Promote adult education and income earning opportunities for parents, especially mothers, to increase their willingness to educate their daughters.

What Governments Can Do to Improve Girls' Access to and Achievement in School: Existing educational systems, with high recurring costs and relatively low returns to investment, are far from cost effective. There are significant recurrent costs associated with present underutilization and drop out. Given the existing investments and the enormous social benefits associated with girls' education, the question is not how much it will cost to better educate girls, but how much it will cost not to.

Cost Savings and Efficiency: Policies should aim to retain all the girls who start in school—there is space for them. Drop-outs imply a heavy cost to the educational system, to girls and to society. Policies focusing on keeping girls in school might include incentive programmes or consciousness-raising campaigns.

Reallocating Resources within the Education Sector: The benefits of education for boys and girls are highest at the primary level. Yet many countries invest too much of their education budgets in higher level education. Shifting some of these resources from higher education to basic education could significantly improve the reach and quality of primary education.

Significant improvements in the number and quality of school places could be also be made by allocating existing resources more efficiently. Reforms might include: double shifting of classrooms, redeploying administrators to teaching, using teacher aides and using satellite schools to reach remote areas. Efforts in several countries have demonstrated cost saving and improvements based on these kinds of reforms.

Selective Expansion: In some settings, increasing the number of places in schools simply by expanding the existing school system would significantly increase girls' enrolment.

- Of 36 million girls out of school in Africa, half could be brought into the system merely by expanding the existing school system. Bringing the remaining half into school will require special attention to redesigning the system and redeploying resources.

Medical Education, Health Policy and Societal Needs of India—A General Perspective: India, with its large population, has many more medical schools and medical students than most other countries in the world. Yet, there is a great need for doctors, especially in rural areas. There is a growing realization that the training of doctors is inadequate to meet the health needs and priorities of the community. Restructuring of medical education and delivery of health care services in India is required. The National Health Policy of India has been formulated based on the needs for health care reform. It identifies the progress achieved, the existing picture and details future directions for medical/health education and health care delivery. It is important for all medical schools and health care deliverers at all levels to adopt the National Health Policy and implement the changes suggested. More research needs to be done to define the health needs of the population on which to base more effective medical curricula.

Medical Colleges in India: At present there are 162 medical colleges in the country of which 158 have been recognized/ approved by the Medical Council of India. Of these 158 medical colleges, 109 are Government medical colleges and the remaining 49 are private. The admission capacity in the above colleges is about 17,000 students per year. Although the existing medical colleges are considered to be sufficient to meet the medical manpower needs of the country on a per capita basis, there is a great need for doctors especially in the rural areas.

There has been an increasing awareness that the training of doctors is inadequate to meet the health needs and priorities of the Indian community. There is a need for an integrated, comprehensive approach to medical education and the promotion of a holistic approach to patients. Medical education in India has to focus on public health and the preventive, health promotion and rehabilitative aspects of health care with less emphasis on a cure-oriented approach. There has to be a restructuring of the delivery of health care services. Based on the recognized needs for health care reform, the National Health Policy was formulated in 1983 followed by more recent revised drafts. It is important for all medical schools and health care deliverers at all levels to adopt the National Health Policy and implement the changes suggested. The National Health Policy of India can be used as a template for all developing countries to formulate their own Health Policies. However, it is one thing to develop policy and another to implement it.

National Health Policy: An important initiative taken by the Government of India to improve health care is to formulate the National Health Policy. The National Health Policy outlines the framework of the goals to be achieved in medical education in India. The policy statements are as follows:

The Constitution of India envisages the establishment of a new social order based on equality, freedom, justice and the dignity of the individual. It aims at the elimination of poverty, ignorance and ill-health and directs the State to regard the raising of the level of nutrition and the standard of living of its people and the improvement of public health as among its primary duties. The goal is to maintain the health and strength of workers, men and women and to especially ensure that children are given opportunities and facilities to develop in a healthy manner.

Successive five-year plans have provided the framework whereby the States may develop their health services infrastructure, facilities for medical education and research. Similar guidance has been provided through the discussions and conclusions arrived at the Joint Conferences of the Central Councils of Health, Family and Welfare and National Development. In addition, central legislation has been enacted to regulate standards of medical education, prevention of food adulteration and the maintenance of standards in the manufacture and sale of certified drugs.

While the broad approaches contained in the successive plans may have generally served past needs, it is felt that an integrated, comprehensive approach towards the future development of medical education, research and health services is required to serve the actual health needs and priorities of the country. It is in this context that the National Health Policy has been developed.

India has a rich and ancient history of medical and health sciences. The philosophy of Ayurveda and the surgical skills enunciated by Charaka and Shusharuta bear testimony to our tradition in the scientific basis of health care for our people. The approach of our medical practice has always been of a holistic nature, which took into account all aspects of human health and disease. Over the centuries, with the intrusion of foreign influences and mingling of cultures, various systems of medicine evolved and have continued to be practised widely. However, the allopathic system of medicine has, in a relatively short period of time, made a major impact on the entire approach to health care and pattern of development of the health services infrastructure in the country.

Progress Achieved: During the last three decades and more, since the attainment of Independence, considerable progress has been achieved in the promotion of the health status of our people. Smallpox has been eliminated; plague is no longer a problem; mortality from cholera and related diseases has decreased and malaria brought under control to a considerable extent. The mortality rate per thousand of population has been reduced from 27.4 to 14.8 and the life expectancy at birth has increased from 32.7 to over 52. A fairly extensive network of dispensaries, hospitals and institutions providing specialized curative care has developed and a large stock of medical and health personnel, of various levels, has become available. Significant indigenous capacity has been established for the production of drugs and pharmaceuticals, vaccines, sera and hospital equipment.

The Existing Picture: In spite of such impressive progress, the demographic and health picture of the country still constitutes a cause for serious and urgent concern. The high rate of population growth continues to have an adverse effect on the health of our people and the quality of their lives. The mortality rates for women and children are still distressingly high; almost one third of the total deaths occur among children below the age of 5 years; infant mortality is around 129 per thousand live births. Efforts at raising the nutritional levels of our people have still to bear fruit and the extent and severity of malnutrition continues to be exceptionally high. Communicable and non-communicable diseases have still to be brought under effective control and eradicated. Blindness, leprosy and T.B. continue to have a high incidence. Only 31% of the rural population have access to a potable water supply and 0.5% enjoys basic sanitation.

There remains a high incidence of diarrheal diseases and other preventive and infectious diseases, especially amongst infants and children, lack of safe drinking water and poor environmental sanitation, poverty and ignorance are among the major contributory causes of the high incidence of disease and mortality. The existing situation has been largely engendered by the almost wholesale adoption of health manpower development policies and the establishment of curative centres based on the Western models, which are inappropriate and irrelevant to the real needs of our people and the socioeconomic conditions obtaining in the country. The hospital-based disease and cure-oriented approach towards the establishment of medical services has provided benefits to the upper crust of society, specially those residing in the urban areas. This approach has been at the cost of providing comprehensive primary health care services to the entire population, whether residing in urban or rural areas.

Furthermore, the continued high emphasis on curative care has led to the neglect of disease prevention, health promotion, public health and rehabilitative aspects of health care. The existing approach, instead of improving awareness and building self-reliance, has tended to enhance dependency and weaken the community's capacity to cope with its problems. The present policies in regard to the education and training of medical and health personnel, at various levels, has resulted in the development of a cultural gap between the people and the personnel providing care. The various health programmes have, by and large, failed to involve individuals and families in establishing a self-reliant community.

Over the years, the planning process has become largely oblivious of the fact that the ultimate goal of achieving a satisfactory health status for all our people cannot be secured without involving the community in the identification of their health needs and priorities. Similarly, the implementation and management of the various health and related programmes cannot be achieved without the commitment of the communities for whom they are intended.

India remains committed to attaining the goal of "Health for All by the Year 2000 " through the universal provision of comprehensive primary health care services. We have missed this goal and require a thorough overhaul of the existing approaches to the education and training of medical and health personnel and the reorganization of our health services infrastructure. Furthermore, considering the large variety of inputs into health, it is necessary to secure the complete integration of all plans for health and human development with the overall national socioeconomic development process. This is especially true in the more closely health related sectors involved with the maintenance of standards and the manufacture of drugs and sales of pharmaceuticals. It also applies to agriculture, food production and protection of the environment, rural development, education and social welfare, housing, water supply and sanitation and the prevention of food adulteration.

In summary, the principles of the National Health Policy must continue to evolve within a fully integrated planning framework which seeks to provide universal, comprehensive primary health care services, relevant to the actual needs and priorities of the community and at a cost which the people can afford. At the same time we must ensure that the planning and implementation of the various health programmes is through the organized involvement and participation of the community, adequately utilizing the services being offered by private voluntary organizations that are active in the health sector.

It is also necessary to ensure that the pattern of development of the health services infrastructure in the future fully takes into account the revised 20-Point Programme. The Programme attributes very high priority to the promotion of voluntary family planning and a substantial augmentation of primary health care facilities on a universal basis. It emphasizes the control of leprosy, tuberculosis and blindness and an acceleration of welfare programmes for women and children together with nutrition programmes for pregnant women, nursing mothers and children, especially in the tribal, hill and backward areas. The programme also places high emphasis on the supply of pure drinking water, improvements in the housing and environments of the poorer sections of society, increased production of essential food items, integrated rural development and the development of universal elementary education.

Population Stabilization: No matter how fundamental the changes in the health care system there will not be significant progress in the health status of the people of India until success is achieved in voluntary family planning with a reduced family size. In view of the vital importance of securing a balanced growth of the population, it is necessary to enunciate, separately, a National Population Policy.

Presently, despite the constraint of resources, there is a disproportionate emphasis on the establishment of curative centres, (dispensaries, hospitals and institutions for specialist treatment), the large majority of which are located in the urban areas of the country. The vast majority of those seeking medical care have to travel long distances to the nearest centre, seeking relief for ailments, which could have been readily and effectively handled at the community level. Also, for the want of a well established referral system, those seeking curative care have the tendency to visit various specialist centres, thus contributing to congestion, duplication of effort and consequential waste of resources.

Future Directions: To put an end to the existing all-round unsatisfactory situation, it is necessary to restructure the health services as soon as possible with the following broad approach:

To provide a network of comprehensive primary health care services which is integrally linked with health education and which takes into account the fact that a large majority of health functions can be effectively handled and resolved by the people themselves. This however, requires the organized support of volunteers, auxiliaries, paramedics and adequately trained multi-purpose workers of various grades of skill and competence. There are a large number of private, voluntary organizations active in the health field throughout the country that could be utilized and intermeshed within the government system.

To be effective, the establishment of a primary health care approach would involve the transfer of knowledge, simple skill and technologies to health volunteers, selected by the communities and enjoying their confidence. The role of the front line workers, selected by the community would have to be related to definitive action plans in the translation of medical and health knowledge into practical action. This would involve the use of simple and inexpensive interventions, which can be readily implemented by persons who have undergone short periods of training. The quality of training of these health workers would be of crucial importance to the success of this approach.

The success of a decentralized primary health care system would depend on the organized development of individual self-reliance and effective community participation and the provision of an organized back-up support in terms of secondary and tertiary levels of the health care services.

The decentralization of services would require the establishment of a well thought out referral system to provide adequate expertise to the community. The extent of this service would depend on the actual needs and problems of the area and thus ensure against the continuation of the existing rush towards the curative centres in the urban areas. The effective establishment of a referral system would also ensure the optimal utilization of expertise at the higher levels of the hierarchical medical structure. This approach would not only lead to the improvement of comprehensive health care services at the primary level but also provide for timely attention being available to those in need of urgent specialist consultation, whether they live in rural or urban areas.

To ensure that the approach to health care does not merely constitute a collection of disparate health interventions but consists of an integrated package of services seeking to address the entire range of health conditions, it is necessary to establish a nationwide chain of sanitary-cum-epidemiological stations. The location and function of these stations would depend on the local situations and other relevant considerations. Each station would have suitably trained staff who would be able identify, plan and provide preventive, health promotion and mental health care services. It would be obviously beneficial, depending upon the local situations, to establish such stations at the Primary Health Centres. For instance, the district health organization should have, as an integral part of its organization, an well-organized epidemiological unit to coordinate and superintend the functioning of the field stations. These stations would participate in the integrated action plans to eradicate and control diseases, in addition to dealing with specific local environmental health problems.

In urban areas, the municipal and local authorities should be equipped to perform similar functions, being supported with adequate resources and expertise, to effectively deal with local preventable public health problems.

The location of curative centres should be in relation to the populations that they serve. This will reflect the density of population, distance and topography of the region and transport connections. These centres should function within the recommended referral system with regard to the general specialties required to deal with local disease patterns and be provided as near to the community as possible. The concept of domiciliary care and the field-camps approach should be utilized to the fullest extent in order to reduce the pressure on these centres, especially in relationship to the control and eradication of blindness, tuberculosis and leprosy. To maximize the utilization of available resources, new curative centres should only be established in exceptional cases at selected locations. The guiding principle should be to provide specialist services as near to the beneficiaries as possible, within a well-planned network.

To reduce government expenditure and fully utilize untapped resources, programmes could be devised to encourage the establishment of practice by private medical professionals depending on local requirements and potential. In addition, encouragement should be given to increase investment by non-governmental agencies to establish curative centres and offer organized logistical, financial and technical support to voluntary agencies active in the health field. While the major focus of attention in restructuring the existing governmental health Organizations would relate to establishing comprehensive primary health care and public health services within an integrated referral system attention must also be paid to the maintenance and centres which provide speciality and super-speciality services. This would ensure that the present and future requirements for specialist treatment are adequately available within the country. The future development of such facilities must take into account a balanced regional distribution and provide services within the reach of all, whether residing in rural or urban areas. India has many health practitioners who encompass a wide range of different approaches to health care including, for example, Ayurveda, Unani, Homeopathy, Yoga, Naturopathy, etc. These practitioners enjoy high local acceptance and respect and consequently exert considerable influence on health beliefs and practice. It is, therefore, necessary to enable each of these philosophies of medicine and health care to develop within the Indian Health System.

Medical and Health Education: The effective delivery of health care services will depend very largely on the nature of education, training and appropriate orientation towards community health of all categories of medical and health personnel and their capacity to function as an integrated team. It is, therefore, of crucial importance that the entire basis and approach towards medical and health education, at all levels, is reviewed in terms of national needs and priorities. Curricular structure and training programmes must be reformed to produce personnel of various grades of skill and competence who are professionally equipped and socially motivated to effectively deal with the communities they will serve.

It is necessary to formulate, separately, a National Medical and Health Education Policy which (i) sets out the changes required in the curricular content and training programmes of medical and health personnel (ii) takes into account the need for teamwork amongst the various levels of health workers (iii) provides guidelines for the education of health personnel on the basis of realistically assessed manpower requirements; (iv) seeks to resolve the existing sharp regional imbalances in their availability; and (v) ensures that personnel at all levels are socially motivated towards the rendering of community health services.

Our standard of medical education in India is high and we train many highly qualified physicians but there are many problems that need addressing. One important area is the attempt to integrate basic sciences in the learning of clinical medicine. There have been many workshops across the nation to address this problem including problem-based learning. However, every country has its own unique needs and although a commonality in education process may or may not be the answer it will not be sufficient in itself to address the health needs of the population. India, with its enormous population, needs more physicians trained to face community and family health needs. Primary health care, together with tropical hygiene and curative medicine play a pivotal role in becoming the focus of educational reform. More research needs to be done to define the health needs of the population on which to base effective medical curricula.

Operation Research: Whatever the economic circumstances and business environment-recession or growth; confident or uncertain-organisations are increasingly calling for better information handling and more informed decision taking. Operational Research (OR) is an essential management tool for understanding and solving the many complex problems that face organisations nowadays.

Operational Researchers work to help manage information effectively, cope with uncertainty and provide long and short term strategies for their organisations. Opportunities for OR professionals have never been better. The demand for OR specialists and the variety of work on offer are expanding rapidly.

One of the attractions of OR work is its variety. As an Operational Researcher you could have the opportunity of moving around and experiencing many different business environments. Operations Research is concerned with optimal decision-making in and modelling of, deterministic and probabilistic systems that originate from real life. These applications, which occur in government, business, engineering, economics and the natural and social sciences, are characterized largely by the need to allocate limited resources. The contribution from the operations research approach stems primarily from:

- Structuring the real-life situation into a mathematical model, abstracting the essential elements so that a solution relevant to the decision-maker's objectives can be sought. This involves looking at the problem in the context of the entire system.
- Exploring the structure of such solutions and developing systematic procedures for obtaining them.

Developing a solution, including the mathematical theory, if necessary, that yields an optimal value of the system measure of desirability (or possibly comparing alternative courses of action by evaluating their measure of desirability).

OR is a profession where initiative, creativity and enthusiasm are every bit as important as technical ability. If you are thinking of a general management career, there are few better ways of getting an early overview and understanding of how organisations operate. Typically, OR teams are involved in projects which draw on a wide range of business skills and have dealings with anyone from shop-floor to boardroom. Whatever your career aspirations, OR will give you a flying start!

OR is an evolving discipline-because the world is ever changing. Over the years, OR has firmly embedded itself in a wide range of sectors, including manufacturing, transport, retailing, marketing, the financial and service sectors as well as local and Central government.

Because the skills of good OR-an analytical mind with an action orientation and sound people skills-are precisely what are needed in all successful managers, OR is a significant recruiting ground for senior management talent. This feature aims to offer a flavour of some of the varied career opportunities that are available to Operational Research people.

Transport and Travel: Growth in the transport sector is often constrained by financial and environmental pressures, government restrictions and the need to maintain safety standards. The result of this is that demands often exceed the capacity of the system and there is always a need to squeeze the maximum possible out of the existing infrastructure and formulate and debate plans for future improvements.

This drive for optimising the use of existing systems and for forward planning, can be helped by OR. For example, OR developed techniques are used widely by airlines and other transport operating companies to offer varying fares and make higher revenues by filling more seats at different prices-an OR technique known as Yield Management.

Retailing: The analysis of market and consumer information is a major and rapidly growing role for OR in the retail sector. In supermarkets, for example, OR has been used to determine which shelf layouts best suit the shopping habits of customers and, so, maximise the outlets sales. Data from store loyalty card schemes is also analysed by OR groups in a variety of ways-for example, to advise on stock holding policies and overall profitability improvement.

Health: Efficiency enhancemen'ts and better patient care are perennial challenges for those providing health services. OR techniques are widely used in the health service. For example, by using OR, appointment systems have been designed that substantially reduce outpatients- waiting times whilst keeping highly qualified medical staff fully occupied.

Financial Services: OR is very active within the major banks and other financial institutions. Operational Researchers address a very wide range of issues from the planning and analysis of high-street customer services to organisation strategy and international finance. They are widely employed in Credit Risk Management-a vital area for lenders needing to ensure that they find the optimum balance of risk and revenue.

Government: There is a demand from the very top of government for the increased use of analysis and modelling to underpin the "Modernising Government" initiative. OR is seen as a key contributor assisting in the development of policies that are based on evidence and will work in practice.

Universities and Research Institutions: OR people teach on a variety of university courses: undergraduate and postgraduate management degrees and diplomas, as well as the more specialist OR and mathematics degrees.

Staff of universities also specialise in the development of techniques and universities encourage people to pursue consultancy work for outside organisations. In addition to providing a source of income, more importantly, this work helps to strengthen the links between the academic and practical OR environments. Specialist Research institutions, such as those in agriculture and forestry, often employ OR trained people. Depending on the institution's needs, these people could be part of a small OR team or attached to a specialist research team.

Defence: As a consequence of the development of very fast, computer controlled, defence systems, computer modelling of attack-defence scenarios has become of paramount importance. This has led to an increased presence of Operational Researchers and there is a strong presence both within the Ministry of Defence and the Defence Research Agency.

Consultancy: Several universities like University of Delhi, Madras, Calcutta, Bombay, Gujarat, Osmania and Punjab hold part-time course for MBA. Part-time programmes are designed to last for 5 to 7 semesters and the classes are held in the evening. Apart from requirement of a good bachelor's degree, part-time programmes also require some experience at supervisory level. While part-time courses are available only to the candidates belonging to a particular city/town where such university is located, MBA courses offered through correspondence/self-instructional method are designed to assist the candidates located at far flung areas. Some universities like Punjabi University, Patiala and Indira Gandhi National Open University (IGNOU) offer such courses. IGNOU is one of the premier institutions which offers MBA programme through a nationwide network of its 170 study centres. Internationally recognized as a centre of excellence for studies, IGNOU offers a 5-semester MBA programme and also provides the facility of counselling. This course is particularly useful for the officers of Armed Forces who retire at relatively younger age and also to those Government servants who wish to seek careers in managerial cadres by seeking premature retirement.

An advantage to do MBA from IGNOU is that the Candidates who, for any reasons, cannot complete the entire programme and are able to pass only a few subjects/papers, are awarded diplomas like Diploma in Management, Post Graduate (PG) Deiploma in Business Management, PG Diploma in Marketing Management, PG Diploma in HRD, PG Diploma in Financial Management, etc., depending on the number of papers passed by the candidates. Another advantage is that the number of seats for MBA programme is determined study-centre-wise which offers a large number of seats at all India level.

The candidates seeking admission in this programme offered by IGNOU must have completed 25 years of age and must have at least three years' experience in the supervisory capacity. There is, however, no upper age limit. The admission is made entirely on the basis of marks obtained in the entrance test which is for two-hour duration and has about 100 objective type questions on comprehension, reasoning, English language, general awareness, data interpretation, quantitative aptitude etc.

Database Marketing: OR techniques have been used to develop programmes which can identify and cluster various customer types. Given the need for companies to target their marketing activities ever more finely, database marketing has become a very important element in many companies- marketing strategies.

Having data capture systems in place, that can identify customer behaviour patterns, helps companies to understand which types of customers buy what kind of products or services.

The task of matching customer needs to stock holding or product development strategy then becomes very well informed.

Clearly, in an operation such as food retailing, millions of transactions can be completed each day. As the point of sale bar-code scanning technology has developed, retailers are now able to capture immense volumes of sales data which, by virtue of loyalty card schemes, they are able to attribute to individual customers. Until recently, it was impossible to analyse such large databases, but new OR techniques have made this achievable.

By applying OR methods to such an immense volume of data, it is now possible to use the information to devise precisely targeted communications about products and services which are most likely to appeal to the targeted customer group.

Business Process Re-engineering (BPR): The ever greater need for companies to increase profitability has resulted in many BPR initiatives. Since improving business processes is a core OR function, Operational Researchers have become heavily involved in helping companies to re-engineer. Many management consultants have Operational Research Groups that are highly skilled in the techniques and application of business modelling and have the essential expertise in analysis and interpretation to deliver a positive impact on their clients-business processes.

Manufacturing Industry: OR has traditionally played a significant role in helping companies to improve efficiency, reduce costs and make the most effective use of capital investment. OR is commonly used to assist with plant logistics, forecasting, planning and scheduling. It also contributes to marketing, personnel and strategic planning work. The types of industry currently using OR are numerous and include brewing, computers, motor manufacture, aerospace, steel production, etc.

Water, Power, Telecommunications and Mining: In these business sectors, the cultural changes brought about by privatisation have tended to emphasise the contribution of OR. The scale of operations in such large organisations means that even a small percentage gain in performance can result in very great benefits. Whilst this may always have been important, such benefits are now crucial in the more profit conscious and service enhancement orientated environment. Operational Researchers take a lead role in working with staff at all levels to negotiate and implement working methods. Many projects involve modelling the complex operating logistics of these large operations, striving for continuous improvement. OR projects in this sector can also focus on marketing, finance, personnel and strategic planning matters.

Medical education in India does not address larger social needs for health care. Medical education is in the news for all the wrong reasons. The government's decision to extend reservations in institutions of higher education under the Centre triggered off a storm of protest, led by medical students. There were spurious arguments on both sides. What has been lost in the heat and dust of the protests are fundamental issues. Is privatisation of medical education hurting the capacity of the system to deliver quality care to the majority of people? Is the distribution of specialisations in post-graduate courses badly skewed? Is the quality of education good enough? And, of course, why is the state health education sector on the brink of collapse? Vibha Varshney has some of the answers.

Short-handed: *Health education should be sensitive to health care.*

That India is short of doctors and paramedical staff in absolute terms is hardly news. But behind bare statistics is another story. There is a big skew in the distribution of health care personnel — for instance over rural and urban areas. And, equally important, there are serious questions about the training doctors receive in terms of its utility for different categories of diseases and, therefore, delivery to different categories of people.

Let's take a look at the big picture in terms of numbers who's *World Health Report* for 2006 shows there is a global shortage of health professionals. The greatest shortfall occurs in south and southeast Asia. India, Bangladesh and Indonesia top the list. The number of registered doctors in India has increased from 61,800 in 1951 to about 645,825 in 2005 — that's 0.60 doctors for 1,000 people.

Compared to this, Cuba had 5.91 doctors for 1,000 people in 2002. The Joint Learning Initiative, a global health network launched by the Rockefeller Foundation suggests that, on an average, countries with fewer than 2.5 health care professionals (doctors, nurses and midwives) per 1,000 population fail to achieve an 80 per cent coverage rate for deliveries by skilled attendants or for measles immunisation.

India has 5.9 doctors, 0.8 nurses and 0.47 midwives for 1,000 people, which adds up to 1.86 health workers for 1,000 people. Apart from the fact that this figure falls considerably short of the desired figure, it also does not indicate the distribution of health professionals and does not, therefore, show how supply relates to demand. The statistics for the state sector reveals a pathetic scenario. According to the Union ministry of health and family welfare's (mohfw's) *Health Information of India*, 2004, the country had 67,576 government doctors: meaning one doctor was serving roughly 15,980 people.

The current availability of doctors does not meet the recommendations of several past committees. In 1946, a committee headed by Joseph Bhore, an Indian Civil Service officer, had suggested one doctor for 1,600 people; another committee in 1948 had recommended one doctor for 1,000; and an Indian Council of Medical Research-Indian Council for Social Science Research joint panel had recommended in 1980 that six general practitioners and three specialists should be available for 100,000 people.

As far as specialists are concerned, the situation on the ground comes nowhere near meeting this figure. The government's estimated requirement of specialist surgeons, obstetricians and gynaecologists, physicians and paediatricians in 2001 for community health centres in rural areas is 12,172, but only 6,617 positions have been sanctioned and 4,124 positions have been filled. An Escorts Heart Institute and Research Centre document prepared in 2005 said India would need at least one million more qualified nurses and 500,000 more doctors by 2012.

Broadband Dream Narrows Down on Economy, Health and Education: Broadband is a global phenomenon and India is on its way to join the big picture. Consider this. Consulting firm Price waterhouse Coopers put together a study on the future of broadband, sometime back. RHK, which has been analysing tech/telecom data for the past 12 years, came out with world rankings of broadband penetration. This was part of its broadband access networks programme. The Federal Communications Commission (FCC) of the US is going all out, analysing whether broadband is being deployed to all Americans. Reason: broadband networks are vital to the economy, healthcare and education....

Back home in India, the Confederation of Indian Industry (CII) recently finalised a broadband economy report: Vision 2010. All in all, it's about the world looking at broadband in a big way!

Speaking of the FCC move, it has sought information on how the Commission should define advanced telecommunications capability, whether advanced telecommunications capability is being deployed to all Americans, whether the current level of broadband deployment is reasonable and timely and what actions, if any, can be taken to accelerate broadband deployment.

Interestingly, it's not India alone that looks at international models before deployment of any new technology, be it direct-to-home broadcasting or broadband. The FCC too wants details on trends in other nations and how America's deployment of advanced telecommunications capability affects its role in a global economy, according to a recent new release issued by the Commission.

Meanwhile, India's vision, as per the CII report, is to make the country among the top five broadband countries in the world by 2010. To put things in perspective, the CII National Broadband Economy Committee has defined broadband as "an always-on network capable of providing interactive voice, data and video services on public networks". If you're looking at speed, the committee has said that there should be at least two tiers of service. While the true broadband would be capable of providing minimum asymmetric bandwidth of 1.5 Mbps, a "lite" version would provide 256 kbps.

Look at the world arena and things are moving fast. According to RHK's World-Broadband-Statistics, broadband lines at the end of 2003 stood at 100.8 million (including DSL and cable), recording an increase of 63 percent over 2002. The report showed that technology-wise, DSL accounted for the largest share with 63.5 percent of total broadband lines. Also, the top three DSL markets globally were China (11.1 million), Japan (10.3 million) and USA (9.3 million). Significantly, country-wise, USA remains the largest broadband market with 25 million lines, followed by Japan (13.6 million), China (13.5 million) and Korea (11.1 million).

Besides analysing the industry trends, the PwC report looks at opportunities, threats and challenges associated with selling content in a broadband-connected world. Its focus is on the US consumer market during 2004 to 2006.

According to the PwC key findings and predictions, the killer application for broadband Internet access between now and 2006 will not be the distribution of professionally produced content such as today's television programmes and movies. Also, the major impact of broadband over the next three years will be the addition of video to existing applications including conferencing, messaging and gaming and the development of new applications that rely on user-and-community-provided video content.

The PwC report predicts that by the second half of the decade, broadband internet will be recognised as a fundamentally new mechanism for engaging audiences because of its unique characteristics. Interestingly, it also points out that to successfully compete with cable, digital broadcast and satellite television as a means of delivering video programming, the broadband Internet will have to deliver content those other systems are incapable of carrying. There's more. During the next few years, broadband penetration in the US is unlikely to achieve the level reached by such countries as Canada and Korea, where deployment has been more aggressively supported and subsidised by the government.

Coming to India, the CII study talks about societal and commercial applications. In societal applications, its focus areas include e-education, e-health and e-governance. Commercial applications are about entertainment on demand, e-commerce and business applications.

As per the demand projections of the CII broadband committee, 350 cities/towns are likely to be covered by 2010 and all cities and towns in urban India by 2020. Among other targets are 7.5 million residential connections by 2010 and 23 to 27 million by 2020. Commercial connections are projected at 1.85 million by 2010 and 7 to 9 million by 2020. In all, total urban connections are estimated at 10.35-10.85 million by 2010 and 32-39 million by 2020.

And the cost? To achieve the targeted goals in India, an investment of $1.4 billion is required by 2006 and $2.8 billion by 2010, based on the DSL on copper model. The fibre-based model would require double the investment, the CII report points out.

Divided Government and Private Higher Education Growth in India: The Role of Federal and State Governments.

India has the second-largest higher education system in the world and the third-largest pool of skilled personpower. The system encompasses approximately 304 universities including 62 "deemed universities," 11 open universities, 14,600 colleges, 10 million students and 0.5 million teachers. Besides these public and private institutions, the exact number of private colleges, international institutions and enrolment involved in Indian higher education training and vocational skills is not yet known.

India's long tradition of private colleges and the current growth in private institutions have been facilitated by the lack of a restraining centralized national government. Prior to independence, many philanthropists and religiously oriented individuals and institutions established centres of higher learning to promote the values of spirituality, human dignity and integrity. The usual orientation of private initiative and private funding was social transformation and leadership rather than monetary gains.

Even after independence, private initiative and households have played a substantial role in supporting higher education. Central government's share of total higher education income in 1950–1951 was just 49 percent. Although its funding rose to approximately 80 percent during the 1980s, since the 1990s government has resorted to cutbacks in higher education in the wake of structural adjustment, paving the way for the rapid expansion of self-financed private higher education. The pattern of government cutbacks and private expansion is familiar in much of Asia. Much less familiar is India's extended experience with college enrolments that were legally private but publicly financed.

Also unusual in India is the fact that central government provides only one-quarter of the funding for higher education, with much of the rest coming from the states. Both the federal and state governments can pass legislation pertaining to education. In case of any conflict between the two, federal law prevails. Though the federal government tried to regulate the private colleges in various states through the introduction of the Private Universities (Establishment and Regulation) Bill in 1995, this effort failed due to resistance from the private sector itself to the requirement of huge endowment funds, free tuition to approximately 30 percent of students and regulation by the federal government. Instead of pursuing this bill further, the federal government adopted a policy of awarding the status of "deemed universities" to private institutions that met the national goals and criteria laid down by the University Grants Commission and other statutory bodies.

Under section 3 of the UGC Act (2000), deemed universities are required to possess viability and a management capable of contributing to university ideas and traditions. Under this scheme, the Manipal Academy, a pioneer in private higher education, has been granted the status of a deemed university. It is the only university that is totally self-financed, as most others have to rely on explicit or implicit public subsidies for their very survival.

Taking advantage of the provision for joint responsibility toward education, some states have passed their own legislation on private higher education recently. Chattisgarh was the first to pass a Private Universities Act, in October 2002. The newly emerged state of Uttaranchal succeeded in getting four private universities during 2002–2003. In fact, there has been a sudden proliferation of private medical and engineering colleges, especially in the southern and western states of India—namely Andhra Pradesh, Tamil Nadu, Karnataka, Kerala and Maharashtra.

For instance, in 2001 Andhra Pradesh had 95 private self-financing engineering colleges and 303 medical colleges in comparison to 11 public engineering colleges and 25 public medical colleges. In many states, private universities have started up in haste without adequate infrastructure and appropriate faculty. Those already functioning have raised fees sharply in conjunction with professional courses or foreign collaborations. Not surprisingly, these developments engendered public demonstrations and resentment, driving the judiciary to intervene.

Recent Supreme Court Judgments: The interventions by the Supreme Court from time to time and its contradictory judgments have only added to the prevailing confusion, however. India's Constitution guarantees various minorities, based upon religion or language, the right to establish and run institutions of higher learning. The idea was to allow these minorities to run educational institutions "for religious and charitable purposes." But shrewd politicians and businessmen took advantage of this provision, raising exorbitant amounts of money, legally or illegally, through capitation fees beyond the reach of many middle-class families.

In Unni Krishnan J. P vs. the State of Andhra Pradesh (1993), the Supreme Court banned the Capitation Fee Act, 1988. Instead, it allowed a number of "paid seats" to be established in consultation with concerned state governments. The idea was to make some families pay full costs toward the education not only of their own wards but also of some others, in the name of social justice. The state governments were also allowed to administer and regulate admissions into unaided and privately promoted institutions providing professional education.

However, in T. M. A. Pai vs. State of Karnataka (October 2002), the Supreme Court reversed its earlier Unni Krishnan stand and gave a green light to financially independent private and minority interests to establish higher education colleges of their choice. Although the court also warned against "commercialization" by private colleges, it was not clear what the practical impact of that warning might be.

In its most recent judgment (August 14, 2003), the Supreme Court has again taken a tough stand against capitation fees and profiteering by the private professional colleges. It has threatened to "de-recognize" private colleges found guilty of charging capitation fees in any form. Again, however, the impact remains unclear; there are reports, for example, of persistent underhanded dealings for obtaining seats in private professional colleges.

Notwithstanding the legal rulings, alliances among politicians, business and academia sustain the commercialization of higher education for private gains. Thus, although democratic India stands out with the role taken by state governments and courts, it joins a powerful international trend of sharp growth in commercial private higher education, some tied to a new and dominant political economic marketplace and some to the lack of a firmer restraining political legal framework.

TEACHING IN SOUTHERN INDIA

In 1986 India's department of education issued a remarkable document that acknowledged, among other things, that "India's political and social life is passing through a phase which poses the danger of erosion of long-accepted values. Not only are the young ignorant of and often contemptuous of, ancient Hindu visions of life, but the 'modern' values of secularism, socialism, democracy and professional ethics are coming under increasing strain." That statement is from the "Draft National Policy on Education," an attempt to chart directions for the 5,200-some institutions of higher learning that have arisen in India during the past century. The document speaks explicitly of "values education." It calls for the fostering of values that "have a universal appeal" and that could help to "eliminate obscurantism, religious fanaticism, violence, superstition and fatalism."

As in others parts of Asia, what happens in Indian colleges and universities is decisive for the future. The median age in Asia is about 17 and going down; in the West it is about 35 and going up. With well over half the globe's population in Asia, it can be regarded as the world's kindergarten, with the West being the world's old-folks home.

This call for more attention to "values" takes place in the context of a general structural revision in Indian higher education. Colleges may, under certain conditions, be granted a new degree of independence from prescribed curricula. Education is gaining independence from the governmental control brought to India by the British and reinforced by the first generation of national leaders who used socialist ideas (mostly Fabian, some Marxist) about centralized planning in a secular state in their effort to establish a modern nation and to keep militant Hindus and Muslims from each other's throats.

These developments arise from the simultaneous failure and success of Indian education. On the one hand, recent Indian educational policy has made Indian doctors, managers and engineers competitive on the world job market. It has also brought education to such a level of strength that scholars, programmes and institutions are able and willing to take more responsibility and be more autonomous in shaping what gets taught.

On the other hand, the educational system has not provided a vision that can inspire the younger generation to a common moral commitment. The editor of *The Hindu,* a widely circulated English-language newspaper, claims that 80 per cent of India's college graduates want to leave the country for one of the Commonwealth nations, one of the Gulf states or the United States to make money. No nation can survive when such a large percentage of its more gifted and trained people want to leave.

Among those most eager to respond to the new freedom and the emphasis on values are some of the leaders of the All India Association for Christian Higher Education, which represents some 2,000 Christian colleges. Under the umbrella of this organization, Christian professors are beginning to develop new courses, new syllabi and new collections of case studies for discussions of ethics. All of these developments are new in several senses. In most places such efforts simply did not exist previously. Elsewhere, they represent a major step beyond the required religion courses which were mostly catechism, only slightly removed from compulsory chapel.

Values education has taken place in India from time immemorial, but often by means of those informal structures of learning by which everyone everywhere is nurtured into specific cultural attitudes about right and wrong, good and evil. And to be sure, in the deep background of these structures were the great scriptures and epics as interpreted by the Brahmins, which have shaped the fabric of the whole culture. More immediately, morality was mediated through the extended family (with all its connections to caste), which remains very powerful in India; sometimes in those temples where pundits gave discourses about the perennial struggles of good and evil; and most frequently by the practical decisions of the panchayat, the intercaste village council of the five leading elders. In recent centuries, law, which is everywhere a bearer of morality, was under the control of the Muslims. Then the British and then the secular government. But none of these structures seems to have effectively generated a moral code for a society in transition.

The new courses are being developed as a kind of unofficial substitute for what is often done by theologians, ethicists and social theorists. In India, theology, ethics and social theory as critical sciences are not widely developed and topics treated by these fields appear in local communities primarily as confessional commentary, caste practice or expressions of communal interests. There are outstanding Indian intellectual leaders in these fields — one thinks of such figures as M. M. Thomas, Russell Chandran, C. T. Kurien, M. N. Srinivas and a dozen or so younger scholars also likely to become known around the world — but in the colleges the concerns for values these names represent scarcely appear.

The new courses and materials are being created mostly by educators in the non-theological sciences — Christian mathematicians, linguists, physicists, biologists and economists who use theologians, ethicists and social theorists as occasional consultants. The class outlines include religion (often based in Bible study), morality (frequently centred in Victorian virtues) and social problems (heavily laced with metaphysical views of Indian cultural history) These topics are being woven into a new mix which includes a dedication to an interfaith sense of the urgent need to reconstruct the spiritual and moral values of the nation.

What was striking to the outside observer in these events was that the inevitable interdisciplinary conversations dealt primarily with the transformations of traditional patterns of life — transformations that seem to some so glacially slow that everything should be done to speed them up and to others so incredibly rapid that people and morality were getting lost in the swirl of change. Of particular concern to many was the shift from a "joint family" structure, with arranged marriages, to a more nuclear family constituted by "love marriages." This shift reflects some increased emancipation of women as well as the transition from a "communal," subsistence-agrarian economy to an increasingly "societal," exchange-urban one. The change has produced enormous anxiety, conflict between the generations and a fear that India will go the way of the West with its high divorce rates, broken families, loss of extended support systems and commercialized libertinism.

Much concern was also expressed about the apparent increase of religious and communal fanaticism in India, as the generation that marched with Gandhi for a tolerant, nonviolent, independent and national spirit fades into history. Several of the teachers of values education believe that only a Christian perspective can renew the foundations of public morality — even in a Hindu context — just as it was the encounter with Christianity that prompted Gandhi (and many of his generation) to revise the dominant understanding of Hinduism. (How Christianity is to relate, as a minority faith, to pluralistic environments is one of the key topics to be taken up at this month's celebration of the 50th anniversary of Tambaram — the meeting in that city near Madras of the International Missionary Council which included the Third World in a way that anticipated the current influence of the "newer churches" in the World Council of Churches.)

The educators are also alert to the continuing problems of poverty, although Indian college students frequently have to be taught to perceive directly what is simply part of the peripheral background of their daily lives. Depending on which figures one adopts, some 40 per cent of the population is below the poverty line (defined here as the inability to get access to 2,200 calories per day). Once the facts are acknowledged, teachers say, the appropriate value responses must still be discussed. Many students see the poverty of some as the natural structure of existence — as the result of inevitable *karma* or as *kismat*. Of course, these ideas are challenged by Christians and Marxists, but neither has yet successfully challenged the *facts* of mass poverty.

As is the case elsewhere around the world, Marxist parties and institutes try to offer an alternative to fatalism, but party leaders appear to be little interested in serious social change. For the most part, the Marxist parties seem to reflect the effort by competing communal groups to form majorities that can keep Hindu and Muslim militancy at bay while taking some modest strides toward a welfare state. Christians are frequently involved in these efforts. Among some academics also, Marxism has provided the common terms of discourse. It supplies not only the slogans of student organizations but also the vocabulary for much analysis of the political-economic situation, especially in Christian circles. However, very few policies in Christian institutions or in public life are actually decided on these bases, in part because class analysis simply does not and cannot take account of the cultural factors that shape much of what is decided.

Teachers say that college students are bored by the analysis of political-economic problems anyway. They want to get jobs with transnational corporations in a big city or, preferably, abroad and join the middle class. They are the "new class" in Indian society. They want to be independent of traditional values, they are suspicious of Marxist parties (even if they vote for them) and of too much piety in church (even if they attend services) Yet they experience a crisis of moral drift. They would like to be inspired, but traditional forms of inspiration simply don't work in the economic, political and social world they are being trained to enter.

What shall guide their lives? Teachers say that many non-Christians think a Christian education better prepares them for the world of urban life, international economics, love marriages and democratic political life than the available alternatives, even if they do not want to convert. (Depending on the college, 60 to 80 per cent of the student bodies and 40 to 60 per cent of the faculties are non-Christian.) "Values education" thus becomes a way of presenting a Christian ethical universalism in non-dogmatic terms. The most important points, it is often said, might also be found in Muslim and Hindu thought even if they are not accented by the traditional representatives of these religions.

The Christian teachers who are taking up these problems read and use the Bible without a sense of the hermeneutical crisis which has preoccupied academics in the West. They then link their interpretations to the sciences they teach, to the culture in which they live, to the expressed needs of their students and (often preconsciously) to the metaphysical questions that the religious traditions of India have posed for centuries. The results echo faintly the stances taken by Puritans, Pietists and Wesleyans, who, in their own ways, were also in controversy with feudal societies and mystical speculations and were simultaneously open to the dialogue between religion and science in an attempt to shape a new future. It would not be surprising if a new "Indian Social Gospel" were to come from these developments. Already slated to be established this year in Tambaran is an institute for research on Christianity and contemporary thought for educating and training leaders in Indian church and society.

No one knows where all this will lead. Only a few examples of the attempt to link values with the arts and sciences have been published. But already evident is a sense of social conscience linked to economic development; a theology of vocation that replaces the ascriptive caste definitions of occupation; a theistically based universalism conducive to science and human rights; and a modernizing, cosmopolitan outlook in a land where the sacredness of the cow signals both the power of tradition and a preference for the agrarian life.

These developments raise a substantive question about the role of the middle classes, a question with implications beyond India. Here, as in other places of the world, the educational fruits of the 19th-century missionary movement produced an energetic middle class that was new to traditional societies. It did this by challenging the religious authority by which elites legitimated their domination and by introducing new religious possibilities that could legitimate new behaviours by those under domination.

Today, modern scholarship is translating and writing commentaries on the great texts of the world's religions at an unparalleled pace. The views of world history's greats are at hand. At the same time, the world church has become alert to the poor and the oppressed who have no voice and many are being given one as we properly offer our prayers, our resources and our time to aid the dispossessed.

How are we to deal with the new and rising middle classes of the Third World, represented by these Indian teachers and college students? They are at the cutting edge of modernization in their culture. What shall Christianity around the world say to those who are neither part of the elite nor in poverty but on the way to new kinds of leadership?

Part of the answer to this question will depend on what role we think the educated middle classes will play in the church and in the future of civilizations and what part we think religion plays in shaping social morality. I suspect that religion deeply shapes social morality and that Christianity implies both a social duty to care for the poor and the oppressed and an intellectual duty to understand the great philosophies of the elites that have shaped cultures for centuries. But the more difficult and ultimately more fateful question is whether Christians can define and refine those basic ethical principles that can support, sustain and guide tomorrow's middle classes (which we want the poor to rise into and the elites to heed).

It may be as much of a sociological law of history as we can presently establish that it is the middle classes who determine the destiny of modern civilizations. When they are strong, democracy, human rights and economic productivity tend to prevail. When they are not strong, the result is the polarization of the rich and poor and a fluctuation between the tyrannies of the right and those of the left.

In their own unassuming ways, simply by trying to be good teachers for their students, Christian teachers in the Christian colleges of India are taking up questions that are the most crucial for Asia's future. They are embarking on a historical experiment — which will surely last more than a lifetime — that tests this question: Does Christianity provide universal values that can be transposed into a new idiom for a new class and thereby influence the reconstruction of a great Asian civilization? Or does Asian change have to pass through the

Maoism of China, the "killing fields" of Indo-China, the tyrannies of a Pakistan or a Korea, or the robotics of Japan? On these matters, the still quite modest efforts in the Indian colleges just might be worth following.

Abbreviations

- A.L.B. — Bachelor of Liberal Arts
- B.A.S. — Bachelor of Architectural Studies
- B.A.A. — Bachelor of Applied Arts
- B.A.A.S — Bachelor of Applied Arts and Sciences
- B.A.Sc. — Bachelor of Applied Science
- B.AgrSc — Bachelor of Agricultural Science
- B.App.Sc. — Bachelor of Applied Science
- B.As. — Bachelor of Asian Studies
- B.A.Econ. — Bachelor of Economics
- B.Arch. — Bachelor of Architecture
- B.B.A. — Bachelor of Business Administration
- B.B.NSc. — Bachelor of Behavioural Neuroscience
- B.Bus — Bachelor of Business
- B.C.A. — Bachelor of Commerce and Administration
- B.Ch. — Bachelor of Surgery (also the name of a postgraduate degree in some universities)
- B.Comm. or B.Com. — Bachelor of Commerce
- B.Comp. — Bachelor of Computing
- B.Comp. Sc. or B.CS. — Bachelor of Computer Science
- B.C.M.— Bachelor of Computer and Mathematical Sciences
- B.D. — Bachelor of Divinity (also the name of a postgraduate degree in some universities)
- B.Des. — Bachelor of Design (Visual design discipline)
- B.Ec. — Bachelor of Economics
- B.Ed. — Bachelor of Education
- B.E.S. — Bachelor of Environmental Studies
- B.Eng. or B.E. — Bachelor of Engineering

- B.F.A. — Bachelor of Fine Arts
- B.G.S. — Bachelor of General Studies
- B.H.Sc — Bachelor of Health Sciences
- B.Inf. Tech. — Bachelor of Information Technology
- B.Inf. Sci. — Bachelor of Information Science
- B.Int. St. — Bachelor of International Studies
- B.J. — Bachelor of Journalism (see the University of Missouri-Columbia)
- B.Lang. — Bachelor of Languages
- B.M. or M.B. — Bachelor of Medicine (also the name of a postgraduate degree in some universities)
- BMASc. — Bachelor of Military Arts and Sciences (used at Royal Military College of Canada)
- BMS. — Bachelor of Maritime Studies
- B.Math. — Bachelor of Mathematics (also the name of a postgraduate degree in some universities)
- B.Mus. or Mus.B. — Bachelor of Music (also the name of a postgraduate degree in some universities)
- B.M.M.S — Bachelor of Multimedia Studies
- B.Ost — Bachelor of Osteopathy
- B.Optom — Bachelor of Optometry
- B.P.A.P.M. (Hons); Bachelor of Public Affairs and Policy Management (used at Carleton University)
- B.P.Ed. or B.P.E. — Bachelor of Physical Education
- B.Pharm. — Bachelor of Pharmacy
- B.Physio. — Bachelor of Physiotherapy (University of Newcastle, Australia)
- B.Psych — Bachelor of Psychology (Commonwealth Usage, Particularly Australia)
- B.P.S. — Bachelor of Professional Studies (University of Mary Washington, Virginia)
- B.R.E. — Bachelor of Religious Education
- B.S. — Bachelor of Surgery (Commonwealth usage, usually as part of a MB BS)
- B.S.E. — Bachelor of Science in Engineering

- B.SE. — Bachelor of Software Engineering (used at McGill University and the University of Waterloo)
- B.Soc.Sc. — Bachelor of Social Sciences (used at the University of Ottawa)
- B.S.B. — Bachelor of Science in Business
- B.S.E.E. — Bachelor of Science in Electrical Engineering
- B.S.F. — Bachelor of Science in Forestry
- B.S.F.S. — Bachelor of Science in Foreign Service (used by the Edmund A. Walsh School of Foreign Service at Georgetown University)
- B.S.S.E. — Bachelor of Science in Science Education
- B.S.W. — Bachelor of Social Work
- B.Tech. — Bachelor of Technology
- B.Theol — Bachelor of Theology
- B.Tour. — Bachelor of Tourism.

3

Role of Education in National Integration

MEANING AND NATURE

As a concept, national integration means the basic oneness of the country. It is the sense of identity and solidarity among all citizens of the nation. Emotional integration is an important and major component of national integration.

Both may even be treated to be identical in so far as the educational process is concerned. Some idea of emotional integration can be obtained from a speech delivered by Pandit Jawaharlal Nehru in October 1955, at Bangalore. The relevant extract, which is stimulating to read, taken out from that speech is quoted below: "We should not become parochial, narrow-minded, provincial, communal and caste-minded, because we have a great mission to perform. Let us, the citizens of the Republic of India, stand up straight, with straight backs and look up at the skies, keeping our feet firmly planted on the ground, and bring about this synthesis, this integration of the Indian people. Political integration has already taken place to some extent: but what I am after is something much deeper than that—an emotional integration of the Indian people so that we might be welded into one, and made into one strong national unit, maintaining at the same time all our wonderful diversity."

It must be stated that integration in a social group is not synonymous with rigid uniformity or total absence of variety. It does not mean a patchwork of similar traits. It does not imply a dull, colourless sameness in all respects. Unity is not uniformity. No one need be required to give up his faith in the religion of his father, his love for the language which his mother taught him, or his pride in the lives and achievements of the great men and women who lived and worked in the part of India he himself lives in. Such faith, love and pride is legitimate and understandable. Such loyalties do not detract from loyalty to the nation; rather they may add depth to it and, in turn, derive meaning and significance from that overall loyalty, which is the nation's due.

National integration is not a negative concept. While allowing for differences in language, race, religion, etc., it is opposed to social disruption and chaos. It implies respect to all creeds, faiths and ways of life and does not conceive of any one of them to thrive at the cost of the other. Thus the concept of integration, like the concept of secularism, is positive. It does not permit prejudices to grow. It fights them as a healthy organism would fight diseases.

We are an independent nation, but it is well-known that nationhood is not merely a product of geography or politics. To be strong, the nation must have a solid basis in the mind of each of its citizens. In a democracy, the members of the society must be citizens; and citizenship is possible only when the individual feels completely integrated with the whole, of which he is a part. The State must not be an amorphous mass but an organic entity.

DISRUPTION ELEMENTS

The Indian people constitute a multiracial, multi-religious and multilingual nation. We have made considerable progress in several directions, since the independence of the country, but we have yet to go a long way. These and other facts give rise to certain disruptive forces which might include the following:

(i) Misdirected religious, linguistic or regional loyalties;

(ii) Imbalance in economic development in different parts of the country;

(iii) Gap in the socio-economic development among different strata of the society;

(iv) Absence of a fully accepted and operative *lingua franca* in the country;

(v) Indiscriminate imitation of the western manners, behaviour and mode of living.

It should not, however, be imagined that national integration is non-existent in India or that Indian society is in a state of complete disintegration. It is true that attention was first directed to the subject when there had been outbreaks of violence, communal frenzy, and linguistic madness in certain parts of the country. But these episodes, tragic as they were, did not prove that the country as a whole was not functioning as an integrated nation. They only emphasised the need for bringing about a greater degree of integration than already existed, and for ironing out such factors in our national life as might, in certain circumstances, exacerbate feelings among sections of the population, create misunderstandings, and thus prevent the country from trying to meet the gigantic challenges facing it. Such factors are not unique to Indian society. They are present in one form or another in most other large agglomerations of human-beings composed of individuals belonging to different religions, nationalities, races and linguistic groups.

Combining Factors

In spite of the forces of disruption, there are a large number of factors which unify us into the Indian nation. Some of these factors may be mentioned:

(i) Our history, culture and emerging value-system;

(ii) The economic development;

(iii) The growth of industries;

(iv) Spread of education and enlightenment;

(v) Impact of science and technology;

(vi) Increasing mobility of the people;

(vii) Effort towards removal of social and regional inequalities;

(viii) All India approach to planning and development.

Nationhood has a strong psychological basis. If political, social and other events convey different meanings to different groups, they may continue to be a source of dissension and disintegration, unless the people are helped to see them in their proper perspective and made to realise that they are warnings from the past rather than guides to thought and action in the present. The most sensible of human-beings are apt to be carried away momentarily by uncontrolled emotions and liable to commit acts which can only lead to a lifetime of remorse. It is necessary to sublimate such passions and canalise the energy they carry in directions likely to be serviceable to the body politic.

There is ample evidence for the fact that national integration in our country is not so acute a problem as is sometimes made out. We may recollect how we behaved during our struggle for freedom, at the time of the Chinese attack on India in 1962, the clash with Pakistan in 1965, and the Indian involvement in the Bangladesh war of independence in 1971. During these incidents, the country witnessed, though temporarily, a high degree of national unity. The presence of an enemy makes people rise above petty considerations. It makes them search for their oneness. But it does not afford a positive and lasting basis for integration.

It should be mentioned that creation or support of the unifying factors is not the responsibility of the Central or State Governments alone. It is the individual as well as collective responsibility of all citizens-politicians, educationists, artists, writers, teachers and students, parents, intellectuals, businessmen, trade union leaders and others.

EDUCATIONAL INSTITUTIONS ROLE

As for a positive and stable basis for national integration, the educational system and educational institutions have an important role to play. They can help the nation achieve a sense of identity and solidarity. Since education helps in making an individual autonomous in the sense that he is able to understand various issues, seek information on them without intermediaries and deal with them intelligently, equality of opportunity should be given the highest priority in educational development. A large section of the population, particularly those belonging to the minority and backward groups are still outside the reach of education.

They are unable, for various reasons, to take advantage of the educational opportunities which are already available.

Consequently, many of these sections remain outside the mainstream of national life and are unable to participate effectively in national affairs. Universalisation of elementary education coupled with the supportive programme of adult education and emphasizing the development of competencies which enable an individual to function as an intelligent and productive citizen should receive importance. Efforts should, in this connection, be made to remove the impediments which prevent women, scheduled castes and scheduled tribes as well as other economically backward groups from having equal access to the educational opportunities.

With a view to breaking down the distinction which exists between those who work with hands and those who are supposedly expected to use their brains, socially useful productive work must become an essential ingredient of education at all levels. In fact one of the major objectives of Basic Education was to promote, through participation in productive activities on a cooperative basis, an understanding among various groups and build a social climate where dignity of labour was charished and not despised.

The curriculum of educational institutions should emphasise the cultural heritage of the country which is characterised by unity in diversity and to which various communities and religions have significantly contributed. The teaching of history, geography and other social sciences assume particular importance in this regard. While the study of differences and divergence in approaches need not be suppressed, it is desirable to deal with them in a broader social and political context which characterised particular periods of the development. The National Council of Educational Research and Training has brought out illustrative guidelines for the teaching of a few subjects.

It should be mentioned in this connection that instead of promoting acquisition of information, education should aim at developing the capacity to think critically. From this point of view, the methods of teaching assume significance.

While it is necessary to develop curricula which meet the specific social and economic needs of certain communities, it is important that a broad uniformity exists in education which is provided in different parts of the country. The adoption of the 10+2+3 pattern of education is thus one of the important measures for bringing about uniformity in the educational pattern and standards.

The "Curriculum for the Ten-Year School: A Framework," which the National Council of Educational Research and Training developed, had emphasised national integration as one of the major objectives to be achieved through education. The Framework stated: "National integration could be achieved only through a proper understanding and appreciation of different sub-cultures of India and the common bonds that hold them together. Discrimination of any kind based on sex, caste, religion, language or region is to be looked at with aversion because it is irrational, unnatural, and harmful to the growth of modern India. All subjects should be taught in such a manner as to foster the spirit of scientific humanism."

It must, however, be stated that the educational institutions are places of learning whose work conforms to the needs of the society. The scope of their work and their role have unfortunately not been spelt out in very clear terms. They are evolving gradually. Two of the functions of the educational institutions are to keep the society in proper shape for change and to equip the individual with useful skills and knowledge.

The first seeks to acquaint the pupils with national traditions and to make them look ahead in order to enrich them. This may be a by-product of good education, but it is advantageous to make a conscious effort in this direction, particularly at the school stage. A reference in this regard may be made to recommendations of the Gajendragadkar Sub-Committee (1968) of the National Integration Council. The sub-committee observed:

"Education from the primary to post-graduate stage should be reoriented, to: (a) serve the purpose of creating a sense of Indianness, unity and solidarity, (b) inculcate faith in the postulates of democracy, and (c) help the nation to create a modern society out of the present traditional one."

It is the children in school today who will be the citizens of tomorrow. It is from among them that we will get the leaders of the future. It is the universities and other institutions which will produce our top engineers, doctors, lawyers, administrators and others who will occupy positions of authority in the country. With the education which they get, they can bring about changes in the society. An educational institution has, therefore, to accept its share of responsibility in promoting national integration. In its turn, the leaders in the society should acknowledge their responsibility to support the efforts in this direction made by the educational institutions and its teachers.

The same thing can be said differently. We all know that there are forces in and around an educational institution which may not be conducive to the development of the ideals of national identity and solidarity. Somebody may even argue that the forces of disintegration outside the educational institutions operate so actively that the effectiveness of the work of the teacher is likely to be negated by external forces. There may be weight in this argument, but this should not lead to despair. To fight against such disruptive forces, the teacher should have courage and hope and, most important of all, should practise in and outside the classroom a behaviour which helps integration.

TEACHERS' ROLE

Teachers all over the world have helped in social reform. They have to inculcate in the young minds in their care a set of values and attitudes which are essential for the growth of a nation from traditional to modern. In order to provide education for national integration, the teacher should bring home to his pupils, whenever the occasion arises, the basic oneness of the country.

It is not suggested that for this purpose he should resort to deliberate falsehood or distortion of facts as, for example, in teaching history, languages, social studies, humanities in general or the Indian contribution to science and technology. What the teacher needs to emphasise is truth and objectivity. He should give correct information and interpret facts, wherever necessary, keeping the objectives of national integration in view. In other words, the emphasis should always be on the desirability of functioning and acting as a single and united country.

It is important to mention that every teacher should have the following specific understandings while teaching any subject whatever:

(i) The Indian nation is composed of people who follow different religions, speak different languages and have different ways of living. In spite of all these differences, they are citizens of the same country and enjoy equal rights. Hence, all that unites us needs to be emphasised and all that divides us ignored.

(ii) The Indian society is on the march towards transforming itself into a democratic, secular and modern nation without sacrificing what is still valuable from the past. This is to be achieved through the building up of a developed and self-generating economy, by routing out poverty and ignorance and by bringing about a just social order. This tremendous task can be accomplished only through the united effort of all the people.

(iii) The people of India are sovereign and masters of their destiny. Their heritage is common, and their problems are common. The latter can be solved only by developing among the people an attitude of love and respect for each other. The development of any part of the country should therefore be, considered as the development of the whole country. A part of the nation cannot develop in isolation of or in conflict with the rest of the country. We all live if the nation survives.

It must be added that national integration like moral education is not a subject on which specific lectures can be delivered to the pupils. The teacher need not have to devote separate teaching periods to clarify the concept of national integration. While teaching any subject, he has to present the facts, as they emerge, in such a manner that parochial attitudes are not bred, that growth of hostility is avoided and that the advantage of functioning as a mature nation becomes self-evident.

A guarantee to the inculcation of national integration among the students can be secured through the teachers themselves practising the same values sincerely and demonstratively. This is however, difficult because the teachers also come out of the prevalent social order and even then they are required to ensure that their pupils are not allowed to fall victim to narrow prejudices. This makes the situation very challenging for them. It, in turn, throws considerable responsibility on the teacher-training institutions and the managements of private and denominational educational institutions.

What has been said for the teachers of any educational institution should apply with greater force to the teachers of teachers. In fact, there is justification for incorporating education for national integration as an element in the syllabus of all the teacher-training institutions in our country. What is proposed to he said now for the adults in general should apply with special emphasis on the managements of private and denominational schools, colleges and other educational institutions.

PARENTS ROLE

Before the child is enrolled in an educational institution, it is completely under the influence of its parents, neighbours, relations and the general community. There are also the most formative and, therefore, receptive years in the life of the child. It is at this stage that the healthiest seeds of national integration should be sown in the mind of the infant child.

The influence of the parents in particular and the adults in general on the younger generation is important otherwise too. For bulk of the time every day and night the growing child lives and develops under the influence of the adults in the community. If a child happens to be under the influence of divisive forces operating in his environments, it makes it rather difficult to inculcate a sense of unity and oneness in his mind while he is in an educational institution. If the parents and others criticise the religions, languages, customs, manners, etc., of others and boost their own, they only contribute to disintegrate the society.

What is being occasionally talked about and has even been observed is that some of our political leaders are also not quite free from coming under similarly undesirable influences. In some cases elections are understood to have been fought on communal religious or even sectarian considerations. Thus in order to achieve a short-lived gain a long-term venom of disintegration is injected in the body politic.

In the context of the multiracial, multi-religious and multi-lingual character of the Indian society, it becomes the bounden duty of every adult not to pull down through words, writing, action or even expression, the religions, languages and other value-systems of any person, whatever. In fact, a more practical approach to the matter would be for each person to appreciate in definite and positive terms the faiths, customs, manners and practices of all persons who belong to religions, languages, etc., other than his own.

I observed in the USA during the fifties a large scale programme of parents' education. The number of couples, in which both the husband and the wife were working for some organisation or individual, was observed to be increasing at a fast rate. In the interest of family happiness, it was considered inescapable to give education to both the parents (and would-be parents) about their responsibilities to look after the young children. A programme of parents' education was accordingly launched.

It included even such elements as how to lift an infant child without dislocating his bones and how to bathe or feed him in a scientific and hygienic manner. The implication was that these needs of the newly born child could be attended to by the mother or the father whosover was present in the house at the particular time.

Although education in the USA, as in India, is a constitutional responsibility of the State governments, the programme of parents' education was financed by the Federal government. Education of parents having become a national necessity, the Federal government offered to find funds to operate the programme.

In India too a similar programme of education for national integration can be launched. Ours will undoubtedly be a more difficult programme to organise and our results may be slower to emerge; because our programme will be directed towards a change of attitude in the concerned individuals unlike the giving of some simple information and training in the case of the programme of parents' education in the USA. We can take up the programme directly as an integral activity under our schemes of adult education or extension education through the colleges and the schools. And what is more important, we can exploit the expanding media of non-formal and informal education.

Role of Text-Books, etc.

When we talk of education for national integration, the role of text-books particularly and other literature generally cannot be ignored. In developing countries like India the books still constitute the most important source of information and of building attitudes. In the case of children specially, the books can create a far-reaching impact in so far as integration or disintegration is concerned.

It is, therefore, necessary that every effort is made to ensure that the text-books do not contain material which is prejudicial to the promotion of a feeling of oneness among the children. The authors of text-books and other literature are all adults. They have to take extra care in writing on such topics (or in interpreting them) which have a more direct bearing on national integration. In this connection, a scheme of orienting the authors should also be considered.

We are adopting the various regional languages as media of instruction at all stages of education. Educationally, this is a very sound policy. But this will discourage mobility of pupils and teachers, which in turn will weaken integration unless counteracting measures are taken. At the stage of higher education this mobility is important even from the educational point of view. Continued use of English as medium of instruction is no solution. English language is important for us and should be taught well.

But it is incorrect to think that English has been or is an integrating force in India, this has only been imposed on us by a foreign rule as the working language of administration and is, therefore, confined to very few people at the periphery of the nation. Hindi is taking time to serve the all-India purpose. To encourage mobility of teachers, pupils and others from one region to another, universities and other institutions should organise short language courses.

By using language laboratory and other modern techniques of language-teaching, any Indian language can be taught to a literate person within a short time. Under a scheme tried out by the Post-graduate Deccan College, Pune, working knowledge in Hindi could be given to American adults in about 20 days by spending about 5 hours each day. I have personally seen the scheme succeed. Several other methods could also be adopted by our educational institutions and other agencies to bring the various Indian languages and religious and cultural patterns nearer each other. These will go a long way to strengthen national integration.

It will be agreed that the institution of sports and games can also be developed as another powerful medium for education towards national integration. The sportsman's spirit is classical. The fellow-feeling among members of a team and even for the opposite team is well-known.

On the field, a sportsman forgets the race, nationality, regionality, religion, language or any other differentiating characteristic of the players participating in the game. It is notable that even the objective of defeating the opposite team or the individual is not associated with any ill-will whatever. In India, therefore, there is a strong case for giving greater encouragement and support to games and sports at various levels through educational institutions and otherwise. This will be good for both education and national integration. The same is true of co-curricular activities too. They constitute an important channel to develop healthy attitudes among the students by promoting cooperative enterprise based on common goals to be achieved by joint effort. Such activities should include the youth leadership camps, social service projects and national integration camps.

Role of the State

The state or the government also has an important role to play in the area of integration. It can provide for, through an efficient administrative machinery, excellent law-and-order situation and thus keep the disruptive forces and anti-social elements under control. Prompt attention to grievances and representations of the people and their quick and satisfactory disposal by the authorities reduces the mental and emotional tension in the population. Through its machinery of planning and implementation as also through appropriate and timely measures for economic development and social welfare the state can minimise regional imbalances and economic disparities and thus strengthen the unifying factors already referred to in this chapter. The state can also organise studies and surveys to discover the factors leading to tension and disruption and to find possible solutions for the same. It can further make a contribution in the same direction by implementing the relevant recommendations satisfactorily.

It may be mentioned in this connection that a National Integration Council was setup by the Government of India in 1961 under the chairmanship of the Prime Minister. This was a large and high-powered body, and its objective was to find ways and means to combat the evils of communalism, casteism, regionalism, linguism and narrow-mindedness. The council was again revived in 1980. But the follow-up of the council's work seems to have been done more at the political level.

Matters connected with emotional or national integration have been studied in some depth by the National Committee (Dr. Sampurnanand Committee) on Emotional Integration in 1962. Such matters relating to school education were looked into further by a panel on National Integration setup by NCERT (National Council of Educational Research and Training). I had the privilege of administering the National Committee on Emotional Integration on behalf of the Union Ministry of Education and of being a member of the National Integration Panel. It may be relevant to draw attention to some of the more pertinent recommendations made by each of these bodies.

National Committee on Emotional Integration

(i) It is necessary to evolve an effective policy in education, the implementation of which will bring the States and Union Territories closer to each other.

(ii) There should be a common pattern of education in the country, which will minimise confusion and coordinate and maintain standards.

(iii) The Government of India should take necessary steps in consultation with the State governments and other authorities to create a pool of competent and experienced educationists and educational administrators, from which the States and the Centre can draw upon for their additional requirements.

(iv) The use of the Roman script may be permitted in certain areas for an interim period to enable persons to improve their acquaintance with Hindi. Throughout India the international numerals must be used. To reduce the burden of three scripts, Hindi may be learnt in the non-Hindi areas in the regional script. At the high school stage Hindi must be taught in the Devanagari script, keeping in view the constitutional provision.

(v) The two link languages—Hindi and English—should be effectively taught at university level so that conditions of emotional and intellectual isolation are not created.

(vi) Schemes to provide continuation of education should be taken up to cater to those children who for reasons of economic necessity leave school between the ages of 11 and 14.

(vii) It is desirable to have a uniform for school children.

(viii) Children should be taught to sing the national anthem in unison and behave in a disciplined way when it is sung.

(ix) National Days—January 26, August 15 and October 2—should be celebrated by schools, with full participation of the teachers and the community.

(x) Special meetings of the school assembly should be held at the beginning of each term. At these meetings children should take a pledge of loyalty to India. The pledge should be of an all-India character.

(xi) The Government should encourage children to go on excursions outside their States.

(xii) If universities are to play an effective part in providing leadership and fostering the necessary climate for emotional integration, they must maintain uniformly high standards through a Judicious basis of admission, and recruitment of staff on the basis of academic qualifications, character and personality.

(xiii) Provision of proper leisure-time activities for college students is essential and should be expanded to cover the entire university population.

(xiv) University students should increasingly participate in social service programmes and work camps so that they can acquire some training in service to the community.

(xv) The selection of teachers on the basis of caste and community should, on no account, be encouraged and universities must make a determined effort to fight casteism and communalism in all their manifestations.

(xvi) Caste or communal hostels should not be permitted. Where separate hostels have been built for Harijans out of funds set apart for their welfare, a certain percentage should be set apart for non-Harijans.

(xvii) The use of Indian languages as the media of instruction from the lowest to the highest stage of education is a matter of profound importance for national integration.

(xviii) It is necessary to have adequate motivation for adult education programmes which should, therefore, be linked with occupational interest of the people.

(xix) Although it is not possible to provide religious education as a part of the curriculum for schools in a secular State, education will be incomplete if students are not helped to appreciate the spiritual values which the various religions present to the people.

(xx) History and geography text-books, as the subjects demand all-India treatment, should be centrally produced.

(xxi) Text-books especially in languages and the social studies imported from abroad for use in India should be screened. Care should be taken to see that no books are suggested for schools which lead to bias or the creation of stereotypes.

THE PANEL OF NATIONAL INTEGRATION

The work of the panel is continuing. Some of its recommendations mentioned below are, therefore, yet to be given a final shape

(i) Text-books and other educational literature prepared at the national level should be translated in all the regional languages and steps taken to see that these are made readily available in the market.

(ii) It is necessary to develop a scientific temper through the teaching of popular science in our schools. This scientific temper is a creator of values and will go a long way in building common bonds among our diverse people. It is an essential part of secularism.

(iii) NCERT may identify suitable centres of cultural activities such as dance and drama or important Yuvak Kendras in different parts of the country where teachers and students can be sent for training to bring about a better appreciation of our arts and to promote cultural integration.

(iv) Text-books in exact sciences such as mathematics, physics, chemistry and biology prepared by NCERT at the national level should be adopted by all the States to ensure common standards and approaches all over the country.

(v) Text-books in social sciences namely, history, geography, civics and social studies at the secondary school stage prepared at the national level by NCERT should he adopted by all States with minor local variations.

(vi) At the lower level there is need for greater local colour and variations reflecting local and regional situations and social and physical environments and culture. Even in this task the States should seek the assistance of NCERT.

(vii) Adoption and adaptation of text-books needs to be further supplemented by the preparation and wider use of teacher's hand books or manuals accompanying the text-books.

(viii) The NCERT should prepare an annotated bibliography of suitable books already available in the market so that the States might be able to approve of them for purchase by every school library.

(ix) A common syllabus and text-books all over the country in order to achieve common standards also presume common educational qualifications of the teachers.

(x) Teacher education for national integration is yet another very crucial area in which the NCERT could play a leading role.

(xi) Common teacher training programmes throughout the country might be developed from the point of view of national integration.

(xii) Implementation of the three-language formulae is another area where the State governments have yet to do a lot of work more effectively and with greater determination.

(xiii) Schools should be provided with copies of patriotic songs from other Indian languages by using the system of transliteration. Students should be required to sing such songs in chorus.

(xiv) So far as the text-books for minority communities are concerned, the States generally find it difficult to select, prepare or publish suitable books for their children. In such cases, the States should either allow their minority schools to affiliate themselves to the boards of their respective languages in other States or they should undertake to prepare and supply books in all the minority languages under their jurisdiction.

(xv) The states should also take full responsibility of training teachers in the minority languages.

(xvi) More schools on the pattern of Kendriya Vidyalays should be opened. In this case, the finances of the schools might be shared both by the Central and the State governments.

In implementing the above recommendations, which mostly pertain to the area of policy, planning, and financing, the State has a basic role to play. The State may find it difficult to implement everything immediately because of the constraints of financial resources. But that should not deter us—the teachers, parents and other adults—to discharge our own responsibilities in strengthening national integration. Many such responsibilities are independent of the State and do not cost money.

4

State Educational Structure

As stated before, one of the more important purposes of the new pattern of education has been to bring about a broad uniformity in education all over the country. It is not that there is something unique or very special about the 10+2+3 pattern through which alone the desired uniformity can be achieved. Any other pattern, for that matter, if successfully introduced all over the country, can produce the same result. However, the determination, the enthusiasm and the vigour with which the Central government had chosen to introduce this pattern had raised great hopes.

It has therefore been expected that all the States and Union Territories in the country will soon have the same pattern of education. An opinion can nevertheless be held that India is too large and complex a country for introducing a uniform pattern. But based on past experience, particularly after the independence, the public opinion has been growing in favour of a broad uniformity at least insofar as the scheme of school and college classes is concerned. It has been considered desirable by one and all that for national integration, which in itself is a great objective such a uniformity is highly desirable.

Before introduction of the new pattern, various States and Union Territories in India were following different patterns. All of them could broadly be divided in two groups. The first group consisted of States and Union Territories where a period of 15 years or more was required to obtain the first degree in general education, and the second group consisted of those areas where the same degree could be obtained in 14 years. These two groups and the structures under each group were as follows:

The 15-year Group

Andhra Pradesh	(10+2)+3
Assam	(12+1 or 13)+3
Bihar	(11+1 or 12)+3
Gujarat	(11+1)+3
Karnataka	(10+2)+3
Kerala	(10+2)+3
Nagaland	(12+1)+3
Maharashtra (Western Region including Bombay City)	(11+2)+2
Meghalaya	(12+1)+3
Orissa	(11+1)+3
Tamil Nadu	(11+1)+3
Arunachal Pradesh	(12+1 or 13)+3
Goa	(11+2)+2 and (11 + 3) (one school only)
Pondicherry	(11+1)+3

The 14-year Group

Haryana	(10+1 or 11)+3
Himachal Pradesh	(10+1 or 11)+3
Jammu & Kashmir	(10+1 or 11)+3
Madhya Pradesh	(11)+3
Maharashtra (Marathwada and Vidarbha regions)	(10+1 or 11)+3
Manipur	(10+1 or 11)+3
Punjab	(10+1 or 11)+3
Rajasthan	(10+1 or 11)+3
West Bengal	(10+1 or 11)+3
Uttar Pradesh	(10+2)+2
Tripura	(10+1 or 11)+3
Andaman and Nicobar Islands	(11)+3
Chandigarh	(10+1 or 10+3
Delhi	(11)+3

It will be noted that except the State universities of Uttar Pradesh and the University of Bombay, the degree course everywhere else was of 3 years' duration. With the introduction of the new pattern of education in Maharashtra, the University of Bombay also changed over to the 3-year pattern.

In the Central universities of Aligarh and Benaras also, located in Uttar Pradesh, the degree course was of 3 years. It was observed that the pattern of high/higher secondary education varied widely in different States and Union Territories.

Its total duration ranged from 10 to 13 years, and it was divided into recognised educational stages in different ways. Thus, the picture was complicated and confusing in the whole country.

PRESENT STATUS

I tried to find out the latest position (year 1983) in this regard. The steps taken by each State or Territory to switch over to the new pattern of 10+2+3 are summarised in the table at the end of this chapter. The paragraphs which follow here briefly elaborate the same position.

Andhra Pradesh

In Andhra Pradesh, the introduction of 10+2+3 structure was completed by the end of the academic session 1970-71. The government has since been trying to consolidate the various steps in this direction and planning to introduce appropriate vocational courses at the +2 stage.

As an interim measure the higher secondary stage has been permitted to be attached to both the schools and the colleges. But it has, as a matter of policy been decided to have this stage ultimately in separate institutions only which have been named as junior colleges.

A separate Board of Intermediate Education has been setup. This board formulated new courses for the plus two stage and introduced them. The universities of the State were duly involved in this matter, and they in turn also revised and upgraded their courses as is shown in the chart.

CHART

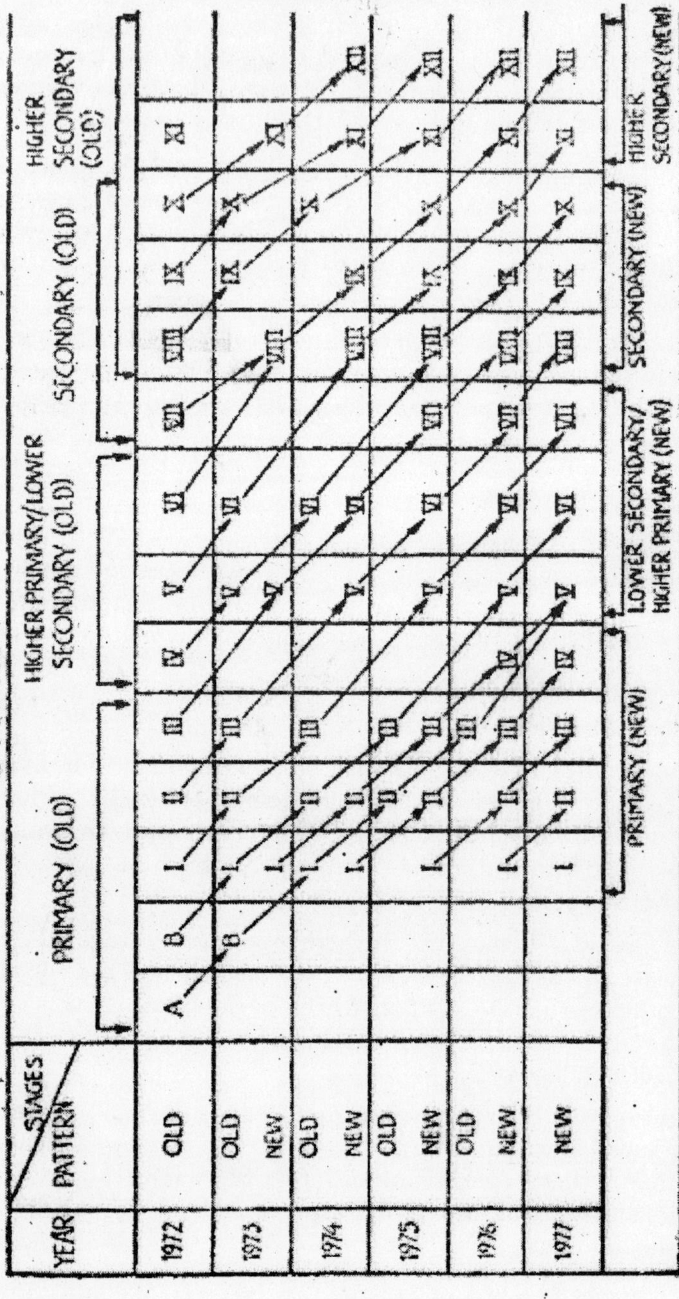
YEAR
STAGES
PATTERN
PRIMARY (OLD)
HIGHER PRIMARY/LOWER SECONDARY (OLD)
SECONDARY (OLD)
HIGHER SECONDARY (OLD)
1972
1973
1974
1975
1976
1977
OLD
NEW
PRIMARY (NEW)
LOWER SECONDARY/ HIGHER PRIMARY (NEW)
SECONDARY (NEW)
HIGHER SECONDARY (NEW)

Assam

The Government of Assam decided in June 1972, to switch over to the new pattern of 10+2+3; and it introduced the same from first January 1973. In order to expedite the changeover from the 16-year pattern to the 15-year pattern, certain school classes were telescoped. In class V, from 1st January 1973, there were two sections in each school. One of these sections consisted of students who were promoted from class IV and the other of those who came direct from class III. For the latter category of students, there was an accelerated programme of instruction which was to be spread over 3 years, so that at the end of class VIII the students who dropped one class would come at par with students of the other category. Similarly, in class VIII, from 1st January 1973, there were two sections in each school. The students passing both classes VI and VII at the end of 1972 were promoted to class VIII. Provision was made for an accelerated programme of instruction for those who came from class VI. Necessary syllabi and text-books to suit the new classes V and VIII were prepared and introduced. Thus the change-over to the 12-year school was to be completed in 1977. A graphic picture of the manner in which some classes have been telescoped to meet the requirements of the new educational structure in the State is given in the chart.

From 1 July 1972, a 2-year P.U.C. was also introduced in Assam. The state government is reported to have taken a policy decision that the 2-year stage, *i.e.* the new classes XI and XII, should be located in schools. But keeping in view some practical difficulties, these classes were in the beginning allowed to continue in higher secondary schools as well as colleges by maintaining the *status quo*. The Assam Board of Secondary Education, to which the higher secondary classes were to be affiliated, had resolved that till it finalised its own syllabi and text-books, the P.U.C. syllabus and text-books as prepared by the two universities (Gauhati and Dibrugarh) would be adopted for the new higher secondary classes XI and XII. The board was to conduct an examination at the end of class XII when the new XI and XII classes were located in the schools. In view of the enlarged responsibilities of the board, a full-time chairman was appointed in place of the D.P.I. who could work as the chairman on part-time basis only.

Bihar

The State government is reported to have introduced the new pattern from the academic session 1979-80. It was however, understood to be in favour of retaining all the 11 classes of its high schools by converting class I into a pre-primary class and renumbering classes II to XI as classes I to X. Introduction of a pre-primary class deserves to be commanded, for it will specially help young children of the backward communities and the first generation learners and it will contribute to raise the standard of education in the State. It is hoped that necessary funds for the purpose have been made available.

Gujarat

The question of the revised pattern was discussed in a joint meeting of the State Advisory Council of Education and the State Advisory Council for Higher Education in June 1972. The consensus in the joint meeting was in favour of acceptance of the 10+2 +3 pattern. The joint meeting recommended the appointment of a committee to work out details of the pattern. Accordingly, the Government of Gujarat appointed in January 1973 a committee under the chairmanship of the State Education Secretary, to study the problem of the 12-years school pattern and make recommendations to the government.

As one of the measures towards the introduction of the 10+2+3 pattern in the State, the Government of Gujarat revised the syllabus for standards 1 to VIII. The latter syllabus was introduced in the academic session beginning in June 1973. The first S.S.C. examination under the 10-year system was held in March 1976. Accordingly, the +2 stage was introduced in the State during the academic session 1976-77 and the first public examination at the end of + 2 stage was given in March 1978. Vocationalisation of the +2 stage is yet to follow.

Haryana

The Government of Haryana had setup a committee to examine introduction of the 10+2 pattern and vocationalisation of higher secondary education in the State. The government then accepted the new pattern in principle and decided to introduce it in the new class IX from the academic session 1978-79. This introduction was, however, done in 1981-82.

Himachal Pradesh

The Government of Himachal Pradesh had also setup a committee under the chairmanship of their Education Minister to go into details involved in the introduction of the new pattern of education in the State. The government then accepted the pattern in principle and decided to introduce it in the new class IX from the academic session 1978-79. This introduction was, however postponed. The +3 stage is already operative there.

Jammu and Kashmir

The Government of Jammu and Kashmir had appointed a committee under the chairmanship of Shri Bhagwan Sahay, the then Governor of the State, for reappraisal of the ongoing educational policies of the State. According to the recommendations of the committee, the primary and middle school education should cover a period of 8 years (classes I to VIII) and the secondary stage of education should be spread over 4 years (classes IX to XII). The committee recommended that the secondary schools should be of 3 types: (a) vocational schools which should have a course of 2 years, (b) general schools which should provide education in classes IX and X, and (c) full-fledged secondary schools having classes IX to XII.

This involved the transfer of P.U.C. from colleges to secondary schools. At the university stage, the committee recommended that there should be an Honours course of three years and a pass course of two years. A number of vocational subjects were also required to be introduced in the pass course to prepare students for different walks of life. This pattern was introduced in class IX of the State in the year 1974-75 and the first public examination at the end of the new class X was taken in the year 1976. The +2 stage in the State has been introduced in selected high schools only. As regards the +3 stage, an Honours course of three years' duration has been introduced in both universities of the State. In order to help in raising the level of instruction at the +2 stage, groups of new higher secondary schools have been attached to the neighbouring degree colleges. The principal and staff of each degree college are required to supervise and help the academic work at the +2 stage of the higher secondary schools attached to their college. This innovation, which deserves to be recommended, can be taken to be an extension of the concept of school complexes to the degree colleges. Consequent to the introduction of the new pattern of education, the State government was understood to have decided in principle that all gazetted posts in the government and every admission to vocational courses like Engineering and Medicine be thrown open to those who completed successfully the +2 stage. It was also provided that in the case of gazetted posts in the government, the selected candidate should be required to undergo a training of three years before appointment. This is another commendable measure and if implemented, it will be in line with the general thinking on the subject, *i.e.* delinking of most of the jobs from the university degree.

Karnataka

The new educational structure of 10+2+3 has been already introduced in the State. The first batch of students joined the 2-year pre-university course in 1971-72 after doing the 10-year S.S.L.C. examination, the curriculum for which had been revised in accordance with the recommendations of the All-India Education Commission (1966). In December 1970, the State government setup a Board of Pre-University Education. The board framed norms for starting new Junior Colleges and decided the staffing pattern, workload, service conditions, pay structure, etc. of the new 2-year P.U.C. It also prescribed courses of study, syllabuses, etc. for these classes.

The new 2-year Pre-University course is being run: (i) in selected higher secondary schools which had the 11th standard corresponding to the one-year P.U.C., (ii) in composite degree colleges which already had the one-year P.U.C., and (iii) in newly established junior colleges which have only 2-year P.U.C. and for which certain norms as given in appendix I have been laid down. The higher secondary schools which were upgraded to have the 2-year P.U.C. were selected after getting them inspected. All the junior colleges which have only P.U.C. classes were in 1972-73 run by private managements. The proportion of the 10-year schools to the institutions having pre-university classes was approximately 4: 1. Whether the 2-year P.U.C. classes are in upgraded higher secondary schools or in degree colleges or in independent junior colleges; the grant-in-aid code, the pattern of fees, and the curriculum etc., are the same everywhere. The State government's ultimate objective is understood to be to take away the P.U.C. classes from the composite colleges and higher secondary schools and form them into separate units, viz. junior colleges. This process of bifurcation was proposed to be initiated from 1973-74 in a phased manner. The pre-professional courses were abolished consequent to the introduction of the 2-year P.U.C. The State universities too took action to upgrade the syllabuses of the degree courses.

The State government has also setup a State Council of Vocational Education in order to give impetus to the recommended vocationalisation of higher secondary education. During 1977-78, 13 institutions in three districts were selected and 21 vocational courses were introduced there. During 1978-79, forty-four institutions throughout the State were proposed to be selected-one in each of the 19 districts, with one more for the city of Bangalore and 24 other institutions in the six districts where the surveys had been completed. So far, vocational courses of only two years duration have been identified so that they can easily fit in with the duration of the +2 stage.

Kerala

The State has already adopted the 10+2+3 pattern. It, in fact, did so before the recommendations of the All India Education Commission were received. The first public examination at the end of the new class X was conducted in the year 1964. There is a pre-degree course of two-year duration followed by a three-year degree course. Everywhere, classes XI and XII have been in the degree colleges only. The first public examination for students completing the +2 stage was conducted at the end of the academic session 1965-66. The University of Kerala has introduced a few vocational courses at the +2 stage. Similar vocationalisation of the new classes XI and XII has been proposed by the other universities too. Efforts are being made to transfer the classes XI and XII from the universities to a separate board.

Madhya Pradesh

The Government of Madhya Pradesh accepted the new pattern of education in principle in the year 1977-78. But the introduction could be done during 1981-82 only.

Maharashtra

The Government of Maharashtra decided around 1970 to adopted the 10+2+3 pattern. Accordingly, the ten-year S.S.C. pattern was introduced in place of the eleven-year school and a new syllabus was commenced in class VIII from June 1972. The first batch of students appeared in the ten-year S.S.C. examination in March 1975. The State government decided that till the restructuring was in process, no new school or college should be started on the traditional pattern.

While the Vidarbha and Marathwada divisions of Maharashtra had 11-year higher secondary schools as well as ten-year high schools followed by P.U.C. and/or three-year degree course, the other division, viz. Western Maharashtra had II-year S.S.C. (High School), followed by 2-year intermediate and two-year degree courses. With the introduction of the new structure, there is a uniform pattern in all the divisions of the State.

The State Board of Secondary Education was reorganised into the Maharashtra State Board of Secondary and Higher Secondary Education and given the charge of the +2 stage too. It was also announced that the degree colleges in the State be allowed to run the higher secondary classes up to the year 1979 only, by which time all the pre-university or pre-degree teachers were expected to be absorbed by the upper classes in the colleges.

The higher secondary classes have, however, continued to be with the degree colleges even today.

Manipur

The Government of Manipur introduced the new pattern in the new class IX from the academic session 1978-79. The first public examination at the end of new class X was accordingly conducted in the year 1980.

Meghalaya

The Government of Meghalaya also has accepted the new pattern and introduced the 10+2 structure in the educational institutions of the State. As a part of the composite State of Assam, Meghalaya has had the same system of education as

Assam. But the degree colleges in Meghalaya are now affiliated to the newly established North Eastern Hill University which has prescribed a three-year course for the first degree in general education. The State government had, therefore, to take decision about introduction of only the 10+2 part of the new pattern.

Nagaland

The Government of Nagaland had also in the past been following the Assam pattern of education. It introduced the new pattern in the new class IX from the academic session 1979-80. According to this schedule, the first public examination at the end of the new class X was to be given in 1981.

Orissa

Till a couple of year back, while bulk of educational institutions in the State were under the 11 + 1 + 3 pattern, there were a few higher secondary schools of 12 years too. With subsequent winding up of the higher secondary system in the State, the operative pattern everywhere became 11 + 1 + 3.

The State universities were considering introduction of a two-year P.U.C. and a two-year degree course. According to this, the State should have had 11 + 2 educational structure. This structure was, however, adopted by the universities of Berhampur and Utkal only.

The third university, namely Sambalpur, followed the 11+1+3 pattern. The State government later accepted the new pattern of education and introduced the same in the new class IX from the academic session 1978-79. The State Board of School Education, which was directed by the government to work oat details of the new structure, completed the assignment in time.

Punjab

After examining the feasibility of introducing the 11+2+3 educational pattern in the State, the Government of Punjab initiated measures to introduce vocational courses in the on-going structure itself. Later however, it accepted the new pattern and decided to introduce the same in the new class IX from the academic session 1978-79. The same was, however, postponed and introduced during 1986-87 only.

Rajasthan

The State government was understood at one stage to have accepted in principle the new educational structure. The thinking was to add class XII to the schools only. The government proposed to close down the pre-university course in the colleges; and in that event the higher secondary stage of 12-years was to he the only channel for going into the universities.

The year from which the 12-year school course was to be introduced was not decided.

The Rajasthan Board of Secondary Education, which formerly used to conduct Higher Secondary Part I examination, abolished it. As a consequence, all high school students and those in class X of the higher secondary schools were to take the Secondary School Examination of the board at the end of class X and until class XII was added, the students were to take the higher secondary examination at the end of class XI.

The Government of Rajasthan then accepted the new pattern and decided to introduce it in the new class IX from the academic session 1978-79. But this introduction was postponed. The +3 stage is already operative in the State.

Sikkim

The Government of Sikkim whose schools are affiliated to the Central Board of Secondary Education accepted the new pattern and introduced it in the year 1975-76 in the new class IX.

The first public examination at the end of the high school stage was accordingly organised in the year 1977 and the first public examination at the end of the +2 stage was conducted in the year 1979.

Tamil Nadu

The task force of the Planning Committee of the State had recommended introduction of the new pattern. After considering the whole matter, the Government of Tamil Nadu accepted the new pattern and introduced the same in the new class IX in the academic session 1976-77. Accordingly, the first public examination at the end of the high school stage was conducted in the year 1978. The State Government has also setup a Board of Higher Secondary Education to plan the +2 stage of education. The Director of School Education is Chairman of the board. At present, the board is a part of the State government machinery but the proposal is to make it an autonomous organisation. The degree colleges have been permitted to retain the +2 stage for five years only. Also during this period, the higher secondary stage is to be affiliated to the Board of Higher Secondary Education only.

Tripura

In the past, all secondary schools of the State were affiliated to the West Bengal Board of Secondary Education and all colleges to the University of Calcutta. The State government accepted the new pattern of education and introduced the same in the new class IX from the academic session 1974-75. The State government also setup its own Board of School Education, which conducted the first public examination at the end of the high school stage in the year 1976. The +2 stage was introduced in selected schools of the State during the academic session 1976-77, and efforts were being made to introduce appropriate vocational courses in selected higher secondary schools.

Uttar Pradesh

The Government of Uttar Pradesh has also accepted the new pattern in principle and decided to introduce the same in class IX from the year 1978-79. The operative structure in the State is already 10+2. In the introduction of the new pattern, however, one year may have to be added to the degree courses in the colleges affiliated to the State universities. In January 1973 a meeting of vice-chancellors of all universities of the State was held. It was agreed in principle to introduce a three-year degree course. The details were being worked out by a committee. Another committee was to review curriculum for the secondary stage and take other preparatory measures including rationalisation of the examinations. In the meantime, the on-going pattern continues to operate.

West Bengal

The Government of West Bengal decided to introduce the new pattern of school education from 1st January 1974, at the beginning of the new academic session in the State. The State Board of Secondary Education had finalised a new syllabus for the new classes IX and X. The first public examination at the end of the new class X was accordingly held in 1976 and the +2 stage commenced in the academic session beginning on January 1, 1977. The State government setup a separate organisation, namely Council for Higher Secondary Education, to which the new higher secondary schools were affiliated and which prescribed syllabus for the +2 stage and was to conduct the examination at the end of that stage. With the help of this body, a few vocational courses have also been introduced at the +2 stage in some selected higher secondary schools. The question about the duration of the first degree course in general education has been under consideration of the State universities as well as the Government of West Bengal. The decision taken in this regard is not known. It is, however, presumed that the universities have agreed to continue with the three-year degree course. It may be mentioned in this connection that the Vishwabharati University located at Shantiniketan in West Bengal continues to follow the three-year degree pattern.

Union Territories

All schools of the Union Territories of Andaman and Nicobar Islands, Arunachal Pradesh, Chandigarh and Delhi are affiliated to the Central Board of Secondary Education. The board had decided that the 10+2 pattern be introduced in its member-schools from the academic session beginning in May 1975. Towards that end, a new syllabus for the new classes IX to XII and a set of text books based on that syllabus were prepared or selected and made available to the member-schools of the board.

The administration of Dadra and Nagar Haveli introduced the new pattern of education in class IX in the year 1974-75. Accordingly, the first public examination at the end of class X was held in the year *1976* and enrolment for the +2 stage commenced in the academic session 1976-77. The administration of Goa, Daman and Diu similarly introduced the new pattern in class IX in the academic session 1973-74. The Union Territory of Lakshadweep, following the Kerala pattern, introduced the new scheme in class IX from the academic session 1974-75.

Progress in Implementation of the New Pattern

STATES

State/U.T. (1)	*Position Regarding Implementation* (2)	*Year of Introduction in Class IX* (3)	*Year in which First Batch took Class X Exam.* (4)	*Year of Introducing +2 Stage Courses* (5)	*Year of Introducing Vocational* (6)
Andhra Pradesh	Implemented	1967-68	1969	1969-70	1975-76
Assam	-do-	1974-75	1976	1976-77	Vocational Surveys were in hand
Bihar	-do-	1979-80	1981	1981-82	1981-82
Gujarat	-do-	1974-75	1976	1976-77	1977
Haryana	Implemented	1981-82	1983	1983-84	1983-84
Himachal Pradesh	Not Implemented the 10+2 part until 1986				
Jammu and Kashmir	Implemented	1974-75	1976	1976-77	1976-77
Karnataka	-do-	1969-70	1971	1971-72	1971-72
Kerala	Implemented	1962-63	1964	1964-65	Kerala University Offers Some Vocational Courses
Madhya Pradesh	Implemented	1981-82	1982-83	1983-84	1983-84
Maharashtra	Implemented	1973-74	1975	1975-76	1978-79
Manipur	-do-	1978-75	1980	1980-81	1980-81
Meghalaya	-do-	-	-	-	-
Nagaland	-do-	1979-80	1981	1981-82	1981-82

Contd.....

Orissa	-do-	1978-79	1980	1980-81	1980-81
Punjab	Implemented from the year 1986				
Rajasthan	Not Implemented the 10+2 part until 1986				
Sikkim	Implemented	1975-76	1977	1977-78	1977-78
Tamil Nadu	-do-	1976-77	1978	1978-79	1978-79
Tripura	Implemented	1974-75	1976	1976-77	Not known
Uttar Pradesh*	Accepted in principle				
West Bengal	Implemented	1974	1976	1976-77	1976

**Already has the 10-year school followed by a 2-year intermediate stage.*

UNION TERRITORIES

(1)	(2)	(3)	(4)	(5)	(6)
Andaman and Nicobar Islands	Implemented	1975-76	1977	1977-78	1977-78
Arunachal Pradesh	-do-	-do-	-do-	-do-	-do-
Chandigarh*	-do-	1976-77	1978	1978-79	1978-79
Dadra and Nagar Haveli	-do-	1974-75	1976	1976-77	-
Delhi	-do-	1975-76	1977	1977-78	1977-78
Goa, Daman and Diu	-do-	1973-74	1975	1975-76	-do-
Lakshadweep	-do-	1974-75	1976	1976-77	
Mizoram	Implemented from the 1982 academic session				
Pondicherry	Implemented	Followed schedule of the neighbouring State**			

**Introduction of the +2 stage has been deferred till the neighbouring States of Punjab and Haryana switch over to 10+2 pattern.*

**Mahe (Kerala Board)-1964; Yanam (Andhra Pradesh Board)-1969; and Pondicherry and Karaikal (Tamil Nadu Board)-1978.*

The Mizoram administration introduced it from the academic session 1982-83. The administration of Pondicherry (comprising Mahe, Yanam, Pondicherry and Karaikal areas) has already introduced the new pattern following introduction of the same in the neighbouring States of Kerala (for Mahe), Andhra Pradesh (for Yanam) and Tamil Nadu (for Pondicherry and Karaikal). Accordingly, the first high school examination under the new pattern was conducted for the Mahe and Yanam areas of the territory by the Kerala and Andhra Pradesh Boards in the years ***1964*** and 1969 respectively. And a similar examination for the Pondicherry and Karaikal schools was held in the year 1978 by the Tamil Nadu Board.

KENDRIYA VIDYALAYAS AND OTHER SCHOOLS

All the Kendriya Vidyalayas (Central Schools) and Sainik Schools, a large number of public schools, convent schools and other all-India secondary schools which are affiliated to the Central Board of Secondary Education adopted the 10+2 pattern of school education from the academic session commencing in May 1975 when the Central Board introduced that pattern in its member-schools, The Council of Indian School Certificate Examination also decided to adopt the new pattern and it introduced the same in its member-schools. The schools affiliated to these two examining bodies are distributed all over the country. A few schools affiliated to the Central Board are also located outside India and they have been following the new pattern since 1975.

5

ADULT EDUCATION IN INDIA

Under the 'Umbrella approach' of the University Grants Commission it has brought adult education, population education, planning forum, legal literacy, rural development and continuing education under one umbrella. Since 1978 the UGC and the Universities and Colleges have been in the field of adult literacy consequent on the introduction of the National Adult Education Programme (NAEP). The involvement became extensive consequent on the introduction of pt. 16 of the new 20-point economic programme by the Govt. of India. It is envisaged to rope in all the Universities and Colleges in adult education programmes by 1985-86. Post literacy and follow-up programmes have also been launched.

Population education clubs have been organised in many Universities, Colleges and Adult Education Centres. Support to planning forum activities have also been enhanced recently by the UGC. As many as 82 Universities are currently involved in the adult education programmes but only 18 are in the continuing education field. The thrust during the 7th Plan period will be on continuing education through its various facets and hence the UGC planned to organise Regional and University level seminars and workshops on continuing education. SNDT Women's University, Bombay organised a four day seminar cum workshop for the Western Region during June 1985 and Madurai Kamaraj.

University organised one for the southern region from 13-16 July, 1985. A university level 6 day workshop on "Colleges in continuing education" was organised at Trivendrum by the Centre for Adult Education and Extension of the University of Kerala inviting Principals and Programme Officers from 30 colleges affiliated to the University and engaged in adult education and/or population education club activities. The Universities of Kerala has done commendable work in the field of adult literacy work, helping nearly 20,000 adult illiterates to become literate and currently more than 20,000 adult illiterates are attending 780 centres run by the CAEE directly and through 33 colleges.

30 Colleges have started population education club programmes with financial support from the UGC. Hitherto the University had not organised continuing education programmes as such, though the CAEE had organised=short courses in adult and continuing education for B. Ed. trainees, school teachers, research scholars etc., and organised workshops for the preparation of neoliterate literature, teaching aids, action research proposals etc. Seminars on 'educational journalism' and orientation courses for functionaries in adult education are not considered 'continuing education' as such. Hence the workshop was a novel one. It expected to clear the concept of continuing education and enable the participants to plan continuing education programmes based on an awareness created on ongoing programmes in other universities so that at least 10 to 15 colleges could launch programmes during 1985-86 itself. The workshop was organised in the Corporation Council Hall of Trivendrum.

The workshop was inaugurated on the forenoon of 15th July, 1985 by Dr. (Mrs.) Rajammal P. Devadas, Director, Shri Avinashilingom Autonomous Home Science College for Women at a meeting presided over by the Vice Chancellor Shri P.S. Habeeb Mohammed, IAS, Smt. Kamalini Bhansali, Registrar, SNDT Women's University, Bombay (Member, UGC Review team) delivered felicitating address. Dr. K. Sivadasan Pillai, Director, CAEE (Director of the workshop) welcomed the gathering and Dr. N.D. Joshi (Project Officer) proposed a vote of Thanks. It was felt that adult education, to be more meaningful, should be followed by continuing education, if not preceded by it, at least in certain contexts.

The topics dealt with included 'meaning and scope of continuing education', 'involvement of universities and colleges in continuing education', 'roles of students and teachers in continuing education', 'strategies and approaches in continuing education', 'psychological factors affecting adult learning', 'patterns of adult learning', 'mass media in continuing education', 'monitoring and evaluation in continuing education' etc. The continuing education programmes organised by the German Adult Education Association in West Germany, by the Extra Mural Studies Departments of the Universities in the U.K., and in Indian Universities with special reference to Madras, Pune and SNDT were presented and discussed.

The programmes launched by Saurashtra and Delhi Universities were also discussed for identifying programmes suitable for Kerala based on the needs of the community and available recourses as well as future possibilities. Slide shows, transparencies and video shows formed part of the workshop. Group and individual sessions aimed at practical work were found more fruitful and attractive. Resource persons from outside the University included Dr. R. Jayagopal (Madras) Dr. Phadke (Pune) Mr. Bernd Pflug (DVV, West Germany) Dr. (Mrs.) Rajammal P. Devadas (Coimbatore) and Smt. Kamalini Bhansali (SNDT, Bombay). The keynote paper submitted by Dr. M.L. Mehta Joint Secretary (Adult Education) UGC, provoked much thought and action.

The participants identified continuing education programmes suited to various localities and colleges keeping in mind the felt needs of the people as revealed through surveys already conducted as part of adult education, and the resources available (men and material) and also avoiding duplication of course in any area, to the extent possible. Individual needs, community needs and the needs and aspirations of the college were integrated in choosing programmes. Thereafter the participants took up the preparations of proposals highlighting the background and significance, nature of the course, possible intake, durations, venue, fees to be charged, if any, course content, resources, financial estimates, possible impact etc.

The courses chosen ranged from scooter repairing, radio mechanism, computer training, typing, coaching classes for competitive examinations, interview techniques, personality development, soil testing, cottage industries, language courses (Arabic, Russian, Hindi etc.) Book binding, film appreciation,

Textile designs, health and hygiene, mother and child care, human relations, banking, tourism, self employment etc. The UGC has a scheme to support upto 5 courses a year for the colleges towards administrative cost, equipment cost and 75% of the programme cost. As a result of the workshop it is hoped that 20 to 25 colleges will launch continuing education programmes during 1985-86 itself.

On the afternoon of 20th July, 1985, Dr. N.A. Karim, ProVice Chancellor delivered the valedictory address and distributed certificates to the participants. Representing the participants Prof. D.A. Stephen (Xian College, Kattakkada) Sr. Joyce D'Mello (St. Joseph's College for Women, Alleppey), Dr. V. Sukumaran Nair (MSM College, Kayamkulam) and Prof. Salahuddin Kunju (University College) spoke on the occasion. Dr. N.D. Joshi presented a report of the workshop and Dr. Sivadasan Pillai evaluated the outcomes of the workshop in the light of the objectives laid down by the organisers and also expressed by the participants in their initial registration forms.

The workshop unanimously accepted certain resolutions for the effective implementation of adult and continuing education programmes with all the wings attached to it. The need for a Faculty of Non-formal Education at the University and a full-time programme officer in the College were highlighted besides suggesting incentives for the functionaries and participants alike. It was felt that 'Continuing Education' alone can make education really 'lifelong', 'realistic' and 'meaningful' 'Learning to be' is what is acquired through a process of continuing education. The workshop not only corrected misconceptions but also gave practical experience and thus created self confidence among the participants.

GROWTH AND DEVELOPMENT

Even after 39 years of independence, nearly 65% of Indians are illiterate and more than 50% are below the poverty line. Why this is so? It is due to defective planning? Discrepancies in the implementation process? Or is it due to the non-cooperation of people? There are difference of opinion. But all these are there. After independence, we have advanced considerably in many fields including education, agriculture, industries, transportation, communication etc. But how far these have been for the poor people? We pleaded for 'Sarvodaya'. But now many have been brought under such programmes? How many have benefited from these? Were there middle men who exploited the poor people? Answer to such questions are all revealing. All these point to the urgent need for conscialtisation among the public. Only then will people participate willingly in the nation building activities.

When we achieved independence only less than 15% of Indians are literate. As per 1981 census, literacy percentage rose to 36.17. May be now it is around 40 or so. Still we have more than 50% of world illiterate population in India. The NAEP, 20 point programme etc., launched massive time-bound programme but could not achieve excepted results. Though it was stipulated in article 45 of the Indian constitution, even in 1986, many children at school going age are outside the school and many dropped out even before completing primary stage.

To improve this situation, point 16 of the new 20 point programme envisaged a three point approach *viz.* ensure hundred per cent enrolment at the primary stage completely avoid dropping out from primary stage and providing non-formal education for the age group 15. In the new education policy formulated in 1986, item 10 provides for expansion of education both formal and non-formal.

There is emphasis on alternative strategies and multiple approaches in the field of education. Village level committee on education also has been formulated in the NEP. The Jan Shikshan Nilayas are supposed to be continuing education centres catering to people of all ages, of all occupations, of all beliefs etc. The strategies laid down in the action plan of NEP, through the different task forces setup for specific purpose is hoped to offer better educational facilities and more and more opportunities for the continuing education of the pupils, who are interested in it.

Adult Education has somehow been equated with Adult literacy in the Indian context. In developed countries, it is really the education of the Adult, irrespective of whether it is for the illiterates, semi-literates, literates, and the educated. Education has since been accepted as a life long process and one has to learn many things, even if he is highly educated, to cope with the demands of the times. So appropriate courses have to be developed to suit the different types of clientele and launched with necessary care and vision.

At the Centre and in each state there are many departments and agencies providing for the development and the welfare of the people. Now the term 'Antyodaya' has come to stay. Even the most backward and the poorest man/family in an areas has to be brought to a considerable level through appropriate steps. However appealing a programme be, if introduced and implemented in isolation, the anticipated results will not be achieved. Hence integration and coordination of developmental activities are essential. This is what is lacking at present and has to be over come. All agencies/Departments interested in the welfare of the people have to put in their efforts in a coordinated way for ensuring maximum effectiveness.

A cadre of extension workers has been suggested for every locality. This could be the village extension worker of the development department, health workers of the health services department volunteers and promoters of National Savings Scheme and Family Welfare Scheme, National Service Scheme volunteers and the NCC Cadets from the colleges and Universities etc. However now-a-days there is a feeling that the adult education functionaries/Supervisors and Instructors of the University sector/Government departments/voluntary Agencies who are working with the community helping them to overcome the hitherto annoying circumstances, be dovetailed for the cause of overall developmental activities. As full time workers are needed for each community to coordinate and oversee allied programmes, the question has to be seen in the right perspective.

Planning commission at the national level, state planning boards, district development committee and block level development committees are in vogue. These are mainly responsible for planning developmental activities for a specified area and period of time. Then these are to be implemented with dedication by a team of workers—paid and voluntary—on priority basis. Certain lacuna exists in the implementation of such programmes. Block level coordination efforts are to be streamlined and implemented with the support and cooperation of all implied agencies. Voluntary agencies have a major role to play. In the field of adult education there are a good number of voluntary agencies. These may be given representation in the BDC's/DDC's etc. and entrusted with the implementation of developmental programmes in a particular area. Effective monitoring supervision and follow up activities are also to be built in.

In most of the extension blocks/community development blocks, functional literacy programmes have been launched. All such blocks have to be covered for the purpose of linking adult education with development. In Kerala we have an organisation, KANFED, which is the sole agency in the state for linking non-formal education with development. As such various measures have been taken and programmes launched with the sole aim of improving the lot of the poor people. Panchayat level units are in existence looking after developmental needs of the locality. People are coming forward to donate land and buildings for establishing regular development network in the respective areas. These, when consolidated will become a great force as the library movement in Kerala or the Kerala Shastra Sahitya Parishad, aimed at popularising science among the masses. Developmental activities should not be mere governmental/departmental activity but should secure people participation.

Adult educators should ensure the necessary linkage between the world of alphabets, through making every one literate and the world of development. They may create proper atmosphere and ensure effective field work. This is how nation's prosperity can be ensured. The adult educators have to pledge for this, realising that it is part of their duty. Development is a process of attaining certain targets which are essential for the well-being of the community and thus prosperity. Let adult educators come to the forefront in discharging this duty.

Role of Adult Education in the Promotion of Science and Technology

The progress of any country depends on the advancement of Science & Technology. Science is a way of life; it is an outlook; it is search for truth; it is the enquiry for new practices and innovations; it is establishing validity of day-to-day life situations through cause and effect relationship or through statistical information. Scientific outlook is needed in the modern world. This is true of the child as well as of the masses. Scientific temper has to be developed among all citizens; this should start from the primary schools. Technological advances establish modern view points and make life more precise and fruitful.

Ideas and ideals can be spread through oral culture and written culture. Oral culture in prevalent even among the illiterate and the most backward sections of the society. Traditional behaviour cannot be changed all on a sudden. It requires proper motivation. It requires the acceptance or atleast the concurrence of all concerned. Knowledge and practices are transmitted to the generations through the family and peer groups. That is why traditional occupations remain the monopoly of a few. But when scientific advances take place, new approaches are evolved.

These are taught in educational institutions such as Engineering College, Polytechnics, Industrial Training Institutes, Industrial Training Centres and Institutes of Technology. This leads to more of practical work, experimentation and verification of hypotheses. Here oral culture is not enough. Education comes in as a formal process. Non-formal approaches cannot be ruled out. This is an ongoing process in workshops all over the community, though at different levels. Written culture becomes inevitable at this junction, to support practical know-how.

In our country, even after 39 years of independence, nearly 65% of in population remain illiterates. It is rampant in North Indian States like Bihar, Rajasthan, Uttar Pradesh, Madhya Pradesh etc. which have very low levels of literacy. In some of these states the percentage of literacy among women is even less than 10%. With this lamentable situation of literacy, how can scientific temper be developed among the people. Illiteracy is one of the major stumbling blocks in the promotion of science and Technology.

People resort to various ways of life due to sheer ignorance. Their beliefs and customs are such that they observe them without questioning. The youth who try to question such unscientific acts are often termed as revolutionaries or extremists and victimised also. Even in this era, where most of the diseases could be cured, many die due to ignorance and consequent maltreatment. Even now there are groups of people who just pray for and do not treat the patient. It is believed that certain diseases occur due to the unhappiness or even anger of gods and goddesses. Without caring for environmental sanitation, people use unclean water and become victims of many diseases.

This is where adult educators can do a lot. They can, at the outset, create an awareness among the people on the need for scientific outlook and scientific pursuits. This need not necessarily be left to the health workers. This can be a part of the work of adult educators who are expected to mobilise the essential resources and adopt integrated approaches. They have to realise that all round development of the masses is their ultimate aim and for that education should become a vehicle. Literacy cannot be and need not be given as mere alphabets or words; instead, they should be made meaningful and presented in relation to life.

For popularising science among the masses, concerted efforts are needed. Voluntary groups/organisations are instituted for this. College teachers and students can give leadership and show the way. This can form a part of their curricular work or at least an extension component. School science teachers can also play a major role in creating scientific outlook and temper not only among children but also in the community. Such attempts are in progress in different countries. People's science movements have gained a sound footing in many states. The Kerala Shastra Sahitya Parisad (KSSP) has won ICSSR award for its meritorial work during 1985. The Shastra Kala Jatha has won it great reputation, not only in Kerala but also all over India. It organised an All India Jatha for the spread of scientific literacy through multiple media.

The KSSP is a voluntary organisation of science lovers. Besides college teachers, school teachers and university professors, a band of Doctors, Researchers, Social activists and students have joined the KSSP. Founded in 1957 the KSSP has grown into a very big organisation. It has branches all over the state and units in most of the schools and colleges. Children are inducted to scientific outlook from the primary classes.

'Balashastram' a monthly and 'Eureka' another science journal addressed to primary school children are published regularly for this group. 'Shastrakeralam' is for high school pupils and 'Shastra gati' for college students. All these appear every month and are read by a good number.

Science Quiz Programme has become an approved programme of the Education Department though it began as a voluntary attempt of the KSSP. Similarly science fairs at which young students, present pieces of innovative experiments, have become not only a regular feature but they have really become 'fairs' attracting people from all walks of life. Science clubs are organising a variety of programmes in Educational Institutions. The 'Science cream series' which the KSSP published are so dear to the science students. The standard and vocabulary are different for different groups and as such a 'grading' has been attempted. The KSSP is also organising lecture series even in remote areas of the state for the masses. The most significant among the activities of the KSSP is its 'Shastrakala Jatha', which through its songs, street dramas, demonstration, etc. attract large audience wherever they stop, without prior notice. The KSSP has by now achieved a lot in popularising science especially among the masses.

These activities have to reach the illiterate people also. So more and more folk art forms are to be introduced. Better still would be to help people become literate. The KSSP is trying it indirectly, but they have to take up such programmes also as part of their regular activities. There are two other major agencies in Kerala. (1) KANFED (Kerala Association for Non-formal Education Development) which is trying to link Non-formal education programme with developmental and welfare programmes, all over Kerala and (2) Kerala Grandhasala Sangham, an association of libraries mainly engaged in the spread of reading habits thus providing opportunity or life long education. KSSP, can in collaboration with these two agencies, do better using the resources available with these agencies, avoiding repetition and ensuring necessary cooperation and coordination.

Anyway, it is essential to create scientific awareness among the masses as a precondition to scientific literacy. Popularisation of science will follow and can result in scientific temper. Adult educators should consider it their responsibility to ensure scientific literacy along with basic literacy and functional literacy. At the stage of planning teaching learning materials and training programme scientific component has also to be taken care of.

In the primer, lessons of science, scientific temper and scientific advancements can be incorporated and even in other lessons, scientific approach can be ensured. In a recent WHO workshop held at Madras on 'environmental health and housing in rural and urban development strategies it was felt that a coordinated approach would yield better results than isolated attempts. Health, hygiene, modernisation, population education, legal literacy, science for the masses etc. should form part of a unified whole-a kit, it was suggested by the workshop. It has also been suggested that extension workers are appointed or deputed in each locality to render essential services. Adult educators have been tipped for this job as they are the torch bearers in the darkness. They alone can light candles as proposed by Welthy Fischer and keep the torch burning so that continuing education will result in the creation of a learning society.

The Departments/Centres/Units of Adult Continuing Education & Extension established in nearly 100 Indian Universities can widen their umbrella and incorporate 'science for the masses' as one of the activities and thus inculcate scientific temper among the students and teachers of the Institutions of higher learning. The scientific attitude and temper can be best-created by a group of scientists especially teachers and researchers taking it as part of their duty. Voluntary organisations can continue their work and new ones may be formed wherever found necessary.

The IUACE (Indian University Association for Continuing Education) has accepted 'science for the masses' as one of its new areas of work. At the state level, Departments of Science and Technology have been established. Attempts like biogas, smokeless choola, cheap latrines etc. are being launched by the Department. Voluntary activist groups are also emerging with the support of enthusiastic and scientists and researchers. Institutes for research and development have to be established and their research findings be disseminated to all concerned and used for nation-building programmes.

Adult educators can not escape saying that science is somebody elses realm of activity. It is also within the purview of the adult education. Hitherto this aspect was not fully recognised and utilised. At least in future, more emphasis has to be given to scientific aspects. It is good that at least now we are collectively thinking of promoting science and technology. If there is a will, there is a way. Let us sort out the strategies and plan our course of action. Every adult educator should feel it his duty to inculcate scientific attitude and scientific tamper among the adults whom they come across.

Mass Programme for Functional Literacy (MPFL)

Yet another experiment aimed at eradication of illiteracy, 'started in May 1986 is heading for a collapse if not subjected to intensive care and treatment. It was in such a haste that Institutions of higher learning were asked to launch a mass programme involving NSS and non NSS students, all over India. The State Resource Centres were asked to prepare large number of kits, which they did with great obedience but without vision and necessary skill and expertise. The time target—was taken care of but not the quality of the materials. This is not true of all SRC's but of atleast the majority. Had they been given enough notice and sufficient time, they could have done better work.

May 1st is an auspicious day. It is the May day ! It is a boon for the workers. But what is its sanctity for starting a mass programme involving student community? May and June are the mid summer vacation months. But in how many Universities are we having vacation during May-June? Many are having examinations during these months. There is no vacation so to say. Very few Universities which could start in May also were not adequately motivated to take up the task.

Yet another lacuna is that MPFL is launched along with the 'Centre Based Adult Education Programme (CBAEP). This programme as well as Centres/Departments/Cells for Adult and Continuing Education Programmes are in vogue in 98 Universities, thanks to the untiring efforts of Dr. (Mrs.) Madhuri

R. Shah, Dr. M.L. Mehta, Dr. S.C. Bhatia and others. 1985-90 being the second phase of the University involvement in adult education programme many colleges are actively engaged in this activity. But the centre Based Adult Education Programme will also be affected by the introduction of MPFL through back doors.

Where the Shoe Pinches?

Lack of coordination between the sections *viz.*, Education and Sports & Youth affairs of the Human Resource Development Ministry is hypothesised by many field workers. The MPFL is channelled mainly through the second one though the first one is also instrumental in its implementation. At the University level the UGC is sponsoring CBAEP, without any increase in the number of centres.

It also has requested the Universities to find out non NSS volunteers to involve themselves in the MPFL. While this is done on the one hand, the NSS Coordinator at the University level and the NSS Programme officers at the college level have been directed to enrol as many NSS and non NSS volunteers, train them and implement the programme. Why this two fold approach? The Adult Education Programme officers in the colleges (some of them are NSS Programme Officers as well) are in a dilemma. The literacy kits prepared by the SRC and handed over to the State Adult Education Departments have been dumped in many colleges and they remain uncared for in some corner or the other. The Masters Training Programme envisaged in the MPFL has become a hoax, not to speak of instructor's (volunteers) orientation.

The prospective learners are to be identified by the volunteer himself/herself. Two cards are expected to be filled in and submitted to the DAEO and the College level Programme Officer concerned. But how many such cards have been received during 1986-87? While the Kerala University Centre for Adult Education & Extension could organise 825 Adult Education Centres directly and through 34 affiliated colleges with an enrolment of about 23,000, it could muster only 1400 non-NSS volunteers from 30 colleges for the MPFL helping 1875 adult illiterates. The NSS sector might have enrolled a good number. However the targets are far away. Even among the enrolled, the results are yet to be monitored. Meanwhile the Government of India Ministry of Sports & Youth Affairs has come forward with an appeal to enrol more volunteers and start the programme in May 1987 itself. The tall claim of enrolment of 1.3 lakh volunteers and making a sizeable number literate through MPFL have to be checked with 'real situations' and not with 'statistics' alone which always remain challenged by 'real workers'.

Unless we have the necessary political will and a uniform approach, eradication of illiteracy cannot be achieved. Multiple approaches are necessary but that should not be within one agency and in one institution. Proper incentives have to be worked out and adequate motivation and awareness has to be built up.

Involvement of students in this programme has to be made compulsory and as a prerequisite for receiving Degrees. Voluntarism will not help in this task. Short term centre based or even camp based programmes might deliver better results. A rethinking. is urgently necessary in the planning, implementation, monitoring, evaluation, feedback etc., of the MPFL if real results are anticipated. In the interest of the nation this should be done before launching the 1987 programme, scheduled for May 1987.

People's Education should have Higher Priority

The development of even the most backward and downtrodden sections of the society should be the aim of any democratic country. This is now termed as 'Antyodaya'. This should be the policy of India, if we want to solve the problems of poverty and illiteracy. In India nearly two thirds of the population still could not read, write and comprehend even their mother-tongue. So also, more than half the population in India lie below the poverty line. Our five year plans aimed at improving the lot of the people have yet to attain the targeted goals, fully. There is marked improvement in many sectors, but they are not upto our expectations. Though there is increase in the percentage of literacy in India, there is increase in the number of illiterates as well. This is not only due to population explosion but due to other reasons as well. These are not acting in isolation. Thus the cumulative effect of a number of serious impediments minimise or adversely affect the development of the country and hamper its progress and prosperity. To ensure effective and real development, people should be educated, or at least made literate.

The illiterate who could not read and understand themselves are denied of the opportunities to act according to their likes and dislikes. They have to depend on others for writing letters filling in forms, preparing applications etc., and hence cannot be on a par with the others. Those who have only the spoken word to their credit, are not fully utilising the resources available to them. They have an inferiority feeling of their own and hence lead a discontented life. They are exploited by the others, especially the educated and are hence are anxious of their future. They lose optimism. They are doubtful about all developmental and welfare schemes. They look up to the Government for anything and everything. They are antagonistic to change of all kinds due to ignorance and bitter experiences.

The messages of 'small family norms', 'saving habits', 'values of life' are not accepted by the weaker sections of the society and especially the illiterates. Hence we have to educate the masses to ensure true benefits out of all plan schemes. Adult and continuing education are needed as priority programmes, but it is not so at present. While we spend crores on the formal system of education, we are rather reluctant in spending even 5% of the education budget for adult education. This is a pitiable situation over which people should not merely lament upon, but work out action plans and implement vigorously.

Unlike the advanced or affluent countries in India adult education is not the education of the adults but it denotes adult literacy. This is rather confusing to man westerners. Actually adult education should mean life long the educational opportunities for the adults to increase the horizons of their knowledge and to strengthen the capabilities. Out-of school education or own-time education as we perceive it, has to be offered to all the illiterate, the semi-literate, the literate, the highly educated etc. But we have not yet achieved adult literacy to a satisfactory level.

In India we should concentrate on providing literacy linked with functionality and awareness of all its citizens, with top priority for the productive age range of 15 to 35 and giving due attention and importance to the deprived and downtrodden sections of the society. Mere literacy is not enough continuing education facilities should also be offered to all. Hence them make use of their leisure hours profitably pursuing academic or vocational studies or equipping better in one's own profession. One cannot say that this is only of secondary importance. We have to prevent people from relapsing into illiteracy. The post-literacy stage thus becomes important. The neglect of the stage is non-excusable.

All educated persons should involve themselves directly or indirectly in the nation building process. Those who have interest and aptitude for adult education work can be tapped in for such work. Making some amount of social service/work inevitable for all graduates (before receiving their first degree), I think, will be ideal in the Indian context. The Universities and colleges have been requested to collaborate in solving the problem of illiteracy. But the response is not upto the expectations. It should be made obligatory on every institution of higher learning to make at least 100 persons literate every year. This, if continued for 5 years, will help in solving the problem considerably. The Corporations, Municipalities and Panchayats can do a lot in the area. They can find money out of their development funds or educational provisions. They should understand that without a learning society, all their attempts at developing the locality will be futile.

A meeting of all local self government personnel under the chairmanship of District Collectors be organised and a time-bound programme and action plan for adult education should be evolved. Peoples' representatives should also be effectively involved in the discussions, planning, implementation and evaluation of the outcomes. Voluntary agencies of reputation should be given a place of pride in the implementation of this programme.

It is my firm conviction that only through proper education of the masses, can developmental programmes be implemented fruitfully. It won't be a waste, even if we fix top priority for peoples' education, to be followed by developmental activities. It should also be noted that social change is an inevitable phenomenon for which people have to be equipped. All kinds of social revolution-green, white or total revolution—will bear fruit only through the proper education and orientation of the prospective beneficiaries or participants. The State and Central Government should liberalise grant-in-aid rules so that local self government agencies can utilise other resources for adult education, which is a pre-condition for any development. Adult educators should even unite to pressurise the authorities concerned to do this, in the interest of the community.

THE PROBLEMS

For the successful implementation of the adult education programmes, frequent visits to the centres, constant dialogue with the instructors and effective monitoring and evaluation are needed. A jeep jatha was organised by the Centre for Adult Education and Extension in Karakulam and Anad Panchayats where 60 Adult Education Centres are directly run by the CAEE. The two day jeep jatha not only helped in evincing public awareness and support, but also in identifying the urgent needs of the community and the problems confronting them. Some of these were eye-openers to the team of 15 adult educators comprising of organisers, researchers, project officers, supervisors and social workers.

The jeep jatha which started from the University Students' Centre at 8 a.m., on 12-5-1984 reached Aruviyode Harijan Colony around 9 a.m. where 2 centres are run for men and women respectively. An emerging colony just outside the city limits, appeared remote and far from developed. The team was whole heartedly welcomed by a gathering of about 150 men and women. "Give us drinking water"—that demand came from all those who assembled there. They took us to a nearby well which was completely dry. The well was deep enough but there was no water. We were taken to two neighbouring places which used to be their solace, but that too had gone dry. Water supply has not reached that area yet. So the colony people had to travel at least 200 metres for a bucket of water. The people-are willing to extend manual labour but the walls couldn't be dug deeper due to mud and sand. But the adult illiterates are prompt in attending classes. They are half-starving, yet they are amenable to change. Which is the priority—dringking water or alphabets, they ask. In a feeding centre attached adult education Centre-crowded to see us and talk to us. The attendance in that people is rather good, mainly due to the food supplied to the young-children. Mothers come with children and are taught health and hygiens, saving habits, first aid pollution, democracy etc., which they are eager to hear and learn. Their demand is that the quantum of food be increased so that mothers need not depend on the food supplied to their-children.

Though the target group is mainly of the 15-35 age group men and women of 50+are found in some centres, eager to learn the alphabets. They are more regular than the youth. But the elderly ones are short of sight and are looking forward to the welfare agencies for the supply of glasses. What they ask is whether there is some provision for 'glasses' for the old, in the scheme of adult education. A question yet to be answered.

When we reached a centre in the same Panchayat, we found that classes were run in the open in the shade of a jack tree. The ground is not plain and there is nothing to sit on. The learners squat on the muddy floor. The roller board supplie to the centre was rarely used due to lack of space for affixin the same. Such a pitiable condition was prevalent in the area. A Harijan Colony of recent origin other facilities were also meagre in the area. But the interest evinced was so high that the average attendance was more than 30. How to construct a temporary shed is their problem.

Though the State boasts of providing electricity in all its villages, we found many centres near which no electric post could be seen. In at least two places due to lack of money, electric connection could not be extended to the centre. Can't this be done as a gift to the learners?

In one centre we found children below 15 years also in the class. They told us that they found the adult education class more interesting than the regular school because of timing approach, variety, freedom etc. However these were only guest learners and not regular learners. On the first day we covered 20 centres within 11 hours and concluded the day visiting centre in a home for the physically handicapped, in the city area. Though not a literacy class in the strict sense, this centre was a non-formal education centre doing commendable work. The journey was so tiring as it was through the village roads steep and dusty without even metal not to speak of tar. Anyway the members of the team were all rejoicing at the sight of the learners who are eager to continuing their learning even at to expense of their leisure time and work.

'On the 13th, as planned earlier, we marched to Anad Panchayat which has about 7000 illiterates compared to the 8700 in, 'Karakulam Panchayat. In either case women illiterates out number men. Centres are also mostly run by women air for women. Half the centres are located in Harijan colonies.

The presence of the Panchayat President in the team-throughout the day was a morale booster. The Problems that were brought to our notice on the 12th were there again. May be this is the situation prevailing in all mofussil areas. On the 13th we covered 25 centres travelling 125 kms. Even after 8 p.m. learners were waiting for the team.

A cashew factory which reopened recently in Anad has posed problems for learners in some of the centres. Their timings overlap. Moreover, after the day's hardwork, with their hands unclean and a foul smell, find it difficult to attend classes. Only Sundays are free for them and they have a lot to do that-day. Having class for continuous hours will pose further problems. How to solve this? Will the factory owner be kind-enough to spare at least half an hour twice or thrice a week for their studies as in the case of worker's education?

Another serious problem posed was on the impact of the programme. Some learners who used to give their thumb impressions for receiving widow pension and other benefits are now denied of the same as they started signing their names. The change in signature has to be accepted by the authorities. This is a laborious task and time consuming. Can't the Project Officers be authorised to declare the new signature of neoliterates as valid and avoid unnecessary troubles?

Adult education programmes, to drive fruits have to be linked with developmental programmes and welfare schemes. Income generating projects have to be linked with adult and non-formal education programmes as well as incentives for functionaries and beneficiaries to be instituted. The needs and problems of learners have to be identified and programmes planned effectively linking these with all possible streams and ensuring proper coordination. The unnecessary and avoidable wastage-both of money and energy—has to be curbed for ensuring desired results. Lack of understanding and coordination among the different implementing agencies is yet another lacuna. Though State and District are not level worth the. Boards are being organised, they Mostly they are namesake and serve no purpose. The recent changes in the norms of financial support are consoling to some extent. Provision of transport and adequate staff for effective monitoring and evaluation still remains a The accountability part also needs special attention problem of all concerned.

A Rural Convocation for Honouring Neoliterates

At a time when in the Kerala University, Convocations have—become an old story, the rural people of a local Panchayat, Karakulam, in Nedumangad Block neighbouring the city of Trivendrum had a unique recognition of receiving neoliterates certificates from no less a person than Hon. Speaker of the Kerala Assembly Shri. V.M. Sudheeran. More than 300 neoliterates (nearly 80% of whom were ladies) receiving their certificates in person, in recognition of their successful completion of 12 months intensive literacy campaign organised by the 'Centre for Adult Education and Extension (CAFE) of the Kerala University. Nearly 100 recipients were presented with a neoliterate book kit in recognition of their creditable performance during their discussions, field work and examination as judged through continuous evaluation and final testing.

The function was organised on 30-3-86 in the Karakulam Government Upper Primary School premises adjacent to the Panchayat Office. The local public cooperated with the CAEE authorities in erecting welcome arches, flower decorations etc., in and around the meeting place. The school hall and even the compound was fully packed with neoliterates, their family members and local people. The CAEE had organised street corner certification ceremonies during April 1985 for the neoliterates of 1984 batch. That was the first year of CAEE's direct involvement in eradicating illiteracy. Karakulam and

Anad were the two panchayats adopted by the CAEE for intensive literacy campaign with a view to completely eradicating illiteracy, at least from the age group 15-35, by 31st March 1990. Nearly 800 illiterates were made literate during the first year In 1985 also centres were run in the same Panchayat for 12 months. Nearly 350 illiterate adults each were helped to become literate in these Panchayats.

With UGC's financial support, the CAEE has been instrumental in making nearly 9000 people literate through 12 colleges during the period 1980-1984. In 1984, the number of collaborating colleges rose to 22 and the centres organised to 590. The neoliterates of 1984 batch came to about 10200. During 1985 the number of colleges increased from 22 to 32 and the no. of centres from 590 to 780. Enrolment also increased considerably. But due to inordinate delays in the release of grants by the UGC, the results did not reach the targets expected, though the number of neoliterates of 1985 batch is also around 10,000. Thus so far the CAEE of the Kerala University has succeeded in helping around 30,000 adult illiterates not only in securing literacy and numeracy skills but also in improving their living conditions and in making attitudinal changes.

The CAEE has also launched 30 college level population education clubs and 225 Adult Education Centre level Population Education Clubs. These are organising a variety of programmes like seminars, discussions, exhibitions, medical camps, competitions, quiz programmes, drama festivals, film shows etc., for creating awareness among the people and college youth on the ill effects of population explosion and the need and importance of family welfare schemes. The CAEE has started 25 such Population Education Clubs in Anad and Karakulam Panchayat areas.

In the CAEE centres, a Primer prepared scientifically by the Unit itself is being made use of. A hand book on the effective use of the primer addressed to the Instructors is also supplied to all the Centres. The learners have learnt by heart the hit-songs in the collection of motivational songs entitled 'Janabodhanaganangal' published by the Literacy Forum, extension wing of the CAEE. There is effective monitoring work through the Supervisors. Each supervisor visits a centre at least once a month and gives necessary support, advice and leadership. Monthly meeting of the Instructors are used to clarify doubts, disseminate innovative trends and suggest ways and means for ensuring local support and cooperation. Thus the CAEE-centres are actually models to other agencies in the field.

Certificates and Book kits were presented to the neoliterates by Hon. Speaker Shri. V. M. Sudheeran after a very encouraging and thought provoking speech. He pleaded for better financial allotment and status for non-formal education programmes. He criticised that developmental schemes are not reaching the real beneficiaries due to their ignorance, illiteracy and poverty. In his opinion commitment alone will succeed in the non-formal sector. He praised the Kerala University for undertaking such a genuine and commendable work. While presenting the certificates Mr. Sudheeran interrogated the recipients on their motivation for learning, their achievements, learning time etc. The Television representatives covered the programme with emphasis on this interview. Dr. A. Sukumaran Nair, Pro-Vice-Chancellor presiding-over the function stressed the importance of education as an agent for human resource development. He stressed the extention role of universities and congratulated the CAEE for its meritorious work under the able leadership of Dr. Sivadasan Pillai.

Adv. Nafeesath Beevi, Former Dy. Speaker stressed on the need for Women's education. She presented certificates to the participants in the 10-day orientation course for rural women-organised by the Literacy Forum with financial support from the Central Social Welfare Board. As a follow up of this; programme it has been proposed to establish an 'Association for Women's Development at Karakulam with the 20 trained women as founding members.

Shri. Somasekharan Nair, Ex. M.L.A. felicitated the neoliterates and requested them to keep the certificates safer than their precious ration cards. Shri. P.I.A. Karim Reader in. Education, also spoke on the occasion highlighting the current importance of non-formal education.

In his welcome address Dr. Sivadasan Pillai, Director CAEE narrated the achievements of the CAFE during the short span of 6 years since its establishment in February 1980. The centre 'is rated very high among the 83 Universities in India which have centres/departments of Adult and Continuing Education, he said. He added that CAFE has been identified by the UGC as one of the five Units for Indo-Danish collaboration in Community education, one of the 12 'units' identified for UGC-UNFPA collaboration in the field of population Education and as one of the 12 centres selected for special support for audiovisual aids.

The innovative attempts of the CAFE like preparation of- a training kit on 55 topics, supply of identity cards to all supervisors and instructors, preparation and supply of comprehensive monitoring registers for all the Adult Education Centres, preparation of proformas like observation schedule, monthly progress reports, instructor's profile, survey form, final evaluation schedule etc., have been approved by the UGC and recommended to the other Universities for adoption. The CAFE proposes to follow the area approach in starting the 780 centres approved for 1986. In Trivendrurn district, Nedumangad, Kazhakkoottam and Trivendrum rural. Blocks have been identified, he said. He also announced the formation of a People's Education Corp's (Janabodhana Sana) enlisting volunteers from among the students and the educated for fighting illiteracy on a voluntary basis agreeing to teach one, two or up to five, within the stipulated time.

It is learnt that the UGC, in recognition of the expertise and experience of Dr. Sivadasan Pillai, has put him as UGC representative in the University level advisory committee of all the Universities in the State of Karnataka. He is also an expert member of the advisory committees of Tamil University (Tanjore), Bharatidasan University (Trichy), Bharatiar University (Coimbatore), Gandhigram Rural University (Madurai), Madurai Kamaraj University, Calicut University, Kerala Agricultural University (Trichur) etc. He is also rendering expert advice and guidance to Delhi University and SNDT University Bombay in the implementation of their Post M.A. Diploma Course in Adult and Continuing Education. He is also attached to Madras University, SV University, Tirupati, Andhra University, Waltair, South Gujarat University, Surat, Punjabi University, Patiala, etc., in various capacities.

Out of the 13 Ph.D.'s so far produced by Dr. Pillai, 4 are in adult education. Currently 10 students are working for Ph.D. under his supervision and guidance of whom 6 are in the field of adult education. Having authored a number of books in English and Malayalam, Dr. Pillai is giving very effective leadership in the CAEE's activities. Dr. N.D. Joshi the only Project Officer attached to the CAFE is a specialist in tribal education and folk arts. The other posts of Asst. Directors and Project Officers are yet to be filled in.

The CAEE is currently housed in the Gandhi Bhavan at Kariavattom Campus. Only in Feb. '86 the new premises was occupied. Till then the CAFE was housed in the University Students' Centre Buildings. The 38th All India Adult Education Conference jointly sponsored by the CAEE, Kerala University and KANFED SRC was planned and organised effectively by Dr. Pillai as its Convener.

The CAFE has completed one UGC research project entitled "Identification of motivation and facilitating factors as well as barriers in the implementation of adult education programme in Kerala with special reference SC/ST and Women". Another study supported by the Directorate of Education, Government of India is in progress. It is entitled 'Adult Education Programmes in Kerala—an evaluative study'. This study concentrating on 1983-84 programmes will be completed by the end of October 1986. Both the Projects are directed by Dr. Pillai. Still it is a pity that the CAEE is yet to be recognised as a research centre for inter-disciplinary researches.

Consequent on a week-long intensive workshop on 'Colleges in Continuing Education' sponsored by the UGC, 29 colleges and the CAEE have formulated proposals for launching continuing education programmes for the benefit of the weaker sections. The proposals are before the UGC for approval and financial support. When this is launched, it will attract more people to the programme, resulting in economic improvement and better life.

Planning Forum has also become part of the activity of the 'Centre/Department of Adult and Continuing Education. The UGC has agreed to grant upto Rs. 4000 each to colleges on a 100% basis for organising such activities.

Newer areas which are being brought under the big umbrella of Adult and Continuing Education include legal literacy, science for the masses, environmental education, national integration etc. The UGC has recognised extension as the third and equally important function of all institutions of higher learning, along with teaching and research. Many Universities have by now established permanent statutory departments for adult and continuing education. Maharashtra and Madhya Pradesh are the states leading in this regard. Other states are being persuaded to follow suit. Kerala State which is providing leadership to other Indian States in many respects, it is hoped will not lag behind in the establishment of a statutory Department/Centre for Adult and Continuing Education in the University of Kerala. The long awaited Post M.A. Diploma Course in Adult and Continuing Education may also be established forthwith for equipping prospective functionaries technically and scientifically.

Appropriate incentives for students instructors, supervisors and college level programme officers have to be worked out and implemented. This would help in recruiting more and more volunteers from among students and e work of and whapproachlto the and follow whole programme, voluntary work will have to be given special significance and this can be achieved only through proper incentives.

MONITORING AND EVALUATION

Adult Education Programme has been given high priority by the Government by including it in the minimum needs programme as well as in the 20 point programme of the Government of India. About 11.5 crores illiterate persons in the age group of 15 to 35 are to be made literate by 1990. While doing this special care has to be given to women, SC/ST rural masses etc.

The programme is being implemented by a number of agencies including voluntary organisations, Universities, etc. besides the State Departments of Education and Development.

The Directorate of Adult Education, Govt. of India is monitoring the entire programme at the national level being implemented by various agencies. It is therefore extremely important for the Universities to send their monitoring returns to the Directorate of Adult Education in the Govt. of India so as to appraise them of the innovative attempts and contributions made by the Universities in this programme.

Aims and Objectives

Monitoring is an essential requisite in any programme and it is more so in the eradication of illiteracy among adults. It is aimed at steering clear of all hazards with a view to achieve the targets. Timely feedback is needed for ensuring proper conduct of the programme and that is the major aim of monitoring.

The monitoring of the programme could be broadly classified into the following heads:

1. Administrative Aspects.
2. Financial Aspects.
3. Academic Aspects and
4. Targets Achieved.

Administrative

To see whether positions sanctioned at the University/ College level including those of supervisors and instructors etc. for the implementation of the programme, have been filled up.

Further, it has to be ascertained whether there is an adequate and timely supply of essential materials as well as provision of space and equipments for the proper conduct of the programme. Whether Advisory Committees at University/ College level are functioning, has also to be found out.

Financial

To ascertain whether funds released are received in time, distributed effectively and made good use of with proper maintenance and audit of accounts.

Academic

To ensure adequate coverage of content areas, proper training and retraining of personnel, evaluation of the impact of the programme and taking up of follow up and research activities.

Targets Achieved

Whether there is an adequate coverage of backward sections of the society, especially women, SC/ST etc., and whether illiteracy packets are identified and special attention given to them have to be enquired into. It has to be seen whether institutions in districts having literacy level below the national average, and whether women's institutions and institutions in the tribal areas have been also involved in the implementation of the programme.

Procedure: Administrative, financial, academic and institutional involvement:

The Universities should periodically (twice a year) appraise the UGC of the administrative, academic and financial position of the programme. Such returns should includes:

(a) details of positions sanctioned, filled up, etc.

(b) details of training and retraining of functionaries involved in the programme.

(c) details of workshops and seminars organised for rent purposes.

(d) materials produced, procured, supplied etc.

(e) evaluation carried out together with results.

(f) research studies attempted.

(g) number of women's colleges involved in the programme.

(h) number of colleges from the tribal areas and from districts having literacy level below the national average.

(i) financial support granted, received, amount released to the colleges (collegewise), amount spent at the University level (categorywise).

Targets

The areas covered by the University/College, the number of illiterates at different age levels, number already enrolled, no completing the programme, no. made literate etc. have to be clearly noted in a proforma. The thrusts, targets, achievements, hazards, if any, also need accounting.

The University will collect all the necessary returns from the colleges and after consolidation, they will be sent to the

UGC and the State Directorate of Adult Education for onward transmission to the Directorate of Adult Education, Govt. of India. Colleges—University Unit—State Adult Education Unit UGC. The following monitoring returns are to be filled in regularly:

(1) Initial Project Report (IPR).

(2) Monthly Progress Reports (MPR).

(3) Quarterly Progress Reports (QPR).

(4) Annual Progress Reports (APR).

It is important to note that:

(i) Initial project report is to be filled in by each college and sent to the University immediately after starting the project.

(ii) Monthly progress report is to be sent latest by the 5th of the following month to the University by all the centres through the respective college/unit.

(iii) Quarterly progress report is to be sent every quarter to the University latest by the 5th of the next quarter.

(iv) And the annual progress report is to be sent latest within a month on the completion of the project.

(v) The University should consolidate the reports and forward to the UGC/State Directorate within fifteen days after the receipt of annual progress report for the colleges.

It is important to adhere to the above schedule of monitoring in all cases.

Evaluation

The Advisory Committee of the UGC has suggested self evaluation and external evaluation of the programmes as indicated below:

Self evaluation-during the 2nd, 3rd year of the programme.

External evaluation-during the 4th year of the programme.

Total evaluation of the impact of the project in the 5th year.

Self-evaluation has to be attempted from different angles *viz.* Instructor, Learner, Learning materials, training methods, etc.

The learner's achievement in terms of literacy, numeracy, awareness, attitudinal and behavioural changes etc., need evaluation at the centre level. The Centre has to be critically evaluated to the learners. Similarly the impact of the programme on the masses has also to be found out. A continuous evaluation of all aspects is needed. The Instructor's Diary and the various proforma and records will themselves reveal some, if not all, of the merits and demerits of the programme.

External evaluation by the University using a common tool with necessary adaptations, with inbuilt statistical analysis may be attempted towards the end of each project for comparative studies and cost benefit analysis.

Important data that the University Unit should always have:

(1) List of colleges involved in the programme along with number of centres sanctioned as well as the number of centres actually organised.

(2) Number of centres organised in different districts.

(3) Number of centres in the backward districts/areas.

(4) Intake in terms of R/U, M/W, SC/ST etc.

(5) List of centres with enrolment, working hours, route to the centre, etc.

(6) Dropout details with reasons, if found,

(7) Impact of the studies.

(8) Involvement of colleges—professional/women.

(9) Teaching-learning materials, records, proforma etc., made available to the colleges.

(10) Register of grants.

Important data that a college should have:

(1) Details of centres, their location, intake, working hours etc.

(2) Area covered—especially backward areas.

(3) Total enrolment—categorywise, dropout, if any etc.

(4) Impact of the programme.

(5) Materials procured and supplied to the centres.

Important Registers to be maintained:

(a) at the college level

1. Register of centres—with all necessary details.
2. Stock register-books and furniture.
3. Issue Register.
4. Acquittance Roll.
5. Accounts Book.
6. Inward and Outward.
7. Programme Register.

(b) at the adult education centre level

1. Admission Register.
2. Attendance Register.
3. Visitors Diary.
4. Instructor's Diary.
5. Stock register.
6. Issue register.

Flow of Communication

The individual Adult Education Centres to send, MPR, before the 5th of the consecutive month. The college to send the IPR immediately after commissioning the centres and a consolidated monthly report to the University unit before the 10th of the ensuing month.

QPR to reach the University before the 15th of the month, after the relevant quarter and the UGC/DAE/State unit before the 20th of the following month. This flow has to be ensured for effective monitoring and feedback.

The APR should reach the University unit within a month after the completion of the project, which on consolidation be forwarded to the DAE and UGC.

Staff

A statistical officer for every 300 centres be provided to all University units for compiling, analysing and reporting periodically to the State Directorate of Adult Education and the UGC.

Vehicle

All those University units having not less than 500 centres be provided with a vehicle (van/jeep) for effectively monitoring and evaluating the programme through frequent visits to the colleges and the adult education centres run by them.

Training

The Statistical Assistance (when appointed) and Project Officers have to be adequately trained for the maintenance of register and reporting of data in relevant proforma and returns.

N.B.:

1. In every University Department/Centre of Adult and Continuing Education, there should be a cell for monitoring and Evaluation with a Project Officer of Statistical Officer in-charge of the unit.
2. The Forms/Proforma and necessary records have to be made available to the Colleges and through them to the Adult Education Centres by the University unit for maintaining uniformity and ensuring regular supply of returns.

ROLE OF COLLEGE STUDENTS ERADICATION OF ILLITERACY

There has been many attempts at eradicating illiteracy before and after independence. The pre-independence attempts could create awareness among the people about the evils of illiteracy and the urgent need for tackling the problem. The post independence approaches were more practical and time bound that the percentage of literacy increased from 14.7 to 36.1 within a span of 34 years. This is commendable when compared with the 7 per cent increase during the 50 year period prior to independence. The current increase has been achieved against the heavy dose of population explosion. But we can't rest satisfied of this. India, being one of the greatest democracies in the world, could not boast of its 36% literacy and sit idle. Hence massive, time bound programme have to be launched with the specific purpose of eradicating illiteracy.

The NAEP (National Adult Education Programme) launched in October 1978 has failed to reach its targets due to various reasons. There was a kind of a 'holiday' for the programme since March 1980 and now signs of a rebirth are there. Eradication of illiteracy has been accepted as a part of item 16 of the new 20-point programme put forth by the Prime Minister. With a view to tackling the problem of adult illiteracy, the new scheme suggests a three pronged approach *viz.*, Comprehensive Access to Primary Education (CAPE), non-formal education for the drop outs (NFE) and adult education, with special emphasis on the weaker sections of the community. If all the three are attempted simultaneously and with a band of dedicated workers, we can be hopeful of better results.

Agencies that could be tapped for ensuring cent per cent literacy are voluntary agencies, welfare agencies, Government departments and institutions of higher learning. Teachers and students from colleges and Universities can play a major role in the eradication of illiteracy as also the voluntary agencies. Let us see how the student community can be commissioned for this work. It may be said that they have to study a lot and hence couldn't do much in this field. On the contrary, we find students engaging themselves fruitfully, in NSS, NCC, Sports, Games etc., Social Service League, Red Cross, Planning Forum. If there is a will, there is a way. So first we have to create a willingness or rather awareness among them.

The fact that more than 50 per cent of the illiterates in the world is in India is not known to the students. Also the fact that UNESCO has criticised our attempts as having only a 'snail speed' and the fact that if things go as at present, India will be the only community having illiterates in 2000 A.D., have to be pushed deep into the hearts of students. Atleast a good number of them, if not all, will rise to the occasion to save their motherland from a possible chaos. When this is done, half the work will be over and the battle can be won easily. Write ups in leading periodicals, speeches and dramatisation through the Radio, Focus on Television (wherever available), Folk art forms and cultural programmes during festive seasons, college days etc. can enthuse the students. If possible, meetings or campaigns can be organised in each institution with guest speakers or artists who can impress the students on their duty and how best they can act.

The College students can organise adult education centres in their locality, after a survey to identify the prospective beneficiaries of the programme and likely resource persons and support. While all the students can take part in surveys, campaigns etc., those who are willing and are interested can take up starting of centres and running them. Classes or discussions are not necessary on all days. It can be limited to 3 or 4 days a week and for 1 to 2 hours a day, in accordance with the needs and convenience of the participants.

Those students who find it inconvenient to start centres can very well be supporters. They can pay occasional visits to the centres which will help to monitor them. In the preparation of teaching learning materials, students can have a key role. Similarly in evaluation too.

Post literacy and follow-up work is another area where the college and University students can employ themselves very effectively. This becomes part of the 'Continuing education programmes'. 'Mobile library system' or 'Bell bycycle system' or 'house to house library distribution on foot' can be attempted according to local conditions. Now there are plenty of neoliterate books (at least in Malayalam and Hindi) though not much of periodicals.

Students can go to the community and address the people on topics of interest to them in a meaningful way. This can be deemed a part of the curricular programme for students from the Degree level onwards. At the Masters' level, regular community work can be insisted upon, thereby linking curriculum with extension. This should be effectively planned and implemented.

The activities of the Planning forum can be enlivened through active student participation. The five year plans hitherto launched can be critically studied with a view to suggesting modifications. Similarly the impact of developmental programmes have to be studied and made known to the public.

The young, energetic students have to engage themselves in such nation building activities whole-heartedly and with dedication. For this, proper incentives have to be planned and implemented. At present only a few colleges are involved in this programme. There too, only a small section of the students are active. Instead, as many colleges as possible have to bee roped in and opportunities for students increased considerably so that no one desirous or taking up such work remains frustrated. Each college should come forward to organise at least 5 adult and continuing education centres every year. There need not be any upper ceiling for the number, but need not go, beyond 100. This is what I feel.

If students are to be involved, teachers cannot remain idler They too have to share their part directly and indirectly. Such a collaborative effort alone can produce drastic changes in the society and result in social progress and prosperity.

Assessment, Evaluation and Problems Faced in the Adult Education Programmes

Unlike the developed and advanced countries of the world, in the Indian context Adult Education refers mainly to the education of the illiterate adults with a view to bringing them to the minimum level of functional literacy enabling them to lead a better and contented life. It includes own-time and continuing education of people who are desirous of pursuing their studies, or bettering their occupation or profession. But in India, it has only secondary importance. The National Adult Education Programme which was started in October 1978 with all pomp and fury also failed to 'deliver the goods expected of it. It aimed at providing literacy and functionality to the participants simultaneously creating the necessary awareness in them. The programme got struck up in the middle and the interim evaluation necessitated drastic changes in its approach, target groups and coverage. Anyway in the new 20 point economic policy adult education has found a place under item 16 along with universalisation of primary education. So far so good. Unless we tackle the gigantic problem of illiteracy from different angles such as (1) ensuring 100 per cent enrolment of children at the educable age (2) completely wiping out the phenomena of drop outs and push outs and (3) providing for the education of all illiterate adults, we cann't attain cent per cent literacy in India even in 2000 A.D. This alarming situation has to be seriously viewed and appropriate remedial measures taken. Adult Educators interested in the future and prosperity of the nation have to think of ways and means of overcoming the drawbacks hitherto experienced and ensure the smooth running of the programme.

Let us first of all try to analyse the problems that confront- the adult education movement, in general. Lack of motivation on the part of the illiterate masses and lack of incentives and recognition to the real workers, are two major lacuna in the field. The half-hearted attempts on the part of the Government, the sporadic attempts of the various agencies, lack of coordination and cooperation among the implementing agencies etc., are some other problems. The interference of political, communal and other anti-social elements of the community, who are not interested in conscientising the people, is also pulling the programme backwards. Certain voluntary agencies which have only money motive and prestige value are not doing their duty well. Teachers' organisations and Trade Unions have been kept away from this task thereby creating a non-cooperative mentality among them. The student community has not been effectively motivated and roped into the programme. The women's organisations which could do wonders in this area, have not involved themselves much in the eradication of illiteracy. So also, the Governments on their part have not taken it up as a committed priority programme which has direct linkage with the developmental activities. Experience shows that wherever such commitment was found, illiteracy is no more a problem. They have solved the problem effectively and forever within a short span of time. Ours is a rather huge problem. Yet we could have achieved a lot, had we really meant it. Lack of dedicated workers is still another problem. Continuance of the workers at least for the duration of a project has become difficult, as they are on the look out for something better in evoluments, social status, acceptance etc., and which are of a permanent nature. The unnecessary rivalry among implementing agencies has also to be viewed seriously.

Any programme should have an in built evaluation scheme. It should be a continuous process. Provision for internal and external evaluation should be there. The programme has to be—evaluated from many angles such as (a) national, state, district and project level (b) project officers, supervisors, instructors and (c) from the level of the learners and the community at large. There can be self evaluation in certain categories coupled with external evaluation. Both process evaluation and product evaluation are needed. Also summative and normative evaluation are essential to have a complete evaluation on the impact of the programme on the community, its cost benefit analysis, feasibility of extension, changes of duplication, changes etc. All these come under evaluation. Experts in the field of evaluation and adult education should sit together and formulate strategies as well as tools. Community development and welfare agencies should also put forth their suggestions on expected results. The results attained have to be compared with expected ones and there will emerge valid conclusions. Reports on evaluation by specially authorised agencies have to be publicised and necessary follow up measures taken. Follow up is an essential ingredient especially of adult education programmes and has to be planned adequately. This can emerge from the evaluation of the programme. Evaluation is then a wide spectrum of activities which require concerted effort of a group of people well-versed in evaluation and aware of the objectives of the programme.

Assessment, however, is of limited scope and concerns only with the learners, instructors, supervisors etc., a specific category of people and for a limited area of activity. What the learners have achieved during the 10 months of their course can be assessed orally and in written form. They can be interviewed and observed. There can be written tests as well. The ability in reading, writing and arithmetic alone is not sufficient. Oracy or the ability to converse with others and express one's ideas truly is another expected outcome. As a result of the programme we expect in the learners certain attitudinal and behavioural changes which are also measurable through appropriate tools. The change that has occurred in the individual as a result of the programme can be assessed and reported.

In the case of the instructors who are the grass root level functionaries, their merits and demerits, achievements and drawbacks can be assessed by higher functionaries and even by the learners and the neighbouring community. How best the instructors motivated the illiterate adults to join the classes, how far they could sustain their interests and prevent drop outs, how far he could inculcate habits, manners etc., and root out blind beliefs and bad habits etc., how far he could win the confidence of the learners as one to whom they can look upto, as a 'friend, philosopher and guide' and thus who will be a community leader and social agent etc., are points worthy of assessment. Here again appropriate tools and techniques have to be developed and properly used. Reporting of results, promptly and objectively is another thing to be borne in mind.

Similar assessment can be arranged for supervisors, project officers etc. All these when pooled together will render enough material for an effective evaluation. That is how the two terms are interlinked. The two are essential as also effective planning, implementation and follow up, in any programme of adult education.

Involvement of Students in the Eradication of Illiteracy

India is wedded to democracy, secularism and socialism. Populationwise we are next only to China. India remains the 11th poorest country in the world with a per capita gross national product of 260 dollars. This is below China, Pakistan and even Sri Lanka. In regard to annual rate of increase in GNP we are below these countries and remain one of the lowest with 1.6 per cent increase. Another drawback of our country is that even after 39 years of independence we couldn't make all our people literate; we couldn't even provide free and compulsory education for children of the age group 6-14. Even in 1986 nearly two thirds of our population remain illiterate. We have more than 50% of the world illiterates in our country. Yet we are the largest and greatest democracy in the world. We are in the forefront of non-aligned countries. We are one of the leading nations in the Science and technology. With all these plus and minus points is it not a shame to have illiterates in India?

The number of illiterates in our country rose from 285 million in 1951 to 437 million in 1981, though percentage wise increase is from 16.67 to 36.23. Nearly 100 million of our youth in the age range 15-35 cannot read and write their mother-tongue. They have rich experience but cannot decipher the alphabets. What a pity! The UNESCO has warned us that our condition will be rather precarious even in 2000 A.D. when almost all other nations might have wiped out illiteracy. We were even accused of the 'snail speel' at which we are moving in the literacy field. In the field of adult education many experiments were conducted, but none achieved expected results.

The night schools of pre-independence period, the social education movement during the first three plan periods, the farmer's functional literacy project of the sixties, the non-formal education movement of the seventees, the National Adult Education Programme of 1978 all were well begun but met with half the success expected or untimely deaths. Pt 16 of the new 20 pt programme gave an impetus to the programme ! But the three dimensional approach was not given necessary importance.

The latest revised 20 point programme has given a boost to education giving it pt 10 position. Education for all is the aim in the New Education Policy and alternate strategies including adult and non-formal education have been proposed in it. The establishment of 'jana shikshana Nilayas' and 'village education committees' proposed in the new action plan together with the proposed involvement of community at greater levels might change the education scene in India. Ideals and proposals are not enough. They have to be properly implemented.

It has been suggested that 40 million adult illiterates will be covered by 1990 and another 60 million by the end of 1995 and made literate. This is not an over ambition plan. This could be achieved if available resources are mobilised and put to use. In the Mass Programme for Functional Literacy (MPFL) proposed by the Government of India, involvement of college and university students and teachers has been proposed at a considerable level for achieving these targets. Currently attempts are in progress to involve 2 lakhs of NSS volunteers and 1 lakh non-NSS students in the MPFL. This is in addition to the Adult Education Centres supported by the Central and State Governments and the UGC. Voluntary agencies are in the field. But Teachers' organisations, Trade Unions and Political parties are shying out of this programme. Why? This has to be overcome.

Each college may be allotted an area-say a village, Panchayat or some wards at least for the eradication of illiteracy. The college should adopt the area for allround development of the people. The University can have an earmarked area for such work. It can mobilise the resources of the college and work on its own. This could be a District, some Blocks or a cluster of villages, but it should be identified and set apart for its work. A university level advisory committee can plan and see over the implementation of the programme. At the college level also there can be advisory committees. Representative to voluntary agencies, Government officials and adult educators of repute be given representation in such committees. Adequate measures should be taken to avoid duplications of energy, time and money by the duplication of such activities by different agencies in the same area. State, University, District, Block level coordination have to be ensured.

It is advisable to make some kind of social work, preferably adult education, a pre-condition for securing first degree Diploma from any Indian University. Only such a step can ensure wilful participation from the student community or else appropriate incentives have to be offered by way of grace marks, preferential treatment in higher studies and in selection for appointment etc., like NSS, NCC and performance in Arts/ Sports etc. If these two are not possible, vacation may be extended and the entire student community be asked to make atleast 5 persons each, literate. Intensive campaign of 10 to 15 days in convenient places bringing illiterate adults in sufficient number and giving them all facilities like food, recreation, rest and even compensatory monetary support is another alternative. These together with necessary follow ups can ensure eradication of illiteracy through student involvement. In this case teachers can also be effectively involved.

TECHNOLOGY AND NON-FORMAL EDUCATION

The linkage of two emerging concepts, or rather growing concepts, is visualised in the title. The first one, non-formal education, is not parallel to but complementary to the formal sector of education which has been subjected to severe criticisms not only from the teacher and the taught but also from the public. Though in existence from the long past, non-formal education gained momentum as an educational experiment or innovation only during the sixties of this century. There are some people who equate non-formal education with adult education in its minimum expectation of imparting the three R's (reading, writing and arithmetic). But actually non-formal education is a wider umbrella embracing education of all ages and all types which are not highly rigid. It includes the education of children below 5+, the age of admission to schools, which is mainly provided by voluntary agencies and individuals.

The opportunities provided for the dropout children between the age range 6-14, the educational and occupational persuits offered to the adults, the continuing education of all concerned—including correspondence courses, open university etc.,—are all parts of the non-formal sector. Education is conceived as life long and as catering to the needs and desires of all, irrespective of age, sex, creed, locality, occupation, hobbies etc. This is life-oriented and meant for the betterment of the living conditions of the people, not merely through economic improvement but through inculcation of habits of reading thinking and action. Non-formal education aims at finding truth. It tries to educate people on topics like environmental pollution, sanitation, public property, democracy, first aid, accounting, saving, citizenship, culture etc., through situational approaches, in their own locality and during their leisure hours. The flexibility in timing,' curriculum, approach etc., are characteristic features of non-formal education.

Though non-formal Education has many salient features, one may have to fix up priorities based on the "Land and the People", their 'needs, aspirations' etc. has been attributed to the education of the adults, non-formal education of the dropouts and continuing education for those who are in the productive sector. It varies from place to place. In a state like Andhra Pradesh where percentage of literacy is below the national average, and where dropout rate is father high, the two problems of non-entrants and drop outs have to be tackled simultaneously. The inclusion of item 16 in the new 20 point economic Policy put forth by the Prime Minister, Smt. Indira Gandhi in January, 1982, is of some consolation.

Involvement of college and university students and all educated persons, irrespective of the field in which they are working or are remaining unemployed will be a step in the right direction. Voluntary agencies also have a major role to play in the eradication of illiteracy, rooting out object poverty, bringing people above the poverty line and providing facilities for better life. Even those who have dropped out of schools after studying one or two classes, are likely to relapse into illiteracy in course of time and add to the number of illiterates in the country. Those, in the productive age group have to be educated on their rights and duties as citizens of a democratic country. This can be done through various sources-women's clubs, libraries, sports and arts clubs, cultural organisations etc.,— and hence inevitably becomes non-formal in, nature. Worker's education is another important area.

In a state like Kerala, which tops the Indian state in regard to percentage of literacy (69.17%) and rather high in educational standards, which has tremendously brought down the fate of drop outs through mid day meal scheme, liberal promotions etc., continuing education is of vital significance. But adult education and non-formal education for the drop outs cannot be ignored at all. This being the case, non-formal education naturally emerges as one of the leading phenomena all over the country. As stated earlier, it is gaining ground in certain areas while in certain others it has spread its roots deep into the soil.

Educational technology is another fast developing area. In the past teaching profession was the monopoly of a few who were higher up in the society by caste or by being rich and hence powerful. The Gurukula system was prevalent in ancient India. Then came the monitorial system, teacher training institutions etc., for the preparation of teachers. Chalk and talk was the main approach to teaching. Though lecture method still prevails, teachers now resort to modern techniques.

The unprecedented expansion in the area of science and technology has brought in not only knowledge explosion but technological upheaval as well. Thus emerged the term 'Educational technology'. It applies equally to the 'hardware' and 'software'. Radio, Television, Tape recorder, Projector, etc., are used in-plenty now-a-days in class rooms as well. Techniques like programmed learning mircro teaching, team teaching etc., and 'teaching machines' have found their entry into the formal system. Some are even afraid that the teachers will be replaced by machines in due course. It is just a hypothetical fear similar to the one which was put forth when computers were about to be commissioned. But what happened? It has not affected the workers much. Instead, sophistication has added to the prestige of the country.

Developed countries all over the world have pressed into use all the results of technological advances into their educational institutions. Educational Television (ETC) in Malaysia is doing very effective work in imparting instruction to students of formal institutions. Like the Radio lessons, these are also preplanned and telecast so that simaltaneous viewing and learning are possible. The distance teaching approaches in advanced countries cater not only to the degree oriented education but to the non-institutional programmes as well. Open universities are functioning effectively in many countries. Here again we find the good use of educational technology. It is gratifying to note that Andhra Pradesh has recently started an Open University in Nagarjunasagar area along the lines of the UK. Open University system. The success of introducing the technology in the formal sector of education is beyond question and it has become an approved fact. But how about the non-formal sector?

'On the Move' is a programme used in the UK for educating the illiterate adults using the medium of Radio and Television. At specified times, twice or thrice a week, lessons are broadcast and telecast. For making an adult illiterate, literate it is not enough if we use only one source. Hearing is not enough; seeing is also needed. Doing can follow and the result would be instruction. One-to-one teaching is also attempted in that country supplementary to this. It has proved very useful. Another, innovative approach there is the 'referral service' where again we can find technology put to use. Any one desirous of becoming functionally literate, has just to remember a telephone number and give a call from any of the public booths to the referral centre where people are available round the clock to help you. All you need to inform is your desires regarding the age, sex, locality etc., of the prospective instructor and whether he/she has to come to your house to help you and at what time. Immediately on receiving this, you will be linked to a suitable person, from among the many who have voluntarily registered with the referral service. People are not willing to disclose their inability to read and write the mother-tongue effectively. Hence the anonymity is maintained but service is rendered timely and usefully. This approach is made possible, as you know, through the technological advancement we have achieved.

CCTV (Closed Circuit Television) is another technique widely used now-a-days. This can be used in the non-formal sector also. Micro teaching, can be effectively used in the training of instructors, supervisors, project officers etc. Team teaching can be used in role play technique. Cassettes and tapes are surely of great use.

The folk art forms which are of great significance in non-formal education can be recorded and presented to small or big groups at their convenience using this hard ware technology. The same person need not be troubled to give the same performances repeatedly on many occasions which will be boring to him as well as time consuming. If we want to simultaneously present such shows, we have no other choice than radio or television. Or else tapes have to be used.

When the SITE programme was introduced in India, it catered to the needs of illiterate adults as well, who were brought under its area of operation. It proved that masses are likely to be motivated and conscientised through this process. Even after the failure of INSAT, the Asiad is being telecast throughout India using improvised techniques. This if continued, can be chanellised for adult and non-formal education as well, community. Listening sets and Radio kiosks are in plenty in India. Why not have viewing sets also? The programme will have to be organised in such a way that they attract the prospective beneficiaries and retain their interests. That is about Television. But there are so many other media.

Recently there was an attempt at preparing neoliterate literature as programmed learning materials, under the joint auspices of the Kerala Agricultural University and the Kerala Association for Non-formal Education and Development (KANFED) a prominent voluntary organisation in Kerala, which runs the State Resource Centre for non-formal education an the state. Fears were expressed in the beginning that in the non-formal sector, such materials are of no use. But when the theoretical and practical aspects were discussed at length, it was decided to attempt the preparation of such materials to be experimented and field tested before mass production. These materials can not have the same use and effectiveness as in the class room. The illiterate adult has rich experience. But he cannot individually learn as a child. He needs some body's help. Then why go after mechanisms and machines? That is a question put forth by mary. Can we rule out the use of technology in the non-formal sector? Definitely not. Then the question is- What type of materials—hardware and software—are needed or are good? How best the functionaries in non-formal education can be trained or equipped for using them? Can we equip the illiterate adults or the semi-literate workers for using these? How about the educated, who are not technologically oriented, to use educational technology, in their 'own-time' or 'Continuing Education'?

I have personally witnessed the happiness that illiterate adults had when they succeeded in writing their names or putting together some simple alphabets to make meaningful words. Similarly the joy or pleasure they derive when their voices are heard through the Radio as a result of an interview or a tape-recorded song or performance, is of immense nature. The neoliterates are rich in many artistic talents which if properly tapped can be followed up and put to effective use. One-actplays, Kadhaprasangas, Villupattu, etc., are art forms which presented in their voices and fed back, will ensure the non-formal education schemes great success, response and retention. In the Radio programmes provision has been made for women, youth, children, agriculture, workers, health, science, etc. Why not find some provision for the learners in the literacy classes at least once a week? Success stories can be made known to the world as also innovations. Their quarries can be answered in public so that many may be able to wipe out their fears.

Starting with the simple mechanism of tape recorder, film strip projector etc., the system can commission sophisticated machines also. The cost factor has to be looked into. A cost benefit analysis will be required before massive introduction of these technologies. Frequent evaluation and feed-back are also essential. To begin with, 'short term experimental projects' are advisable—comparative effectiveness of these media in the formal and non-formal sector can also be studied.

In Kerala, KANFED recently brought out a documentary film on non-formal education-its need difficulties in implementation, the role that can be played by voluntary agencies, the impact it has on the society as a whole and for the individual participants etc. This has been well received and demand is there for dubbing the same into other languages. The films also have a major rọle in non-formal education which cannot be ignored or seen in a lower perspective.

Slides can be prepared rather cheap and will definitely be of great value in non-formal education. Flash card forms another effective material, when used in small groups.

Machines are doing many things for men. But teaching machines or any of the sophisticated teaching aids, I doubt, can take the place of teachers. These machines and accessories can only supplement teachers and teaching but can not replace them. This is true of both formal and non-formal education. When time and distance are being defeated by scientific and technological inventions, how can we allow the, technological advances to keep aloof from the masses. At a time when people are after accessories and utensils of latest technology, there is no point in keening formal or non-formal education away from these. Integration of educational technology with education is inevitable. Before long it has to take place and get established.

Non-formal education can not escape this inevitable phenomenon. It can be safely said that technology has come to our rescue at a time when we are trying to arrest drop outs from the non-formal sector and to sustain the interest of adult learners. Let us try to rise upto the occasion by wilfully making good use of technology oriented non-formal education.

In order to have a fruitful discussion on the methodologies of training, it is necessary to identify certain other aspects *viz.*, training 'for whom', 'why' and 'for what'. Only then will arise the question 'how'. Since the participants of this seminer are drawn from various agencies—Government, semi-government and voluntary—engaged in training, social service or welfare activities, solely or partly, there cannot be any uniform approach. However, one thing is common. All are interested in the progress and welfare of the community, the upliftment of the downtrodden and deprived sections of the society and implementing developmental activities in the respective areas. The common aim of training should hence be equipping the personnel to take up welfare activities in an effective way. This can be through the provision of adult education programmes *viz.*, adult literacy, non-formal education for the dropout, vocational training, rural development and self employment schemes etc. Popularising scientific and technological advances among the masses and inculcating reading habits among them form other areas of work. This dichotomy has to be kept in mind while thinking of the 'how' of the training of cadres.

The 'how' will very depending on the category of personnel involved *viz.*, full time paid workers, part time paid workers, volunteers, social workers etc. Though there are commonalties, a uniform type of training cannot suit all these. The background involvement, experience in the field, chances of sticking on to the field etc., are factors to be considered in the preparation of training strategies. Another point to be clarified is the 'why' of the training. In the preparation of teachers we now use the term 'teacher education' instead of 'teacher training'. It is argued that only animals and birds can be trained and not men and women. Training can, however, take place in mechanical fields such as physical training, pilot training, type writing etc. Only if similar situations and environment are anticipated, can we train people to act in the same way. In the case of human beings, it is rather difficult. What is possible is some kind of orientation or preparation or guidance for the successful discharge of one's duties. That too has to be attempted scientifically and whole-heartedly.

Training is generally of two categories: (1) pre-service. *i.e.*, training imparted prior to one's entering a job or profession so as to equip him sufficiently and (2) in-service *i.e.*, on the job training to revamp the abilities or reorient a person to the desired goals in the light of changes or trends in the profession or to keep oneself abreast of the times. There will be marked difference in the planning, organisation, conduct and evaluation of these two programmes. Not only duration and content will differ but difference will exist in the aims and objectives, resource personnel and materials, approach, outcome etc. When the personnel involved in any ongoing programme have to be reoriented to the changed trends and objectives, refresher training programmes are launched on a massive scale within time limits to cover all the different levels of functionaries.

The three major phases of any training programme are planning, implementation and evaluation. All are equally important and deserve special attention in all its innumerable aspects. Prospective trainees have to be oriented to the programme sufficiently early and to the extent possible background reading materials have to be supplied prior to the starting of the programme. A tentative programme schedule can be drawn up for discussion with the participants, immediately on arrival with a view to making necessary changes in response to their expectations, background and experiences. The trainers and resources persons will also have to be brought together for necessary briefing in order to avoid possible duplication, difference in interpretation and consequent confusion and monotony among the participants. Field work, practical sessions, group and individual assignments etc., require adequate planning as also the provision for interaction among the participants and talent shows. Necessary records and documents should be procured in sufficient number. A reference library is a must. Emphasis should be on participatory approach and not on stereotyped lectures and demonstrations. Newer techniques have to be experimented with adequate preparation, feedback and follow up. For the success of any training programme a combination of theory and practice is needed. Frequent evaluation by participants and consequent changes in approach and programme must be the policy to be adopted in any good training programme.

Micro teaching is one of the modern techniques that could be effectively tried in any training programme, especially of the formal type. In teacher education programmes, this has been found very useful, but in the non-formal sector this cannot be of that use due to the flexibility of the approach and diversity of content and personnel. A shortened programme (in duration, no. of participants and content area) with possibilities of repetition, review, revision and resultant refinement is the crux of micro teaching. Team teaching is another approach possible in training programmes. Instead of a single person handling a subject through lecture, discussion, demonstration etc., a team of experts well versed in the subject, and having mutual understanding and qualities of adjustment take part in this. This ensures integrated approach which is essential for the success of development-oriented programmes. The members of the team should have prior discussion on the areas each one has to cover and an agreement should be reached so that any member can interfere in the presentation if some additional point has to be made or clarifications are needed. Whenever areas or topics of an interdisciplinary nature are tackled, this approach will be very useful.

Role play is yet another modern technique very effective with the masses. Purposive enactment of 'roles' by different individuals to enter into fruitful discussions on topics of vital importance is the crux of the technique. The 'actors' need not necessarily be prefixed; they can emerge spontaneously and participation of trainees will be maximum in this case. Different persons can try different roles so that resultant discussions will vary and can lead to appropriate decisions. Dramatisation is different from role play in that the latter is spontaneous and oriented towards identified problems requiring immediate solution. Need reduction and problem solving should result from any developmental and welfare programme whether it is educational or not and here role play can be a successful technique. The 'street drama' form yet another approach.

Discussions-leaderless and with leader as well as planned and spontaneous-can enlist group activity and feeling of participation among the trainees. Small group discussions help in persuading even the introverts to speak out. So in every training or seminar ample opportunities should be provided for group discussions, preferably small group sessions followed by pleanaries. These should help the trainees acquire the necessary abilities to organise, demonstrate, evaluate and follow up discussions on their own.

Brainstorming and buzz sessions are also of great value in training programmes. This will help to ensure participation of all the members of the group.

Practical sessions should be given appropriate provision in any training programme. We need theoretical and practical orientation. Planning things at the top without trying to understand the feelings of the masses is a major drawback in our country. People are interested in doing armchair researches; but they often hesitate to go to the field. Unless one goes to the field, he cannot have a clear picture of the situation; he can't establish rapport with the people without a proper dialogue. So every one interested in social or welfare work, has to gain adequate mastery in surveying, collecting data, recording the same, tabulating, interpreting, and communicating as also establishing proper human relations. The way to win the support and confidence of the people has to be found out. An understanding of adult psychology, an idea of their needs and problems, aspirations, behaviour patterns etc., together with approaches for motivating them and sustaining their interestes is essential for any trainer and hence should form a part of any training programme for key, middle level and grass root level functionaries.

Preparation and use of teaching learning materials, improvisation of teaching aids, procurement of materials should find a place in the training schedule. Evaluation of the entire training as a programme (process) or a product is also essential for future guidance. The technical jargons used by various agencies differ considerably and hence require discussion. For higher level training, supervision, administration, finance etc., should also form part of the total programme. Initial and final inventories to be administered on the trainers need to be prepared. Necessary publicity before and after the training will enthuse public interest, opinion and even criticisms which are all needed. There can only be a common frame of reference and not a uniform pattern for the training of cadres. Naturally there can't be any one methodology. Salient features of all good ones have to be integrated fruitfully to make the programme a real success.

Language Simplification for Neoliterates

Post-literacy and follow-up measures are highly essential to retain the level of literacy among the neoliterates and to prevent them from relapsing into illiteracy. However much an adult learner is motivated to acquire the skills of literacy and numeracy, it has to be followed up carefully to sustain their interest and create reading habits among them with a view to ensuring a learning society. It has been alleged that even among the educated, reading habits are deteriorating; not to speak of teachers most of whom depend upon their own lecture notes and prescriptions of the good old days. Even in Kerala, where there is a good library movement with a network of more than 4000 rural libraries, it has been reported that there are not many readers, who really read standard books. Novels, short stories, dramas etc., are liked by people but not scientific, technological and reference books. So good reading habits have to be inculcated among the neoliterates through properly directed and guided reading. For this appropriate books are needed.

Who is a Neoliterate?

Any one who did not or could not make use of the available educational opportunities, on time, and who at a later stage acquired the skills of reading and writing through formal, informal and non-formal approaches, can be said to be a neoliterate. He/She was hitherto unable to read and comprehend the printed or written word but can, now, with fluency or with difficulty, read and understand the print media. A neoliterate can be described as one who has acquired the ability to read and write his or her mother-tongue, rather late *i.e.*, after acquiring adulthood or even in old age. The reading speed and power of comprehension might differ from person to person and appropriate reading materials are needed for them.

Are there Reading Materials for Neoliterates?

Yes. There are. In most of the Indian languages and in English. But many have confused neoliterate literature with children's literature and hence most books that we find in the market are not meant for the target groups. Books for neoliterates should have certain specific qualities and hence should form a separate category.

The Government of India organised competitions for the neoliterate books with a view to ensuring the production of books of quality that would attract the neoliterate adults. By now, a cadre of neoliterate writers have emerged in Kerala, thanks to the attempts of the Kerala Grandhasala Sanghom and KANFED (Kerala Association for Non Formal Education and Development). Nearly 100 books have been produced by the Sanghom and KANFED has to its credit more than double this number. Both the agencies published books for neoliterates not as a business concern but as service. The established booksellers and producers (including the SPCS—Sahitya Pravartaka Cooperative Society) have yet to enter the field. The Award winning neoliterate books also do not possess high standards as only few dare to submit their scripts for scrutiny and not many are aware of the competitions, though 23 years have passed since the system was introduced. In Malayalam we have about 400 books which are classified as neoliterate books, of which at least half the number are worth that categorisation. Others need thorough revision.

Not only books, but pamphlets and periodicals are also there addressed to the neoliterates. The 'Saksharakeralam' weekly published by the Sanghom for 5 to 6 years (not now) and 'KANFED `News' published by KANFED since 1978 are worth mentioning. A monthly wall newspaper 'Nattuvalicham" published by KANFED serves not only neoliterates but the elite as well, as a conscientising piece of immediate use and attraction. But the regular newspapers and periodicals are yet to start setting apart a column at least for the neoliterates.

Qualities Expected of Neoliterate Books

The following are some of the general guidelines:

(1) Neoliterate books should deal with their immediate surrounding needs, aspirations etc. They should easily attract the attention of the reader and tempt him to read more books.

(2) The vocabulary should be in accordance with that of the neoliterates and the style of presentation, simple. Small sentences with familiar words should be preferred. The narration should be interesting. Unfamiliar objects and situations should be illustrated. Care should be given in avoiding factual errors in the books.

(3) The books should convey the massage of better living and social progress. Taboos and superstitious beliefs have to be rooted out gradually through appropriate measures. Conversational style and familiar situation have to be preferred.

(4) The books should be graded according to the vocabulary content etc., and readability, from the point of view of the learner. All neoliterate books need not be of the same difficulty level. There should be books on Science and technology, occupations, places of importance, legal aid to the poor, health and hygiene, democracy and citizenship etc., besides stories, travelogues, biographies etc. Folk songs, abridged versions of epics, etc., may also be attempted.

(5) The format and lay put should be designed properly to attract the neoliterates. Convenient size of the book and use of bold types facilitating easy reading should be preferred. The number of pages may range from 24 to 60.

A neoliterate book should be such that at first sight one should be tempted to take the book and examine it, read it at a stretch and read it again and again till it is fully comprehended. The cover, paper, illustration etc., are all contributory factors; but major emphasis should be on the content and presentation.

CAEE Workshops on Neoliterate Literature

The Centre for Adult Education and Extension (CAEE) with the support of its Extension wing, the Literacy Forum organised a series of workshops during 1980 and 1981 for evolving criteria for the preparation and evaluation of neoliterate books. The workshop has recommended the following criteria:

Group I—Relevance of the content, Relationship of the theme with the neoliterate, type of letters used, length of sentence, simplicity of language, sequence of ideas, style of presentation, reality, values, message.

Group II—Mode of presentation, evidences, propriety of examples, possibilities of expansion, printing.

Group III—Clarity, truthfulness and number of illustrations, size of the book, paper used, column used, cover, lay out, preface and cost of the book.

The 25 categories listed above are given a maximum weightage of 5 (first 10), 4 (for the next 5) and 3 (for the last 10) respectively if the quality is rated as 'good'. For an 'average' response, one point less and for a 'poor' response, one more point less was suggested yielding a maximum of 100 points and a minimum of 50. In the grading of the neoliterate books using the above criteria, the following categorisation has also been recommended by the workshop.

Scores	51—60	Poor
	61—70	Average
"	71—80	Good
"	81—90	Very good
"	91—100	Excellent

The workshop which evaluated 60 neoliterate books selected at random could find only 10% as 'excellent' and another 15% "very good".

These criteria were effectively used in the evaluation of a series of 'Science Cream' books published by the Kerala Shastra Sahitya Parishad, which could identify 10 books for bulk purchase by the Development department for post literacy and follow up work.

KANFED organised evaluation workshop involving neoliterate writers for grading their publication and improving the quality of the books. Though there are plenty of books, they have yet to be scientifically screened.

Qualitative Improvement Needed

On a perusal of the neoliterate books published in Malayalam by various agencies, and the award winning neoliterate books, one is tempted to comment that qualitative improvement is an urgent necessity. Though the books are mostly prepared in workshops and scrutinised and edited by special committees, flews are not few in many respects. The authors have their own style of writing which can be pruned only to a limited extent. Hence it becomes necessary to evolve norms regarding the language to be used in books for neoliterates. Here it lies the significance of the present seminar.

How to Simplify the Language?

Different writers mean different things while using the term 'simple language'—so many the length of sentence is the major factor. To some others, the vocabulary matters much.

Familiar and often used words are preferred by most writers. This they do to simplify the language. Compound and complex sentences make comprehension difficult for the neoliterate. I however doubt whether such sentences can be completely avoided. In science and technology it requires special ability to bring down the technical aspects to the level of the neoliterate. Many have succeeded in this area as well.

There is a tendency to count three alphabets as one word. It is doubtful whether this can be applied to neoliterate literature? The State Institute of Encyclopaedic Publications. The State Institute of Languages etc., have come forward with this 'three alphabet-word' formulae. Simple words which are frequently used by the illiterates have many more alphabets. Hence this restriction, I feel, is applicable to neoliterates.

Length of sentence can be a criterion, especially in the neoliterates series. Colloquial terms make comprehension easier for the particular group bit not as a whole. In print form generally acceptable and understandable words and phases are to be preferred. Conversational style and narrative approach will be more appealing to the neoliterates. Even highly technical knowledge can be simplified using familiar situations. Dialogue of ordinary style can evoke keen interest among the readers. Certain simple expansions of joy, fear, exclaim anxiety surprise etc., also can be attempted.

Idioms and proverbs of local use can make things clear easily instead of giving long, scientific explanations. Comparisons with local conditions and specifics also may be attempted. The neoliterate adults are rich in experience. What they lack is the ability to read and write. If properly motivated, they will not hesitate to read anything presented to them, even if it is difficult to pronounce and comprehend.

Suggested Procedure for Preparing Neoliterate Books

Through a survey among the prospective readers, areas and topics of interest have to be identified first. A perusal of such a list will help one to fix up priorities in line with financial and allied matters.

Announcements inviting scripts from writers, be given in the radio, press etc. The respondents may be assigned topics or titles of which the script should be made ready before a specified date. A workshop of all script writers may be convened at a suitable place with adequate number of resource personnel. The participants may be grouped based on fields or subjects.

Each script writer may be asked to read his script while others listen and comment on the language, expression, style etc. Constrictive criticisms are needed and the writer may be given chance to defend his viewpoints. Each writer has to pass through this ordeal and then comes the revision process.

The writers rewrite the script based on the suggestions and once again present the same before the group for approval. Having approved the scripts go to a scrutiny committee for editing, illustration, publishing etc. The publishing concern has to took for the design, format, type, colour, cover etc., as well as quality of paper and printing beside pricing.

The question of language simplification comes at the workshop level or even when directions or guidelines are issued to writers of neoliterate books. These cannot be a uniform pattern for all Indian languages, bit certain common guidelines can be evolved such as the ones suggested in the previous section.

Any book produced for neoliterates should not wait for a reader. It should be in great demand. Readers should come in search of the book.

Let us see how best we can ensure this.

TRAINING TECHNIQUES OF NON-FORMAL EDUCATION

Although India accounts for only 2.4% of the total world area, it contains about 15% of the world population. India is- the second most populous country in the world, with China at the top with 21.72%. The population of India as on 1st March 1981 was 683,310,051 (Males 353,347,249 and Females 330, 462,802) according to provisional census figures released by the Government.

On of the ironies of the Indian literacy situation is that while the percentage of literacy has been increasing every decade,: the total number of illiterate has also been increasing.

Literacy Percentage

Year	*Persons*	*Males*	*Females*
1951	16.67	24.95	7.93
1961	24.02	34.44	12.95
1971	29.45	39.45	18.69
1981	36.17	46.74	24.88

Between 1971 and 1981 the literacy percentage has increased by nearly 7 per cent. While this increase is reflected in the increase of literates by about 82 million, the illiterates have also increased by 48 million.

Kerala, with a literacy percentage of 60.42 stood first among the Indian States in 1971. It recorded a 14.48% increase during 1971-81 and showed a literacy percentage of 69.17, thus keeping its topmost position. Kerala, a small state in the South west corner of India has an area of 38,863 sq. km. which represents only 1.03 per cent of the total area of India. But it has a population of 25,403,217 which is 3.71 per cent of the total population in the country. The State has the maximum density of population of 654 per sq. km., among the Indian States.

	1961	1971	1981
Literacy rate (both the sexes)	46.85	60.42	69.17
Males	54.97	66.62	74.03
Females	38.90	54.31	64.48

Agencies Engaged in Adult/Non-formal Education

Government, Semi-government and voluntary agencies have been and are in the field contributing to the rather high percentage of literacy and educational level in the State. While the Departments or Development, Education and Social Welfare come under the Government Sector, the Universities of Kerala and Calicut come under the Quasi-government sector.

Agencies like Kerala Grandhasala Sanghom, Kerala Shastra Sahitya Parishad, Kerala Association for Non-formal Education and Development (KANFED), Mitraniketan, etc., are the major ones in the voluntary sector.

KERALA GRANDHASALA SANGHOM

Started in 1945 with 47 rural libraries in the erstwhile Travancore area of the present Kerala State, under the able leadership of Mr. P.N. Panicker, the Kerala Grandhasala Sanghom had on its rolls nothing less than 4000 rural libraries. This voluntary agency aimed at spreading the message 'read and grow', providing opportunities for all the literate people to read books and periodicals at a very nominal subscription on even free of charge.

Gradually it opened up women's section, children section, arts club, sports club, book club etc., and established radio listener's forums, free tuition centres, guidance bureaus etc. Science corners, Agricultural corners etc., were also formed in most libraries and thus extended their activities to the masses. In 1970, when the Sanghom celebrated its 25th year, a survey revealed that illiteracy is rampant in many parts of the state and that new readers have to be found out for the effective use of the libraries.

The Sanghom then resolved to extend its area of work to the field of eradication of illiteracy. It launched experimental functional literacy projects with financial support from the Government of India during 1971-75 with the help of an Expert Committee. The Sanghom received honourable mention for Krupskaya Award in 1975, in recognition of its meritorious work in the field of adult education. The Sanghom has published 7 primers, 98 neoliterate books, a literacy chart and 2 guidebooks besides an evaluation report of its literacy activities. A weekly for neoliterates "Saksharakeralam" was published by the Sanghom for about 6 years.

Since the taking over of the Sanghom in 1977, the Sanghom has confined its work to procurement and distribution of books. Since most of these libraries have own buildings, they continue to serve the community to a considerable extent, though not upto expectations. In the retention of literacy and in inculcating reading habits, the Sanghom's role is unique and commendable. A public library bill is being formulated to streamline the activities of the Sanghom and to effect more Governmental control, not only in financial matters, but also in administration.

Kerala Shastra Sahitya Parishad

This is another voluntary agency of Scientists and people interested in the spread of science among the masses. For its very useful work this agency bagged the 1982 ICSSR (Indian Council for Social Science Research) Award. Besides organising science fairs, science exhibitions, science corners, corner meetings, jathas etc., recently they launched cultural programmes of the folk type which proved great success.

They publish 4 science magazines meant for primary school children, high school pupils, college students and the public respectively. Their wall chart has acquired the appreciation of many. A scientific culture has been developed even among the masses through the activities of the Parishad.

The science quiz programmes launched among pupils, have resulted in developing Scientific interest and fostering scientific aptitude. Most of the volunteer workers are science teachers and college lecturers/Professors dealing with science. A series of books under the common title "Science Cream" have been published by this agency.

Though with major emphasis on science and technology, the Parishad has been doing efficient work in popularising Science among the people. Scientific literacy is their secondary objective. Programmes for the 80's have been worked out at its annual conferences and are being implemented.

Kerala Association for Non-formal Education & Development (KANFED)

This agency was setup for the sole purpose of propagating non-formal education linked with developmental activities. It is the successor organisation of the Kerala State Adult Literacy Council formed as part of the Kerala Grandhasala Sanghom by a few leading social workers and educationists. Registered under the Travancore Cochin Charitable Societies Act 12 of 1955, on June 30, 1977, KANFED has its headquarters at Trivandrum though it has state-wide jurisdiction.

The objectives of KANFED are:

1. To promote the educational, cultural and economic development of all sections of the people.

2. To help universalisations of education by propaganda for it and by the institution of non-formal education activities as supplementary to the formal education systems.
3. To establish institution for research and training in all aspects of non-formal education, publishing houses for the production of literacy materials, and centres for the eradication of illiteracy.
4. To plan and carry out projects in continuing education, correspondence course and research.

On June 30, 1983 KANFED completed 6 years of fruitful work. In the anniversary celebrations the State Governor, Ministers, Vice Chancellors, Pro-Vice Chancellors, Ex-Ministers M.L.As. and leaders from various walks of life praised the activities of KANFED, which included the following:

1. Training more than 10,000 workers for organising and running adult education centres on a long term basis.
2. Creating awareness among all concerned on the need for concerted efforts for eradicating illiteracy and ensuring a learning society.
3. Preparing and publishing 15 primers, 30 technical books and more than 200 books useful for neoliterates.
4. Publishing 'KANFED news', a weekly for neoliterates, Anaupacharika Vidyabhyasam fortnightly for functionaries and Nattuvelicham, a monthly wall paper for conscientising people.
5. Running two correspondence cum contact courses for workers entitled 'Janavidya Pracharak' and 'Janavidya Pravesh' for graduates and undergraduates respectively.
6. Taking a short film on non-formal education narrating KANFED's programmes for liberating people from illiteracy.
7. Organising street Jathas, exhibitions, corner meetings, seminars etc., for equipping people to cope with the modern trends in science and technology.
8. Running model centres and continuing education centres on its own.

The Government of India reorganised KANFED and entrusted the State Resource Centre for non-formal education with it. The SRC is functioning since July 1978. The German Adult Education Association has selected KANFED as one of its 18 projects all over the world with financial support for specific items such as training, publication and publicity. Awards for social workers were first instituted by KANFED to honour dedicated volunteers behind the agency.

A scheme was discussed at the Sixth anniversary meeting to, eradicate illiteracy completely from the age group 15-35 in Kerala before 1990, through copoperative and concerned efforts.

KANFED had been instrumental in making at least 50,000 illiterates, literate during the last years with the reasonable estimate of 50 per cent success in its centres. The KANFED centres are made permanent as Vidyabhavans with mini libraries, guidance facilities and as centres of help for all needy people. It is hoped to start at least 10,000 such centres in Kerala within five years, under the banner of KANFED. Though started as late as 1977, KANFED has won great reputation not only in Kerala but all over India and even outside.

Centre for Adult Education and Extension, University of Kerala

When this author returning from U.K. after undergoing advanced training in non-formal; education in the United Kingdom with a Government of India fellowship in 1976, the University of Kerala started imparting courses for specialisation in adult and non-formal education at M.Ed. level in its Department of Education. Provision for Doctoral work in non-formal education was also made the same year, under the guidance of this author. Three candidates have already secured-their Ph.Din non-formal education and 6 number of personal researches on relevant topics have also been completed by submitting his thesis shortly). A this author.

In 1978, the Government of India launched the National Adult Education Programme (NAEP) with a target of 10 crores illiterates to be made literate within a span of five years. The University Grants Commission prepared necessary guidelines and directed all affiliated Universities to involve their students and teachers in the eradication of illiteracy. The University of Kerala also rose to the occasion and decided to collaborate in the fight against illiteracy. Thus a Centre for Adult Education and Extension (CAEE) was started in February 1980 with the following objectives:

(1) To coordinate the adult education programmes taken up by the colleges land other institutions of higher learning.

(2) To train the different level of effect on and Student teachers (Project Officers), instructors.

(3) To prepare teaching learning materials like Primers, guidebooks, workbooks, teaching aids etc.

(4) The evaluate the outcome of the programme attempt comparative studies.

(5) To carry on and guide research studies taken up by academic and grossroot level workers.

(6) To organise short courses, extension lectures, seminars, exhibitions, workshops etc.

The CAEE has completed 3 years in February 1983. It had been instrumental in training 100 college teachers as Project Officers, a similar number of graduates as Supervisors and more than 1000 students as instructors. At least 10,000 adults have been made literate through the literacy or people's education centres run through college students. A CAEE Primer has been prepared through workshops, field testing, evaluation etc. A guide book for instructors and a workbook for learners have been prepared. Survey forms, evaluation sheets, observation schedules, interest inventories etc., have been developed. Through a series of workshops criteria have been evolved for the preparation and evaluation of neoliterate books. The workshops organised for the preparation of teaching learning materials—especially aids—were of unique importance being the first of its kind in India using waste materials and local natural resources. Short courses were organised for college and school teachers, research workers, professional students, social workers etc., on adult and continuing education action research etc. The CAEE has been rendering able support and cooperation to various Government departments, welfare and voluntary agencies in the state and even outside.

According to the new 20 point economic policy promulgated by the Prime Minister of India, Smt. Indira Gandhi on 14 January 1982, the country hopes to eradicate illiteracy at least from the age group 15-35 by 1990 and ensure cent per cent enrolment and prevent dropping out of children, thus ensuring reduction in the number of illiterates. Kerala has every chance to achieve this target. The CAEE has resolved to do the needful involving all constituent colleges in the programme so that its legitimate role could be played as effectively as possible. A coordinating body is envisaged to monitor the programme properly and ensure best result.

NATIONAL EDUCATION POLICY

Nearly 20 years have passed since the Education Commission headed by Dr. Kothari submitted its report. Some of the recommendations have been implemented either fully or partly but many remain untouched. Still it was felt that education in India needs a thorough overhauling in order to Indianise it. Indian heritage and culture are not taught to the emerging generations, who are to shape the destiny of India in the years to come. Children are taken away from the realities of life and are given bits of information and knowledge unrelated to daily life situations. Values of life are not inculcated among the children, it was alleged by educational reformers and thinkers alike. All these led to the preparation of a document entitled 'challenges of education' as a source book for elaborate discussions all over the country, which, it is hoped, would result in a new educational policy.

The document has been severely-criticised, by many as a hastily prepared document lamenting on 'pitfalls and 'under achievements rather than suggesting course of action for bettering the provisions for and conditions of education. The truth that targets and aspirations have not been achieved even in quantity has been categorically conceded by the document writers. However a realistic analysis on the difference between expectations and actuals has been attempted for the first time in the history of Indian education. The projections by agencies like UNESCO & UNICEF have also been incorporated in the report. The recommendations made ate mostly in general terms and not in concrete terms with the result the process of implementation will be an uphill task, if at all atleast some of these are to be implemented. There is neither an acceptable policy not a plan of action in the policy frame. It is however consoling to note that the document was made available to the public in English, Hindi and in the regional languages. So fat so good. But the discussions were rather sporadic, halfhearted and not properly planned and organised. Only the elite had opportunities to express their opinions on the documents; the common man was left out. The trio in education—the teacher, taught and the patent-have not been given enough chances for discussing the proposals. Laymans' point of view on education has not been enquired into and incorporated. The state legislatures have not given due consideration to the document. Political rather than ideological differences have been found dominant in many such discussions. State policies reflect only pro and anti central government directives.

A uniform policy on education formulated at New Delhi cannot do justice to the various states and regions of the country. Flexibility in tune with local conditions and peculiarities has to be ensured, without affecting national unity and sovereignty. National integration has to be ensured at all costs. The education offered should aim at this. The condition prevailing is fat from satisfactory. So there should be drastic changes in the national policy of education. In order to implement this, teachers have to be orientated properly providing appropriate in-service education and offering relevant refresher courses so as to enable all teachers to do their job well.

In the light of the new education policy, aims and objectives of education at all levels will undergo changes and will have to be reflected in the content and methodology. To equip the teachers (both current and prospective), necessary changes have to be incorporated in the teacher education programme starting with the selection of teacher-trainees and teacher educators. Qualified persons with the necessary aptitude towards teaching profession have to be attracted to take up the task. Now this is not done. At least some people take to teaching as the last resort. Some others consider it a stop gap arrangement and will always be looking for a change. This has to go. Hence the selection of prospective teachers itself is a problem and a challenge.

There was a time when teachers were considered as "paid agents hired to bring light into the dark corners of the world". Teaching was the privilege of a few in olden days. Now quantitative expansion has taken place and to cope with the ever expanding needs, teachers ate needed in large numbers. There ate not enough trained teachers, thought in certain subjects unemployment is also a problem. Correspondence courses, contact cum correspondence courses etc., were started to meet the backlog of trained teachers.

With the advent of new technology in the class rooms and consequently in teacher preparation programmes, teacher education has gained mote importance and respect. Micro teaching, team teaching, programmed instruction etc., have become the order of the day in most of the Regional Colleges of Education and University Departments of Education. Some of the teacher education institutions are still lagging behind. Radio and Television ate widely used in the preparation of teachers. With all these modernisation techniques, in the years to come teacher education will have newer challenges.

The role of the teacher will undergo drastic changes as it cannot any mote be confined to the class rooms or only to the students brought before him. Instead, he has to work with the community, understand peoples problems and help them solve the problems playing a leadership role. The teacher has to understand the problems of the community and help them solve the twin problems of poverty and illiteracy simultaneously. The gigantic problem of illiteracy in our country has to be—affectively tackled. For this the teachers have to take up a key role, though they have not hitherto been engaged in it. Here starts the great challenge before educators. Teachers should emerge and act as real 'social engineers'. It is not their competencies that matters most; but it will be their commitment to the profession and interest in the welfare of the society. People complain of deteriorating 'teacher status'. But who is to be blamed? Mainly teachers themselves are responsible for this peculiar situation. They alone can save their face. This will be another challenge.

Introduction of a parallel stream of non-formal education to overcome the deficiencies of the existing formal system and to provide education for all, which is directly related to daily life situation is expected-to put, forth another challenge to teacher education. This is an inevitable thing. Teachers and teacher educators have to take up this challenge and equip themselves adequately in the non-formal sector also. Open University system will also pose problems in the education field. But there-is no escape. This will be a boon to the toiling masses who were either denied of educational opportunities or couldn't make use of available ones.

The 'teacher is the emerging society' has to be a different, person than the present one. He has to be a real 'friend, Philosopher and guide'. He should be enriching his knowledge and skills through continuous learning. He cannot close his eyes towards technological advancements. He will have to face the problems of the community at least around him and with all the resources at his command try to solve—the same. He should be an organiser, leader, conscientiser etc., besides—being a preacher and philosopher. Action and applied researches, he should undertake. He should voice the concern of the masses, especially of the poor and the down trodden and help in their liberation. He should both be an and rogogue and a pedagogue. If these and many more expectations are to be fulfilled, teacher education will have to face many more challenges in the years to come. In future the teacher may not have to 'teach', but only to 'direct learning' as and when requested for by the learners. This will definitely be a difficult job when compared with the old 'banking system of education'. No more can a teacher be 'trained', he can only be 'educated' learning the choice before him to preach, teach or cheat. In the years to come, the teacher will be confronted with a new set of students preparing themselves for life in the 21st century when computers and automation will be the rule of the day. If everything will be available on pressing a button, what is to be learnt is only to 'identify' the correct button. Here 'trial and error', or 'insight' can work. Then what will be role of teachers? What kind of teacher education will be needed? To think along these lines is itself a challenge? Let us face it.

ENVIRONMENTAL EDUCATION

Education is a life-long process. It starts at the time of birth and goes on upto the time of death. It is not a time-bound process. It cannot be fully institutionalised and formal. It has to be partly out of school and non-formal. Even for the educated, continuing education is needed to keep themselves abreast of the times. This can be own-time education using multimedia approaches.

In olden days education was equated with the proficiency in the 3 R's (reading, writing and arithmetic). This is only basic literacy in the contemporary world. Now, consequent on the explosion of knowledge, especially in the field of science and technology, one has to learn a lot. The ability to comprehend, apply and arrive at valid conclusions is essential for all those who wish to lead a successful life. For this education has to be life-centred and modernised in outlook and content. The new education policy being finalised and implemented in India aims at this.

Illiteracy Stands in the Way

But the pity is that nearly two thirds of India's population are illiterate. They cannot even read or write their mother-tongue. They cannot decipher the alphabets and they cannot comprehend even regular day-to-day affairs if presented in written form. There are nearly 43.75 crores of illiterates in India. Out of these, nearly 10 crores are in the age group 15 to 35. It is consoling to note that in the Action Plan based on the New Education Policy, the Government's firm desire to eradicate illiteracy atleast from the age group 15-35, by March 1995, has been reiterated. Unless the people are made literate, they cannot be real partners in the nation-building process. The welfare measures launched by various Governments remain far away from them and the middlemen usually exploit them.

Education is the process which enriches human beings with knowledge, skills etc. In order to create awareness among the masses, we can use mass media including Radio and T.V. But the messages do not reach the real clientele if it is in the print form as many find it difficult to read them and comprehend. This is true of citizenship as well. The rights and duties of citizens are not known to them. The relation between the individual and society is not clear to them. A sense of 'we-feeling' can be aroused only through proper understanding of the society. Similar is the case with environmental consciousness. In many countries people are aware of the need to keep their surroundings neat and clean.

In advanced countries nobody will spit on the road or throw away cigarette butts, match sticks, food materials, waste paper etc. This is ensured not only through legislation but also through conscientising the public on the need for doing so. But how alarming is the picture in our country! 'Even in Kerala which is the most literate and educated state in the country, people do not observe such essential social manners. Environmental health is conducive to the health and well-being of people. Though pupils are taught science in different compartments, its domestic use in relation to public health and everyday life is not stressed, Science is taught not in relation to daily life problems but apart from actual situations. This has to go. In the new education policy signs of progress are there as subjects are to be related to immediate neighbourhood and needs of the people. This is possible more in the adult and non-formal sector than in the formal system.

Ways and Means of Disseminating Information

Environmental information is not lacking. But the print media is not accessible to the public as majority of them are illiterate. Radio programmes are useful in motivating people, but the message is not lasting long. Television is just reaching the interior parts of the country. Common people cannot afford to use this medium effectively. The way out is to provide public T.V. sets in community centres, libraries etc. Folk art forms can be fruitfully used in disseminating values and habits expected of the masses. Exhibitions, Padayatras, campaigns etc., are acceptable methods in communicating the desired behaviour patterns.

Knowledge of facts, concepts, figures, theories, etc., is not enough for establishing norms of behaviour conducive to environmental health. Attitudinal changes have to be brought in the minds of people, which would naturally result in behaviour modifications in the desired direction. These can be achieved only through a well planned education system, implemented whole-heartedly and with commitment. In the formal sector this cannot be achieved as the educative process is stereo typed and the system, rather rigid. Nature study should form a part of the curriculum at the school level. From the preschool stage, sensory training should be emphasised. Opportunities for observation, analysis and derivations if provided to the learners, lasting influence of these will result. These are needed in environmental health and hygiene.

Worthy Models Needed

Housing is a real problem to the masses, next only to food and clothing. It is said that poverty and illiteracy, are the twin problems that face India today. Kerala showed a model to. Indian states introducing the one lakh housing scheme. This was a boon to the homeless working class and deprived sections. Now-a-days low cost housing schemes are in plenty, especially for the benefit of the weaker sections of the society. The slums in cities and towns are now being cleared and flats are being constructed. But people living in these apartments are not made aware of the need to maintain these properly. In a newly started multi-storeyed hospital in Kerala, the patients used to spit from the top floor thus spoiling the beauty of the whole building and simultaneously polluting the air and spreading contageous diseases. If this is the situation in Kerala, one can dream of the situation in those states which are far behind in literacy level and civic consciousness. It is not enough if we provide the poor with new buildings and premises; they have to be told of the need for maintaining the surroundings neat and clean. Herein comes the need for educating the masses. Through specific examples the people should feel it their duty to keep one's family in good condition and persuade the neighbours also to be so. People throw all rubbish either in the road or in the neighbour's premises. Why so? If the other person also does similarly what would happen? This is the question to be posed to such people. If they answer after a pause, or fail to give an answer, the community or social worker can treat this as an entry point and make good use of the same. Social worker should provide examples and thereby persuade the masses to follow suit. Adult education is the solution here.

BENEFITS OF COMMUNITY EDUCATION

Community education is emerging as an inevitable phenomenon in the developing countries. Local Education

Authorities or Village Education Committees mentioned in the New Education Policy can plan the education needed for the people in a locality and try to offer the same. Local variations in curricular and co-curricular activities are essential; so also is change in education system at regular intervals to cope with the demands of the society based on emerging trends.

Tools and Techniques to be Used

Through a comprehensive survey awareness, information, knowledge, skill etc., of people in different aspects of environmental health can be ascertained. How these differ in rural and urban areas, how these are related to rural and urban development strategies etc., can be found out. The variations thus perceived will throw light on the special emphasis needed in each area. When these are ascertained, 'how to tackle the situation' will be the next problem. Questionnaire, checklist, interview, observation are the tools and techniques in securing information level on environmental health of people. This base-line data can help in evolving the content and approach of an education system, preferably non-formal, with a view to improve upon prevailing practices.

Conclusion: Doctors and para medical personnel can help in this endeavour. Personnel from the Health Services Department can deliver the goods. In their absence properly trained social workers can be engaged. The system of barefoot doctor's in China is an example. In the field of population education, it has been suggested that India has to follow Chinese example. In environmental health, we may look upto China, Singapore, German, Japan, etc.

The do's and dont's in health have to be instilled in the minds of young and old alike. If one misses the bus at the young age, he has to catch the bus at a later point, say through adult education. Health care, should become an essential comparent of education at all levels. 'Health is Wealth'. Personal hygiene alone is not enough, environmental health is equally or more important. It is the duty of every individual to ensure this. This could be achieved only through education. Hence the linkage. People's movements alone solve the problems of environmental health.

Use of Language in Formal and Non-formal Education

Language is a divine gift to human-beings. Unlike other beings like birds and animals, human beings can communicate both through symbols and sounds as well as language. Mother-tongue is the most favourite language for any one. In India people speak different languages, of which 14 are approved by the constitution for official purposes. Hindi has been accepted as the national language and English, the link language. Pupils study 3 languages 'at the school level. Opportunities are there to study foreign and Indian languages, if they: desire to do so. With this background let us examine the position of language education in India.

Language is taught even from the Pre-school stage,, though it is expected to be taught only from, the, Primary stage. This is mainly because of the parents insisting on teaching alphabets and numbers at the pre-school stage in addition to sensory training, song and dance, physical exercise etc. The first lessons in language starts when the child learns to address father arid mother in the "local tongue." This is even before the child is 1 year old. There e is no formal teaching; it is purely inform informal.

The first lessons are thus acquired from the parents, siblings and peergroups.

In the Primary stage, instruction is mainly in the mother-tongue, if not otherwise insisted on by the parents. The clamour is now for English medium schools. The 'mumy-daddy' culture is thus imbibed in the children from early years, thus paving the way for developing a hatred towards India's heritage, values and culture. This is notable phenomenon in Kerala and other metropolitan cities.

The Three Language Formulae

The Indian Education Commission headed by Dr. Kothari recommended the three language formulae and insisted that mother-tongue or regional language should be given the pride of place in the entire system of education. It was suggested that the regional language should be the medium of instruction even at the college level and language institutes were established to publish books for use in Institutions of higher learning.

Official language commissions were formed to ensure the use of local languages in the administrative set-up. Thus every effort is being made to use regional language even in courts of law. However, the common man is even now, that is after 30 years of the formulation of linguistic states in India, deprived of the use of his mother-tongue in every day life situation.

Print Medium, Monopoly of a Few

If language is the vehicle of thought and an inevitable medium in the communicative process, it is not available to the majority of Indian people, at least in print or written form. The oral culture is there; but the written one is the monopoly of a few. In India nearly 64% of the population remain illiterate. These people can express themselves; but the alphabet in written form is not accessible to them. Though they are also citizen in India who take part in the decision making process through their elected representatives, cannot read or write even their mother-tongue. The all India percentage of literacy is only 36.23% according to 1981 census. Kerala has 70.42%, being the highest among the Indian states. Tamil Nadu has 46%, with almost same level in Maharashtra. The Hindi belt has only less than the National average with Rajasthan, Bihar, Madhya Pradesh, Uttar Pradesh etc., accounting for the majority of the illiterates. Even after 39 years of independence many children are out of schools either as non-entrance or as dropout. This situation has to be tackled effectively and at the earliest opportunity.

Yet another dismal picture is that in India nearly 10 crores in the age group 15-35 are not able to read and write. For this group non-formal education is the only panacea. This group is able to communicate in oral form and understand when expressed orally. The spoken language is rather difficult from the written one. Local dialects is easily accessible and known to the masses. Regional variation exist even in the case of local languages. These are points to be borne in mind while discussing issues in language education.

NAVODAYA VIDYALAYAS

Consequent on the announcement of the New education Policy a new controversy has arisen. In the Navodaya Vidyalayas proposed to be established in each district the medium of instruction is in question. It is in the fitness of things to have the regional/local language as the medium in these vidyalayas. Hindi and English should form additional compulsory languages, but not the medium of instructions. Hindi has to be spread as the national language but it should not be imposed upon the non-Hindi speaking people of India. Even when the three language formulae was in vogue, north Indian States didn't care to teach any south Indian language. It should be a common policy in India to study 2 Indian languages and English at the school level. For the Hindi speaking areas, one south Indian language should be made compulsory. The South Indians are bound to study Hindi. Naturally there is a fear that the Hindi speaking areas will have an upper hand in All India Examinations where Hindi is the medium. It would be rather difficult to have examination simultaneously in all the 14 approved languages. It is in the context that English comes to the rescue. How far can we go like this?

In the formal system the medium of instruction for non-language subjects is in question. Whatever, be the medium it will have an upper, hand. The classification, or placement of language as first, second and third is creating difficulties not only in allotting number of periods per week—but also in specifying the level of importance offered to it. In the teaching learning process much difference exists.

Language in the Non-formal Sector

In the non-formal system the question of language is not that serious at least at the basic literacy level. In can only be the mother-tongue or regional language. No are will go in for literacy in English without adequate background in one's own tongue only as the hierarchy goes up; the medium will be in question. In open universities usually the local tongue is the medium of instruction. English can be the alternative. In correspondence and own time education, medium is of one's own choice.

Education has since been accepted as a lifelong process. If one really wants to have lifelong education, he has to be proficient in at least one language wherein—he can find enough books for reference. The concept of lifelong education is-rather new and attributed to the informal sector. Educated persons will have to continue their studies in their respective fields to be abreast of the times; he has: to master allied areas if he wishes to be a really educated person.

Modern Techniques in Language Education

Thus in all sections—formal, non-formal and informal—there is need for language. The language should be such that one can comprehend without another person's help or intervention.' It should persuade him to probe deep into the subject-of-study or enquiry. Language can gradually lead one to literature which has its own beauty rhythems etc. Language styles are different for different writers. Appreciation is a quality that has to be developed through language education teaching Modern Language has contributed micro-teaching, metholaboratory for remedial and effective teaching. Audio cassettes are now available for studying languages; short courses have been developed for acquiring mastery of languages. A language can be learnt in about 30 days with the help of should cut and another language medium. Gramophone records enable learners to follow self-study methods. This is a boon to the literate people.

For the illiterates, a ten months' course was first evolved. Then finding it difficult to retain the learners for such a long period, the period for basic literacy has been limited to 8 Months. Experiments are on for reducing even this time span it is proposed to offer literacy in 4 to 5 months. In the—each one teach one programme, nearly 150 hours have been suggested for making people literate. In all these, the non-formal sector teaching has its peculiar approaches. This is common for most Indian languages.

A Laudable Example

The Department of linguistics of Kerala University under the able leadership of Dr. V.I. Subramonian (then Prof. & Head of the Department and former V.C. of Tamil University) developed language courses to be completed in 24 days for people having competence in at least one languages. This techniques have to be evolved for all Indian languages will help promote national integration.

Children could be taught as many languages as possible Bible while they are young. The formative stage has to be properly used. The teachers handling language,: at different levels have to be trained, orientated or re-orientated as envisaged in the new education policy and its plan of action. The Indianness envisaged in the new education policy can be provided only through the mother-tongue of its citizens. Linkages may be established through link language and national language, the teaching of which also should be properly planned and implemented.

Conclusion

Heredity and Environment are two factors that affect education and development of people. If this is accepted, as a natural corollary, education at all levels should be through the mother-tongue. For those who want to acquire additional language skills, adequate provisions may be made for the same. Language and literacy skills have to be developed effectively. Newer methods and strategies have to be evolved for ensuring language proficiency at appropriate levels. There are some who believe that language teachers as a cadre are inferior to other teachers. This disparity should also go and teachers should all be equal in status and emoluments irrespective of whether they teach any language or non-language subject. Specialisation at higher levels in language education may also be offered in all Universities as an inter-disciplinary branch of studies. Non-formal education can inculcate valuable and lasting language skills among the learners. Language is thus equally important both in formal and non-formal education.

DEVELOPMENT AND NON-FORMAL EDUCATION

"Development concerns not only' man's material needs. but also the improvement of the social conditions of his life and broad human aspirations. Development is not just economic growth, it is growth plus change."

"Development is a total process, in which all aspects of human life aspirations-education, health, nutrition etc.—are involved and evaluated on the touchstone of economic growth and living standards."

"It is a social process which results in a cumulative increase in levels of consumption." It is "the evolution of a different art of living and working together". It is "all round growth of the economic structure to attain substantial and continuing increases in the standards of living of the population".

The foregoing explanations clearly indicate the dimensions of development-that it embraces all aspects of social behaviour—law and order, business, family relationships, literacy, use of gadgets etc. Thus development comprises of social and economic change. Development is not just a matter of having plenty of money, nor is it purely an economic phenomenon. Development is more than economic growth. It is a kind of modernisation. It is rather a 'remaking of society'. It is need based and resource based. It is concerned with all sections and strata of the society.

It is to be noted that development cannot be imported. It is a process of change that must be sustained indegenously by the people. It should result in the benefit of all.

It has been widely accepted that the most important investment any country can make is in its human resources. Development is impossible if it does not take place in the minds of the man who build the nation. Thus the people become the most important factor in any developmental process. They are the real objects. But many people in India belong to the exploited, downtrodden, weaker section who are also suffering from illiteracy, poverty, ill health, poor or lack of housing lack of employment etc. Any attempt at national development should try to uplift these people through proper education, employment and social status.

Human resource development has become a term of frequent use at the administrative and implementation level. Though there is no Minister for Education with cabinet rank in the Central Ministry. There is one for Human Resources Development which comprises of Education, culture, youth affairs, sports etc. The nation's intention to develop human potential is seen in this. In terms of population we are the second largest in the world with around 75 crores, leaving China alone ahead of us. Population growth in India is so appalling that by 2000 A.D. we may have 100 crores. We are pledged to provide 'health for all' by 2000 and basic literacy for all people up to 35 years by 31-3-1995. The feasibility of these targets are to be seen in due course.

Currently, nearly two thirds of Indian population are illiterate. It is more than 50% of the world illiterate population we have been rightly cautioned that if we proceed along the same times that we followed ever since attaining independence, illiteracy will continue to increase and in 2000 A.D. India will be the only country having illiterates. For India, which has established its leadership and supremacy in many respects among the world nations, this is no more tolerable. Further illiteracy is indirectly effecting our developmental and national building activities.

People who are unable to comprehend the written word are taken away by the false promises and propaganda of a section of the society. They become blind followers and not participating masses. This is not enough.

Development is a process aimed at uplifting even the weakest sections. That is what we mean by 'Antyodaya'. Once we pleaded for 'Sarvodaya'. What we now need is 'Antyodaya'. "This is possible only through educating the masses. This we can designate as people's education, community education etc. All these form part of non-formal education.

Non-formal education is not merely non-formal in approach. It is life oriented and need based. It is provided so as to suit ones aspirations, abilities, aptitudes and facilities. It is own-time education provided at convenient place and time. This—can be basic literacy, post literacy, continuing education etc. It is a boon for the dropped outs and even pushed outs. It is a solace for those who had to discontinue studies due to reasons beyond their control. The reasons may be economic, health related or socio-cultural. Irrespective of these reasons and the age level, they have to be provided with necessary alternate strategies and courses to be pursued at their own speed. Those who join non-formal education courses including correspondence courses and Open University System, are more mature, really motivated and better disciplined.

Many Indian Universities are engaged in different types of non-formal education programmes. Correspondence courses had an early start. Then came the open University system; which was first introduced in Mysore University following the footsteps of the U.K. Open University established in 1969. Adult and continuing education as well as extension programmes gained importance in the University sector only recently-due to the initiative taken by Dr. Mohan Sinha Mehta and followed-up with full vigour. by Dr. Mrs. Madhin R. Shah as 'chair-person of the UGG. Now 98 Indian Universities have Departments/ Centres/Cells for Adult, Continuing and Extension education. These have not only reached out to the community, but have started assuring their needs, aspiration, problems etc. and helping them solving these on a priority basis.

The development awareness among the masses is rather meagre. They have to be told and convinced about the impact of developmental activities during the post independence period. There are people who still believe that it is the duty of the Government to supply every thing to the people. The need for cooperation and participatory work are, not felt by them, not to speak of their active involvement. Here in comes the need for non-formal education related to development.

In the real sense of the term, non-formal education is expected to create awareness among the public-all factors—on their rights and duties, need to involve themselves in nation building activities, need for safeguarding public property, forming good habits etc. The levels of presentation and modes of approach have to differ. But the ultimate aim is the same—*viz.* all round development of the individual—body mind and spirit as envisaged by Mahatmaji. As the society in, constituted of individuals and the nation by different groups of, people, the development of every citizen is important.

Through formal education, we cannot do much to develop,. Awareness among the learners on developmental activities. Only when go from 'File to the field' can we face real situation and tackle them effectively. Such programmes are now being launched, thanks to the vision of service minded bureaucrats and administrators. Target oriented, time bound, life related' programme launched through dedicated workers, monitored and evaluated gestifically by appropriate personnel alone can deliver the goods and bring in desired changes. This can be Non-formal in approach but not completely avoided formalities.

Public accountability should not be lost sight of. Separate frames of reference appropriate to different sections of the people, localities, geographic and cultural backgrounds have to be developed and content for such non-formal education should be highly flexible and diverse to relate it closely with development.

Books for Neoliterates in Malayalam

Who is a Neoliterate?: A 'neoliterate' is one who has acquired the ability to read and write his/her mother-tongue, 'rather late'. In other words, any one who didn't or could not make use of the available educational opportunities, on time, and who later on acquired the skills of reading and writing through some means or other (formal, informal or non-formal) can be said to be a neoliterate. He/she was hitherto unable to read and comprehend the printed or written word but can, now, with fluency or with difficulty, read and understand the print media. The reading speed and power of comprehension might differ from person to person and appropriate reading materials are required for them.

Do We Need Separate Books for Neoliterates?: The books already available in the market are either meant for the literate, educated, elite group or for children of different age levels. These are in no way appropriate for the neoliterates, who have enough of experience and maturity, but reading habit has to be inculcated in them through appropriate steps. Books for neoliterates should have certain specific qualities. Children's books are offered to neoliterates who find nothing challenging for them both in content and narration. The bold letters used is the only common criterion. The simple illustrations do not attract the adults. The reading interests of adults have to be taken care of and themes catering to their interests have to be published. The content should be such that they get something new from their exercise of reading a book. Hence it is inevitable to have separate books for neoliterates.

Certain Misconceptions

There are some-people who believe that any book can be given to anyone who can read and that proper reading habits can be cultivated in due course. This may be true of children and in the case of 'guided reading'. But generally, this is not the case with neoliterates. Many books printed and published for the 'neoliterates' are quite inappropriate for them and even curb the reading interests of such people. Books for 'continuing education' are considered by some as useful for neoliterates too. This alarming situation is doing more harm than good.

Qualities Expected of Neoliterate Books

The following are the guidelines that are generally accepted:

1. Neoliterate books should deal with the immediate surroundings, needs, aspirations etc., of the neoliterate. They should easily attract the attention of the reader and tempt him to read more books.
2. The vocabulary should be in accordance with those of the neoliterates and the style of presentation, simple. Small sentences with familiar words should be preferred. The narration should be interesting enough and not boring. Unfamiliar objects and situations should be illustrated. Chapters should deal with relevant aspects of the main theme. Care should be taken not to permit factual errors in the books.
3. The format and lay out as also the cover should be designed properly. The size of the book should be Demi 1/8 or RA 5 size. As far as possible, 12 or 14 point. bold type should be used. Still bigger types may have to be used for chapter headings. The number of pages in each book should be not more than 48.
4. The books should convey the message of better living and social progress. Taboos and superstitious beliefs have to be rooted out, gradually, through appropriate measures. Conversational style and familiar situations have to be preferred.
5. The books should be graded according to the vocabulary, content etc., and readability, from the point of view of the learner. All neoliterate books need not be of the same difficulty level. There should be books on science and technology, occupations, personalities, places of importance, jurisprudence, health and hygiene etc., besides short stories and dramas. Folk songs may also be attempted.

In conclusion, a neoliterate book should be such that at-first sight one should be tempted to take the book and examine it, read it at a stretch and read it again and again for ensuring better comprehension. Care should be taken in selecting paper, type, ink, illustrations, cover design, etc., and even in fixing the cost of the book within the reach of the prospective beneficiaries.

In the Name of Awards

The Ministry of Education and Culture of the Government of India has been organising prize competitions for neoliterate books for the last two decades or so. Every year 5 or 6 books in Malyalam also are given awards. These are not, any way, of a high standard. It is true that out of the entries the better ones are selected. Only few submit, manuscripts for the competition. Some are not aware of it due to lack of publicity. At times extension of time limit is given at the last minute and many could not make use of this extension. As one who has examined the books many times, I can say that many more books are there in the field which deserve to be honoured through awards. Provision should be made for entry of published works and fees should be abolished. The Ministry should get necessary copies of all neoliterate books published every year and select the good ones for the award. Further, criteria for evaluation should be scientifically fixed and selection made only on that basis. Awards shouldn't be for the sake of awards, but it should be for motivating more people to write neoliterate books which are of a better standard.

Kerala Grandhasala Sanghom: On successful completion of the first pilot project on functional literacy, the Kerala Grandhasala Sanghom resolved to publish 1000 books for neoliterates and a list was prepared along with some guidelines. Workshops were organised and 150 scripts were prepared out of which nearly 100 have been published so far. Due to lack of financial support, the books are not attractive; most of them are substandard and not much useful for neoliterates when viewed from their level of vocabulary and reading ability. Anyway, being the first concerted effort, the work deserves all praise.

KANFED: When KANFED was formed in 1977 exclusively for linking adult and non-formal education with development through spreading literacy and creating a learning society, it decided to publish a set of 1000 books for neoliterates. Nearly 150 have been published so far with financial support from the German Adult Education Association. Here too, workshops were organised and writers paid better than the Sanghom. Books have been made more attractive and rather cheap. In an attempt to produçe a number of books within a short span of time, unnecessary titles have also come up which tempt one to remark that KANFED books are more for 'continuing education' than for the neoliterates who have just acquired the skill of reading. Anyway KANFED books, in general, are superior to those published by the Sanghom, in may respects. Only a Scientific Study at comparing and evaluating the available neoliterate books can lead to valid conclusions.

(a) Kerala Gandhi Smaraka Nidhi has published some books which are mainly meant for people's education. These can't be termed neoliterate books.

(b) The State Institute of Education also has published a number of books which again are of the continuing education type. These are not claimed to be neoliterate books.

(c) The Kerala Shastra Sahitya Parishad through their popular science series are spreading science among the laymen. The books are meant for the literates but if simplified, can be used for neoliterates.

(d) The Children's literature series published by many agencies can be modified to suit the neoliterates.

Sporadic attempts at preparing and published books for neoliterates are in progress. These have to be pooled and encouraged. Formation of a Neoliterate Book Publishing Society has to be thought of so as to improve the production of neoliterate literature.

6

EDUCATION IN THE FIVE YEAR PLANS

PREINDEPENDENCE EDUCATIONAL PLANS

We are mainly concerned with education at the college level. We shall, therefore, restrict ourselves chiefly to the college/ university education, and that too general education under these plans both in the pre-independence and post-independence period. The first effort in planning in the private sector for national development was made in 1938 under the Chairmanship of Pandit Jawaharlal Nehru. Two sub-committees were setup under the Chairmanship of Dr. Radhakrishnan and Dr. M. N. Shah to draw up the educational development plans. Nothing tangible could be done by these commissions due to the turn of the political situation in the Congress ministries going out of office. This was thus the first Planning Commission for the national development to set the ball rolling. Though it proved abortive and could not achieve anything worthwhile it certainly served the country by its failure. This non-official effort to draw up an educational plan for the country prompted the Government of India in 1943 to prepare a plan of post-war development for all sectors. Sir John Sargeant was then the Educational Commissioner to the Government of India. A Committee under his chairmanship was given the responsibility to prepare a comprehensive plan of the educational development in the country.

The plan was approved by the Central Advisory Board of Education in 1944 and with some modifications it was submitted to the Government of India. The plan was popularly known as the Sargeant Plan after the name of the chairman of the committee. It was pointed out by the committee that the universities in India had not yet realised the full aims and aspirations of university education in the highest sense in spite of the best attention that had been devoted to the university education and the valuable contributions they had made to the human knowledge. In order to improve the standards of education at the college level it was recommended that.

(i) Conditions for admission may be revised so that only those students join the colleges as are capable of benefiting from the university courses.

(ii) The present intermediate course of two years after matriculation my be abolished. The first part of this course may be shifted to the high schools and the second part to the colleges.. Thus there will be eleven-year school and three-year degree college.

(iii) The tutorial system may be largely extended so that better personal contacts could be established between the teachers and the students.

(iv) Research of a high ratequality may be done at the post-graduate level.

(v) Salaries of teachers both in the colleges and universities may be suitably enhanced so that better teachers could be attracted to colleges/universities. The conditions of work and service too may be improved.

(vi) A University Grants Committee may be setup which could coordinate the functioning of various universities and allocate grants to the universities for their over-all improvement.

(vii) In order that no poor child of ability was excluded from higher education, liberal assistance in the form of fee, scholarships and stipends should be made available to them throughout the course.

(viii) The number of existing training institutions being inadequate, more training colleges may be setup so that training facilities could be extended to suitable boys and girls who could become really competent teachers in secondary schools.

But the plan was not accepted by the people at large for various reasons.

It's implementation was spread over a long span of forty years. The plan was prepared by the alien government which was not fully conversant with the economic and social structure of the country and also did not take into cognizance the political aspirations of her people.

The changed political pattern of the country laid more stress on expansion of education at all levels whereas the Sargeant plan laid stress on quality. In fact it is always better to attend to quality after the adequate expansion has taken place. The plan did not take into consideration the possible sources of income of the country. It was considered a very costly plan and thus could not sustain. The plan was prepared without adequate data and the projections of the population growth had not been taken into account.

It is true that the plan could not be implemented in full in the post-independence period but many of these recommendations were incorporated in the reports of the Commission and Committees that were setup later and on the basis of which the five year plans of Free India were formulated.

THE FIVE YEAR PLANS AND EDUCATION

The importance of 'planning' cannot be overemphasised in any sector of life. Educational planning "formulates a systemwide philosophy general goals and instructional objectives". It organises the relevant available data, projects into the Future, determines personnel and material requirements and establishes priorities in accordance with the resources and requirements.

The essence of planning is to attempt more than what plain prudence dictates. This is where the element of faith, determination and adventure come in. A plan is a charter of the progress of people who go ahead courageously in spite of numerous problems and handicaps. Immediately after the adoption of India's constitution in 1950, the government embarked upon the systematic planning for the development of the country. So far we have completed Six Five Year Plans and are in the midst of Seventh Five Year Plan. Education being the most important component of the growth of a nation, it has held a key position in these plans. The destiny of a country is determined more by its educational programmes than by any other single factor. It is through planning that we have been able to make achievements which are the envy of most of the countries.

First Five Year Plan

The First Five Year Plan document as prepared by the Planning Commission prefaces with the brief task of educational planning which can be summarised as below:

(i) To make available in the various fields, personnel of suitable quality.

(ii) To satisfy the cultural needs of the people which is so essential for the healthy growth of a nation.

(iii) To stimulate the growth of creative faculties.

(iv) To increase the capacity for enjoyment and developments spirit of critical appreciation of arts, literature and other creative activities.

We can have a true picture of the progress made during the post-independence period if we could look at the position of post-matric or college education before we launched the first five Year Plan. Considering the size of the country and population of the country the overall provision of educational facilities was very inadequate. The literacy was hardly 17 per cent and there was provision of education for only 0.9 per cent for the age groups 17-23 years. This in simple language means that only nine persons out of a thousand could avail of college education. It was still felt that education was "top heavy". The provision at the secondary stage was considered properly proportional to that at the primary stage. But the provision at the university stage was believed to be much larger than the base structure could possibly support.

Therefore in the field of higher education the problem was of consolidation rather than of expansion. However, it was felt that educational facilities were not properly distributed between urban and rural areas. At the university level facilities were not properly distributed. They were practically non-existent in the rural areas. The reasons were obvious. The British rulers did not want to carry education to the rural areas where 80 per cent of the people of the country lived. They wanted to educate only the elite so that they could help them in running the administration.

Undue emphasis was laid on the academic and theoretical aspects of education which led to a lot of wastage. Due to the absence of facilities for technical and vocational education, the outputs of the colleges and the universities depended too much on employment by government or commercial concerns which could absorb only a limited number of them. Higher education was considered very costly. Only the affluent people or the big landlords could afford to send their children for university education. Many a talented youth who could benefit and could be source of strength to the society were deprived of the privilege of higher education. Another major defect of the educational system was the emphasis on examinations.

The First Five Year Plan, therefore, set out to strengthen and improve, higher education. The Ministry of Education had appointed a University Education Commission in 1948 to examine the entire question of university education under the chairmanship of Dr. Radhakrishnan. This Commission made a number of recommendations to improve the quality of education at that level.

Most of these recommendations were envisaged in the First Five Year Plan. The Planning Commission recommended the setting up of a University Grants Commission which came into existence in November 1953. The Commission visualised that this organisation (UGC) will advise the Central Government on:

(a) the maintenance of high standards of teaching and research in the universities;

(b) the establishment of new universities or the expansion of the existing ones; and

(c) allocation of funds for grants to the universities.

Excepting three institutions directly administered by the Central Government, universities were a state subject and therefore the all-India aspects were likely to be neglected. There was a great disparity in the quality of administration in various universities. The function of the UGC therefore included the ensuring of maximum standards of teaching and internal administration in the various universities and securing of proper attention for the national aspects of university education. The UGC was expected to bring about improvement in the university education and to coordinate the post-graduate work at the various universities which would bring better results and better economy. The establishment of the UGC has really proved a boon in boosting the talent of the youth and for bringing about numerous worthwhile reforms at the university level.

To bridge the gap between the urban and rural areas as far as university education was concerned, the University Education Commission (1948) had recommended the establishment of rural universities. The First Five Year Plan supported the establishment of at least one rural university before the close of the plan period. It was not considered feasible to setup a rural university and instead rural institutions were setup in various parts of the country. The rural institutes were to offer a three-year diploma course which was considered at par with the degree conferred by universities as far as the recruitment to government jobs was concerned. Unfortunately this idea did not catch the imagination of the people in general. If the rural institutes could have become the order of the day, a metamorphosis must have come about in our rural life.

Some other recommendation made by the Radhakrishnan Commission were endorsed for a follow up in the First Five Year Plan.

(1) Residential life in hostels should be provided, facilities for private study may be provided through correspondence courses, radio lectures.

(2) This would reduce the overcrowding in college and help the students to enter life early.

(3) Admission to colleges and universities should be made selective and the recruitment of the teaching staff should be done through competitive tests.

(4) Standards of teaching should be improved.

(5) The number of working days in a college be raised to at least one hundred and eighty.

(6) An atmosphere of discussion and free thinking should be encouraged through seminars, teachers' and students' camps.

(7) One-sidedness of present university education should be corrected so that arts students may have basic scientific knowledge and science students the essential knowledge of the humanities.

(8) The age limit of admission to colleges may be raised.

(9) Guest speakers may be invited to colleges.

(10) Vocational guidance and aptitude tests are in an underdeveloped stage, steps should be taken to make up this deficiency as early as possible.

In order to develop a more balanced outlook, personality and habits of cooperation and self-help, students should engage themselves in such activities as community cleaning, making and repairs of roads within the college compound, gardening, visits to the countryside and slums, etc. These activities will have the additional advantage of reducing the maintenance of a college.

There were no programmes of expansion for higher education at the Ministry of Education level. However the state governments did have their own programmes for university education. Schemes at the state level included opening of new universities and colleges and improvement and expansion of existing colleges. Improvement schemes mostly consisted of improvement of buildings and equipment. Expansion, schemes involved opening of new classes for new subjects, mostly scientific subjects. Provision for scholarships to meritorious students and for research was also made.

The outstanding features of the First Five Year Plan were:

(1) UGC was setup.

(2) The gap between the urban and the rural areas was bridged to some extent.

(3) Facilities for private study were provided.

(4) Provision for scholarships to meritorious students was made.

Second Five Year Plan

The recommendations of the university education commission; Secondary Education Commission and a number of committees which had been setup during the first plan period or a little earlier were available for the guidance of the framers of the plan. The weakness of the educational programmes and the ways and means to strengthen them as pointed out by these commissions and committees were taken care of and in the light thereof further programmes were formulated.

The Second Five Year Plan provides for a greater emphasis on basic education, expansion of elementary education, diversification of secondary education, improvement of standards of college and university education, extension of facilities for technical and vocational education and implementation of social education and cultural development programmes. The rapid increase in the number of students in universities and colleges during the post-independence period in particular had largely affected the standards of education. At the end of the first plan period the total enrolment was estimated to be 720,000 as compared to 420,000 five years before. The number of students qualifying each year in degree and higher examinations in arts and science had risen during the period from 41,000 to 58,000. The Government of India took a number of measures through the UGC to improve the quality of education at the university/college level.

The three year degree course which had been recommended by successive commissions had not been implemented as yet in spite of very cogent reasons for the proposal. It was during the second plan period that this institution of three year degree course was initiated throughout the country by the UGC and organisation of tutorials and seminars was emphasised by the universities.

Introduction of diversified courses at the secondary level was another landmark to improve the college education. A large number of students after the school stage could divert to various vocations instead of rushing to the colleges. The scheme of multipurpose or multilateral schools was launched. A multipurpose school was to provide various types of courses for students with diverse aims, interests and abilities. This helped the students to develop their natural aptitudes and inclinations in the special courses of studies chosen by them. Above all, this change in the curricular programme gave them a dignity of labour and manual work. The courses of study included both general and vocational subjects and the pupils bad the opportunity to choose from both the streams according to their needs or aptitudes.

A great importance was given to the improvement of college and university plants. Improvement of buildings, laboratories, libraries, provision of hostel facilities, stipends for meritorious students and scholarship for research and increase in the salaries of teachers in the universities were some of the salient features of the Second Five Year Plan. The total provision for the university education in the plan was about 57 crores (22.5 crore at state level and 34.6 at the Central level out of which Rs. 27 crore were allocated to the U.G.C). This was against a provision of about Rs. 15 crores in the First Five Year Plan. Thus there was an increase of 280 per cent outlay in the Second Five Year Plan. In fact there was emphasis more on consolidation than on expansion except of technical and scientific education in the universities. The planners stressed that university education should acquire greater purpose and direction. It should fit more closely with the plan of economic and social development through suitable action at the secondary as well as the university stages and through appropriate changes in the conditions and methods of recruitment to public services. The outstanding features of the Second Five Year Plan were:

(1) Three-year degree course was initiated.

(2) College teachers' salaries were improved.

(3) There was expansion of technical and scientific education.

(4) A great importance was given to the improvement of university and college plants.

Third Five Year Plan

The main emphasis in the third plan, as visualised by the Planning Commission, was on the provision of facilities for the education of all children in the age group six to eleven years, extension and improvement of teaching of science at the secondary and the university stages; development of vocational and technical education at all levels, expansion and improvement of facilities for the training of teachers for each stage of education;

increase in scholarships, freshens and other assistance. There was to be a special emphasis on the education of girls and the disparity in levels of development in education between boys and girls was to be substantially reduced. At all stages of education the aim was to develop both skill and knowledge and a creative outlook; a feeling of national unity which stands above region, caste and language and an understanding of common interests and obligations was to be boosted. With the expansion of elementary and secondary education, there was a great demand for higher education. The number of colleges rose from 772 in 1955-56 to 1050 in 1960-61. During the plan period about 70-80 colleges were to be added every year to meet the rising aspirations of the people. Over the past decade covering the first two plans the number of universities had increased from 27 in 1950-51 to 32 in 1955-56 and to 46 in 1960-61 and about a dozen more universities were likely to be added during the third plan over the decade 1951-61. The increase in the number of pupils was unprecedented.

To meet a host of problems which were likely to come in the wake of more colleges and more universities the planners suggested that:

(1) Physical and teaching facilities may be added commensurate with the expansion of university education.

(2) Suitable criteria for admission be worked out.

(3) Proposals for evening colleges and corresponding courses be prepared.

(4) Large facilities may be provided for diverting students to vocational and technological education.

The number of training colleges in the third plan was expected to increase from 236 in 1960-61 to 312. In fact there had been a significant addition in the number of training college in the second plan too. There were only 53 training colleges in 1950-51. This large increase had diluted the standards of education in the colleges and the schools where their (training colleges) outputs were posted to impart instructions. The existing training colleges were therefore to be strengthened by the introduction of new techniques of teaching and evaluation and audio-visual education and the organisation of research.

A greater emphasis was laid on science education during the third plan. The third plan envisaged that out of the increase of about three lakh of students at the university stage about 60 per cent should be in respect of science classes bringing the proportion of students taking science courses to over 42 per cent. Large provision of scientific equipment and appointment of science teachers was made. It was proposed to prepare lists of scientific equipments for the guidance of the educational authorities. Schemes were also to be initiated for the manufacture and supply of such equipment at low cost. A large number of scholarships were to be provided to the meritorious science students and continuing review of standards of teaching and examination in science and technology at all levels was also to be carried out. Preparation and publication of standard text-books for use was to be undertaken.

Post-graduate studies and research in science was to be further expanded in the third plan. Assistance had been given to the colleges and universities for the development of special fields of scientific studies such as geophysics, astronomy, astro-physics, applied geology, oceanography, applied physics and animal genetics. In humanities, departments of Buddhistic and African studies and institutions or departments for studies in Hindi, linguistics and social sciences and for archaeology, and music had been setup in the second plan. These programmes initiated during the earlier plan were to be continued and further developed during the third plan. The UGC was also to assist universities and colleges in the development of post-graduate studies and research particularly in the field of science. For this research fellowships were also initiated. It was expected that the number of post-graduate studies in science would increase by seven thousand and the number of research studies will increase by about a thousand.

Shortage of educated women available for taking up various occupations pointed to the need of increasing the proportion of women students in colleges and universities.

The proportion of women students to the total enrolment in Indian universities was about 13 per cent in 1955-56 and about 17 per cent in 1960-61 and was expected to be about 21 per cent in 1965-66. Courses of special interests such as home science, music, drawing, painting nursing etc. had been introduced in the Second Five Year Plan. These facilities were further to be expanded in the Third Five Year Plan. During the Second Five Year Plan UGC provided liberal assistance—for women's colleges and womens' hostels. This was to be continued in the Third Five Year Plan. Further in order to encourage women students special scholarship were to be continued. In view of the Report of the National Committee on Women's Education special efforts were to be made to boost the girls' education.

A proposal for setting up an institution for training women in organisation, administration and management was to be under active consideration of the government.

Three-year-degree course had been introduced in the Second plan. Other necessary reforms such as improvement in the teacher-pupil ratio, introduction of tutorial system, improvement of libraries, laboratories and instructional buildings were to be continued, periodical conferences, seminars, summer schools and refresher courses were to be continued for teachers in various subjects. Teachers were also to obtain special grants for visiting centres of research for short periods.

Among additional amenities for students during the second plan were the:

(a) Provision of hostels,

(b) Hobby workshops,

(c) Health centres,

(d) Non-resident students' centres,

(e) Counselling, and

(f) Student aid funds.

All these programmes were to continue in the third plan also.

Expenditure on scholarships rose from about Rs. 3.5 crore in 1950-51 to Rs. 8 crore in 1955-56 and to 11 crore in 1960-61. The number of scholarship holders rose from 3.6 lakh in 1950-51 to 8.8 lakh in 1956-57 (out of this 7.8 lakh were in schools and one lakh in colleges and universities), and to 11.8 lakhs in 1960-61. In addition to this by 1956-57 free studentships and financial concessions were available to 50 lakh of students, 1.5 lakh being in colleges and universities.

The proportion of students receiving scholarship rose from 9 per cent in 1950-51 to 16 per cent in 1960-61. An important scheme for scholarships is the one relating to post-matriculation scholarships for scheduled tribes, scheduled castes and other backward classes. State plans also were to provide for the extension of existing schemes of scholarship. Among the schemes of scholarships undertaken by the Ministry of Education the scheme of national scholarships for outstanding students at the post-matric stage, scholarship for overseas studies and a wide range of scholarship offered by foreign countries and international agencies to Indian students need a special reference.

It was emphasised in the third plan that the state governments also should revise their existing schemes of the award of scholarship so that the scholarships enable the promising students in need of assistance to complete their education and that they should not be discontinued at some intermediate stage. Attempts were continued to improve the economic and social status of teachers. During the first two plans a number of research institutions had been setup at the school level. They were to be continued in the third plan. In addition to these, extension departments were setup in the training college.

The UGC had setup Examination Research Units in three universities, further research work was to be organised in the third plan in more of the universities. Evaluation personnel were to be trained in large numbers so that the examination reforms could be implemented in right earnest.

In the sphere of youth activities grants were to be given for the construction of stadia, swimming pools, open-air theatres etc. Steps were also taken for the promotion of the activities of the National Cadet Corps, Auxiliary Cadet Corps, Bharat Scouts and Guides and the National Discipline Scheme. The first national college of physical education at Gwalior was setup in the second plan which was to be continued in the third plan. The National Institute of Sports had to be developed in the third plan so as to provide for all the major games. With the help of the coaches trained at the Institute, a national coaching scheme providing for widespread coaching facilities was to be introduced so that the standard of sports could be gradually raised. The National Physical efficiency drive was to be further intensified.

The salient features of the Third Five Year Plan were:

(1) Girls' education was greatly emphasised.

(2) More scholarships and fee concessions were allowed in universities and colleges. The National Scholarship Scheme was instituted.

(3) Examination Research Units were setup in some universities.

(4) National Institute of Sports was to be developed.

Fourth Five Year Plan

The plan could not be started in 1966. (There was a plan holiday for three years.)

During the third plan period, there had been a substantial expansion in enrolment at all levels of education in India. But the expansion of numbers had been accompanied by a certain measure of deterioration in quality. According to the draft outline of Fourth Five Year Plan.

"The Indian educational system has not been sufficiently geared to economic development, insufficient attention having been paid to vocational and agricultural education, girls education has still a long way to go before it can catch up with that of boys. The high proportion of failures, the third classes at the university stage especially in regard to pass course bear evidence of the need for improvement in quality." The statement thus directs to the points of main emphasis in the Fourth Five Year Plan. It may be pointed out that in the previous plan no realistic efforts had been made to introduce schemes of 'national education'. What was done was mostly the extension of existing pattern. Several models in various sectors of education were borrowed from USA, UK and Russia which hardly fitted in our situation.

It had been observed that the plans at the Central level and at the state level were framed by the high-ups on the basis of their own idiosnycracies, having no knowledge of the practical difficulties of the teachers or the heads of the institutions in most of the cases. The teacher, at any level, who was the crux of the situation was altogether neglected. These plans therefore did not emerge from the grass roots but filtered down from the top. In the words of J.P. Naik these plans were like on inverted pyramid having a narrow base and a heavy top. The slant was changed in the Fourth Five Year Plan. The three preceding plans had no clear vision of the goals of education and thus they failed to steer in a definite direction. The main emphasis was only on the achievements of targets in enrolment and expenditure. The planners aimed at providing more funds and the consumers' attempt was to spend the provided amounts to the last rupee. In fact the educational officers were taken to task if they failed to achieve the targets of expenditure without caring about the net results. The author had to pay through the nose when he objected to the spending of a few lakhs of rupees placed at his disposal towards the fag end of the year by the state education department. In some cases the money was just dumped in obviously unproductive projects. This weakness was taken care of in the fourth plan.

The Fourth Five Year Plan attempted three major tasks in the field of education *i.e.*,

(1) to remove the deficiencies in the existing educational system,

(2) to link it more effectively with the increasing demands of social and economic development, and

(3) to remove internal stresses and strains in the education system which had developed as a consequence of rapid expansion during the first three plans.

Framers of the fourth plan at the Centre and the state level stressed that investments in education should seek better returns by avoiding wastage and improving the quality at all levels. High priority was to be given to consolidation, diversification and work orientation. Training of the technical personnel was to be given high priority. The emphasis at the elementary stage was to be on free and universal primary education, elimination of wastage and stagnation. At the secondary stage the provision of vocational education of a terminal character and the strengthening of the science teaching were to be given special attention. At the post-matric and university stages the emphasis was to be on diverting the students to vocations, technical and professional channels and on extending facilities for science and post-graduate teaching and research work. Quality of teaching was to be improved with the greater insistence on the training of teachers and by linking increase in status to improvement in qualifications. Summer institutes were to be organised to provide in-service education to the college teachers. Research in curriculum and methods of teaching were to be intensified. To boost the economic development of the country great emphasis ways to be laid on extending adult education and functional literacy.

Book production in Indian languages received greater attention. A number of state university textbook boards were setup in various states to produce college/university level books in the regional languages. Translation of books on science and technology in foreign languages was encouraged. This provided a great help in making the regional languages, the medium of instruction at the undergraduate level or even the post-graduate level. Lack of suitable books on scientific subjects in the regional languages was a great handicap in imparting education. The scheme of loan scholarships was instituted in the Fourth Five Year Plan. This was a big step towards the democratisation of education. The objective of the scheme was to enable every student of merit to study upto the highest level. Loan scholarships prompted the students to keep up their performance and to shun agitations and anti-social activities. Special attention was to be paid to the education of the members of the scheduled castes and tribes through these loans and many more concessions.

The plan envisages the steps to slow down the number of students for arts and commerce courses and to extend the facilities for science, agriculture, technical and medical education. No new universities were contemplated during the fourth plan. Instead preference was to be given to setting up of university centres for post-graduate studies each embedded in a complex of colleges with a large enrolment. Such centres were to have adequate laboratory facilities, libraries and a number of university teachers. Later on most of the these centres developed into independent full-fledged centres/ universities. Better results were visualised by insisting on large sized institutions (particularly technical), maximum utilisation of buildings, libraries and laboratories for longer hours, part-time and correspondence courses. Efforts were also to be made to mobilise local resources and to establish a close relationship between the educational institutions and the community. It was also proposed to link the institutes of rural higher education with developments in rural area, through suitable adjustment of courses and admissions.

The expansion of universities and the increase in the number of persons enrolled in colleges and other institutions of higher learning is a striking feature of the years since independence. Enrolment at the university stage in science, arts and commerce faculties has gone up from 0.3 million in 1950-51 to 1.1 million in 1965-66. While during each of the first two plans the enrolment increased by 0.2 million, it is estimated to have risen by 0.4 million in the third plan, whereas the target of increase in enrolment for the fourth plan was 0.5 million. An important sector of post-secondary education in the fourth plan is the training of teachers for elementary as well as secondary schools.

The importance of teacher education was to be largely emphasised during the fourth plan due to the unprecedented increase in enrolment at the elementary and secondary stage. It was felt that investment in teacher education would yield rich dividends. Unfortunately the professional education of teachers had been comparatively neglected in the first three plan periods though its importance had largely been stressed by various commissions. By and large, training institutions had remained isolated from the main stream of academic life, of the university as well as from the daily problems of the schools.

In the fourth plan the additional requirements of teachers were estimated to be 779,000 (500,000 for additional enrolment and 279,000 for replacement at the rate of 3 per cent) for the elementary stage and 209,000 (152,000 for additional enrolment and 57,000 for replacement at the ratio of 4 per cent) for the secondary stage. To meet these additional needs of teachers more facilities for whole time teacher education and for correspondence and short term courses were to be made available. The plan was to provide for 140,000 elementary teachers and about 17,660 secondary teachers. For whole time trainees, additional places were to be found largely by expansion of existing institutions rather than by opening new ones.

Short-term courses were to be organised to help the teachers improve their knowledge of particular subjects. The universities, state institutes of science education, state institutes of education, summer institutes and correspondence courses etc. were to be utilised for the purpose. An intimate connection was to be established between teacher training institutions and the universities. The universities were to be encouraged to setup departments of education or schools of education. Incentives in the form of cash awards and special increments in salaries were provided in the plan for teachers to enhance their academic and professional qualifications.

An important step towards the improvement of teacher education was to setup comprehensive teacher training colleges where teachers of different disciplines were to be provided teacher training in the same institutions. This was to be a very healthy measure to break the artificial barriers between different categories of teachers and to help in building up sound traditions for the profession. Besides, large institutions could be more economical and in a better position to employ well-paid staff and to provide more chances of promotion. But unfortunately the comprehensive colleges were not very much welcome and ceased to exist in most of the states in the years to follow. The salient features of the Fourth Five Year Plan were:

(1) The educational plans began emerging from the grass roots. A new direction was thus given to education.

(2) Great emphasis was laid on avoiding wastage and improving quality.

(3) In-service education programmes were boosted.

(4) Teacher education became a part of the mainstream of academic life.

Fifth Five Year Plan

The thrust of the plan was mainly in four directions:

(a) *Ensuring of Equality of Educational Opportunities:* This was to include, besides other measures scholarships, freeships and remedial coaching for students from weaker sections and a provision of non-formal education for those who were forced to enter life early.

(b) *Linkage with Employment and Development:* For this the curriculum was to be reformed and the vocational courses were to be introduced as a part of general education at the university stage.

(c) *Quality Improvement Thereof*: The major programmes under this were to include the examination reform, the teacher training including in-service training, improvement of text-books and improvement of physical facilities and improvement in teaching and learning methodologies.

(d) *Linkage with Social Environment:* To build up social consciousness among the youth, social service was to be an integral part of the curriculum at the undergraduate and the post-graduate level.

The main problems confronting university education were the rapid expansion of higher education without corresponding increase in physical facilities, lack of coordination with the social life; widespread lowering of standards consequent on rapid and unprecedented increase of the students' body; deterioration in the quality of teaching and increasing incidence of unemployment among university graduates. The main strategy for the development of University education was, therefore, to be such as to ensure that on the one hand the rising expectations of the newly emerging socio-economic group continue to be met and on the other, indiscriminate expansion is not allowed to further dilute the standard of university education.

The courses of study were also to be restructured so that the students completing the education were enabled to become productive members of society. The admission to the colleges was to be rationalised keeping both these factors in view. The Indian economy had neither the resources to meet the expansion of higher education at this rate nor did it have the capacity to absorb all its outputs. The admissions therefore had to be suitably streamlined. The following steps were suggested to restrict the admissions.

(i) Vocationalising of higher secondary education.

(ii) Limiting admissions to regular institutions following some well-defined standards.

(iii) Providing evening colleges, correspondence courses and private study.

(iv) Formulating suitable recruitment policy—not emphasising on the university degrees where they were not essential. The effort, was to meet 50 per cent of the demand for additional facilities in regular institutions, 20 per cent through evening colleges, 20 per cent through correspondence courses and 10% through private study. Special attention was to be given to the expansion-of facilities for higher education in backward area.

Post-graduate Education and Research: Admissions at the post-graduate level were to be selective. It was emphasised that as for as possible facilities for post-graduate education and research should mainly be available in the universities and in the post-graduate centres located in places with a cluster of colleges. The various universities in a state were required to collaborate to provide post-graduate facilities in various subjects at a fairly high level of excellence and to avoid unnecessary duplication.

Scientific and technological research in the universities and other institutions of higher learning were to be supported on an adequate scale so as to develop first rate research capabilities within the educational system. The existing programmes of improvement of physical facilities, curricular and examination reform, production of improved text-books, especially in the regional languages, promotion of innovations and improving teacher competency were to be continued.

The curricular reform was to aim at making the courses more flexible by allowing considerable freedom in the combination of subjects. The employability of the graduates was to be increased by linking the courses with practical problems and social utilisation. The programme of examination reform already started by the UGC was to be speeded up during the fifth plan. Some selected institutions were to bee recognised as autonomous colleges for promoting innovations in curriculum, methods of teaching, evaluation of students etc.

Student Services: A number of schemes were included to provide basic amenities to the students at the university stage. These included increased provision of hostels, day-student homes, health centres, cafeteria, book banks etc. Creative channels for utilising the energy of the youth were provided through stepping up programmes of games and sports, cultural activities and the involvement of the students in the task of social and economic development. Employment orientation courses were to be introduced and guidance services expanded. No new conventional universities were to be established. Post-graduate centres were to be setup to meet the post-graduate and research needs. These centres could be developed into universities in due course of time. The experiment like that of the open university was to be tried. To encourage talent and to overcome the handicaps of the weaker sections considerably, increased emphasis was to be laid on scholarships in various fields. According to the draft fifth five year plan, the supply of teachers at the school level was been adequate in number, except in some states in the eastern region. Therefore in the fifth plan the emphasis was laid on consolidation and improvement of teacher education programme. The following programmes of quality improvement in teacher education were proposed in the fifth plan.

(1) Reorientation of curricula and examination reform in training institutions for better academic and professional preparation of teachers.

(2) Provision of refresher courses for teacher educators.

(3) Comprehensive programmes of in-service training of existing teachers.

(4) Establishment of extension services department in training institutions for regular guidance of schools.

(5) Setting up of State boards of teacher education in the states.

(6) Development of a few comprehensive colleges of education in order to break down the isolation between the various types of teacher-training institutions.

(7) Improvement in teaching and learning methodologies in the training institutions.

(8) Improvement of physical facilities in the training institutions.

(9) Encouraging research, experimentation and innovation in teacher education.

(10) Increased use of educational technology and mass media.

But as no funds had been set apart for teacher education, most of the programmes of quality improvement remained on paper only.

Some of the national, state and local organisations did make some contribution in their own way to bring about quality improvement in the teacher preparation programmes but no breakthrough could be made in this important area which plays a very important role in producing quality teachers for secondary and elementary schools.

The following are some outstanding features of the Fifth Five Year Plan:

(1) Remedial coaching and more scholarships for weaker sections of society.

(2) More emphasis on non-formal education and scientific and technical research.

(3) Stress on level of excellence in the matter of post-graduate studies.

(4) Some selected colleges were to be recognised as autonomous colleges; open university was to be tried.

(5) Emphasis was laid on consolidation and improvement of teacher education programmes.

Sixth Five Year Plan

The education system during the last four: decades has recorded a phenomenal growth. By 1979-80 the total number of schools had increased to about 8 lakh from 2.9 lakh in 19:0-51. The corresponding increase in enrolment was from 255 lakh to 1060 lakh. The number of colleges rose from 542 to 4460 during this period. In the case of colleges the enrolment went up from 3.60 lakh to 26.18 lakh.

Enrolment in higher education rose to more than 35 lakhs in 1984-85. The total Government expenditure during the Sixth

Five Year Plan was around Rs. 2901 crores. This is about 115 per cent of the total Sixth Plan outlay on education (based on India 1984: Compiled by Ministry of Information and Broadcasting, Government of India).

In all the previous five year plans education was taken to be a social service rather than an input in the development process. There was a change in emphasis beginning with the Sixth Plan wherein it has been considered to be pivotal in the social and economic development of human resources. Priority has been given to the programme of universalisation of primary education and eradication of illiteracy in the age group 15-35. Both the programmes are covered under the revised 20-point programme.

Efforts were made, during the Sixth Plan for the consolidation of existing institutions and to equip universities and colleges with essential facilities within the limited resources available. Other important programmes taken up during the period included restructuring of undergraduate courses, improvement in standards of teaching of science and the humanities, strengthening of post-graduate education and promotion of research within the university system. A one-hour daily telecast on higher education was also initiated for the benefit of colleges. On the recommendation of the Science Advisory Committee to the Cabinet, a new scheme was introduced in 1983-84 for the strengthening the infrastructure facilities for research and post-graduate education in science and technology within the university system.

Special Features of the Sixth Five Year Plan

(1) Programme of universalisation of Primary Education.

(2) Eradication of Illiteracy in the age group 15-35.

(3) Rural bias to educational programmes.

(4) Improvement in the quality of teaching.

(5) Restructuring of undergraduate courses.

(6) Strengthening of post-graduate education and promotion of research.

Seventh Five Year Plan 1985-90 basedon the Second Vol. II of Seventh Five Year Plan published by Government of India.

The Seventh Plan provides for reorientation of the education system so as to prepare the country to meet the challenges of the 21st century. The main thrust areas in the Seventh Plan would be:

(1) Achievement of universal elementary education.

(2) Eradication of illiteracy in the age group 15-35.

(3) Vocationalisation and skill training programmes at different lelvels of education.

(4) `Upgrading of standards and modernisation at all stages of education with effective links with the world of work and with special emphasis on science and environment and on value orientation.

(5) Provision of facilities for education of high quality and excellence in every district of the country.

(6) Removal of obsolescence and modernisation of technical education.

University Education

The main emphasis in higher education will be on consolidation, improvement in standards and reforms in the system to make higher education more relevant to natural needs and to forge forward and backward linkages of higher education with employment and economic development. Expansion of general higher education facilities will be carefully planned so as to take care of the need to provide larger access to the weaker sections and first-generation learners from backward areas. In doing so emphasis will be laid on providing access to existing institutions through appropriate reservation, scholarships, provision of hostal facilities, etc. A net work of facilities will be provided through open universities correspondence courses, part-time education to meet social demands and the needs of continuing education.

The need and urgency for the restructuring of undergraduate courses so as to bring in the necessary concern for relevance and use, application, orientation, flexibility and diversification is well recognised. The guidelines for the restructuring of courses of study indicated by the University Grants Commission provide for addition of groups of courses that may be relevant and useful according to the local or regional needs. Extension activities will be developed as components with each subject/discipline, beneficial linkages will be developed between colleges and development institutions and programmes.

Application-oriented Programmes will be Given due Emphasis: The Indira Gandhi National Open University which is being established as a pace-setting institution, will besides offering courses in higher education based on the principles of the open learning system, be also responsible for training of personnel, production of programmes and development of material for utilisation through the electronic media. The National Open University will function as a nodal resource centre for coordination of programmes and development of models for distance education, documentation and dissemination of information and organisation of appropriate support programme.

In the area of post-graduate education and research, emphasis will be placed on promoting quality programmes, interdisciplinary studies and on new emerging frontiers. Research within the university will get due emphasis and be coordinated with national research efforts under the science and technology programme. The programme of strengthening infrastructure facility for research and technology and of post-graduate education with the system which was started on the recommendation of the Science Advisory Committee to the Cabinet will be further developed.

Training of Teachers in higher education is another area: which needs special attention in the Seventh Plan. The faculty improvement programmes will be designed to impart knowledge of new methods and techniques of teaching, learning and evaluation to develop a national value system and to prepare the teachers for the task of restructuring undergraduate courses.

Many of the reforms initiated earlier such as autonomous colleges, examination reforms seem to have faced obstacles and delays in the process of implementation. The Seventh Plan will give high priority to the speedy implementation of the various reforms initiated and to the modernisation of university administration. Besides concerted efforts to increase the enrolment of scheduled castes/tribes students, the most significant programme for these students will consist of remedial, preparatory training and special coaching. These programmes will be implemented on a larger scale by institutions with sizeable student population drawn from scheduled castes tribes and other weaker section. These institutions will be strengthened to impart a better quality of education. The scope of these institutions will also be enlarged to include training for employment, coaching for competitive examinations for recruitment to various services and adult and continuing education programmes.

Special Features of the Seventh Five Year Plan

(1) Universalisation of elementary education.

(2) Eradication of illiteracy in the age group 15-35.

(3) Quality education and modernisation at all levels.

(4) Provision of facilities for students of scheduled castes/ tribes and weaker sections.

(5) Emphasis on non-formal and distance Learning.

(6) Linkage of higher education with employment and economic development.

(7) Linkage of research with institutions of work.

Seventh Five Year Plan

Human resources development has necessarily to be assigned a key role in any development strategy, particularly in a country with a large population. Trained and educated on sound lines, a large population can itself become an asset in accelerating economic growth and in ensuring social change in desired directions. Education develops basic skills and abilities and fosters a value system conducive to, and in support of, national development goals, both long-term and immediate. In a world where knowledge is increasing at an exponential rate, the task of education in the diffusion of new knowledge and, at the same time, in the preservation and promotion of what is basic to India's culture and ethos, is both complex and challenging. It is, therefore, appropriate that the commencement of the Seventh Plan coincides with a comprehensive review of the education policy.

The resolution on the National Policy on Education adopted in 1968 pointed out that the great leaders of the Indian freedom movement realised the fundamental role of education and, throughout the nation's struggle for independence, stressed the unique significance of education for national development. The Resolution further declared that the radical re-construction of education as envisaged involved (i) a transformation of the system to relate it more closely to the life of the people; (ii) a continuous effort to expand educational opportunity; (iii) a sustained and intensive effort to raise the quality of education at all stages: (iv) an emphasis on the development of science and technology; and (v) the cultivation of moral and social values. According to the Resolution, the educational system must produce young men and women of character and ability, committed to national service and development.

There has been a great deal of accomplishment in the field of education since 1947. Any number which may be picked up as a parameter to define growth in education will show the magnitude of the massive quantities expansion that has taken place (Annexure 10.1). The number of recognised institutions has increased from 2,31,000 in 1951 to an estimated 7,55,000 in 1984-85. The total enrolment over the same period in these institutions increased from 24 million to nearly 132 million. The national stock of educated manpower is estimated to have increased from less than 4 million to about 48 million at present, the annual increment to the stock now being of the order of 3.5 million. It is significant to note that facilities have not only increased but also diversified at all levels and in different subjects. The enrolment for postgraduate studies, for instance has grown from a mere 20,000 in 1951 to over 300,000 by 1984-85 while that in science subjects is estimated to have increased from 4,400 to about 73,000. Extensive facilities are available for education in a variety of branches of engineering and technology. The output of this system has contributed significantly to our achievements in areas like atomic energy and satellite communication and provides the trained manpower for our economic development.

The expansion of educational facilities has also helped to some extent in the correction of regional and other imbalances and in achieving progress towards equality of educational opportunity and social justice. The annual non-Plan expenditure on education from the Central and State budgets has increased more than fifty times over the last 35 years, from Rs. 114 crores in 1950-51 to more than Rs. 6,000 crores in 1984-85.

Although the Indian education scene since independence has been characterised by massive quantitative expansion at all levels, it is still to undergo the kind of transformation envisaged in the National Policy. It is faced with a staggering backlog; the level of illiteracy is as high as 63 per cent; to achieve universal elementary education, as enjoyed by the Constitution, there will be need to enrol fifty million more children; vocationalization of secondary education has yet to make headway; there is very significant pressure on the higher educational system and a decline in the standards of quality. There is an urgent need for a new design for education. The Approach to the Seventh Plan has emphasised that one of the primary tasks is the harnessing of the country's abundant human resources and improving their capability for development with equity. It is recognised that programmes for alleviation of poverty, reduction of social and economic inequalities and improving productivity can and should be integrated with educational development. Further, the strategies for educational programmes and training and their organisational designs should particularly focus on women, youth and economically weaker groups so that they can make increasing contribution to the socio-economic development of the country.

Elementary Education: Overriding priority will be given to realising universalization of elementary education for children in the age-group 6-14 years by 1990; this will continue to be part of the Minimum Needs Programme. The emphasis will shift from mere enrolment to retention of pupils in schools and to the attainment by them of basic elements of learning. The objective is sought to be achieved through a combination of formal and non-formal methods, focusing sharply on the needs of girls and of children belonging to the economically and socially weaker sections.

The enrolment at the elementary stage is estimated to have reached nearly 112 million by the end of the Sixth Plan period. For achieving the goal of universalization by the end of the Seventh Plan, over 50 million children will have to be additionally enrolled. A projection of enrolment in full-time elementary schools. Increasing enrolment in full-time schools beyond this level of 137 million in classes I to VIII might not be feasible due to socio-economic reasons and other factors. Even to achieve this level effectively, sustained efforts will have to be made to reduce the number of dropouts.

Non-formal education would be the other important programme for the achievement of universalization of elementary education as this can be useful to those who are not able or willing to attend full-time schools. The number of children to be covered by the non-formal programme is reckoned to be of the order of 25 million. Non-formal education in the Seventh Plan will, therefore, have to be expanded at a fast pace and made acceptable with a variety of forms to suit the varying needs of the target groups. Non-formal system should be made flexible and appropriately linked to the formal system. Adequate textual material with area-specific background and supplementary reading material would be developed and made available to students. Adequate teacher-training arrangements will be made for teachers participating in the non-formal system. For optimum use of resources, the schools, the non-formal education centres and adult education centres should develop linkages and be educationally integrated with development programmes.

The enrolment projections in paras 10.24 and 10.25 are indicative figures, worked out at the macro-level and desegregated to the State level. Specific operational targets will require to be worked out by the State Governments concerned block-wise and village-wise through decentralised planning. Once such targets are worked out for the catchments area of each school or a cluster of schools, it would be expected that the authorities responsible for the achievement of the target would adopt the most appropriate strategies of implementation and monitoring of progress.

The role of the teacher is most crucial in achieving universal elementary education, especially in the motivation of children as well as their parents. They can play a leading role in improving the quality of primary education, bringing in environment and health education and value orientation. In-service training of teachers thus becomes a programme of high priority. The training of teachers will include, apart from pedagogy, the use of mass media, science and technology, planning and curriculum design for local environment-based courses, mobilisation and use of community resources and other relevant subjects. There will also be special emphasis on teaching methods and other measures particularly required for first generation learners and for reducing the number of dropouts. Teacher training institutions will be developed and strengthened accordingly.

Facilities will have to be created for the training of additional teachers required during the Seventh Plan period. There is as yet no infrastructure in the country for training of teachers in non-formal and early childhood education. Training of such teachers would have to be organised by suitably strengthening the existing teacher training centres.

Considering the numbers involved (over 2.5 million teachers), institutionalised in-service education of teachers will be difficult to organise not only due to the huge costs involved but also due to lack of facilities for training. It is therefore, necessary to think of a variety of training arrangements. Among others, these would include:

a. In-service education by utilising the mass media, as was done during SITE;
b. Adoption of schools of lower levels of education by institutions of higher levels for upgrading of teacher competencies;
c. Despatch of teacher guidance notes by training schools;
d. Publication of bulletins informing teachers of new developments; and
e. Use correspondence course materials supported by occasional contact.

Drop-outs and non-attendance of children at the primary stage of education are due to poor school facilities, unrelated curriculum, poor methods of teaching and poverty. The reorientation of teacher training referred to above will help to a large extent in tackling these factors. In addition, suitable supportive programmes for the provision of incentives, the improvement of facilities, increasing community awareness, curricular reforms, adjusting of school timings, utilisation of local community resources and earn-while-you-learn scheme, etc., will be introduced or expanded selectively according to local requirements.

Enrolment of girls has been lagging behind despite special measures taken in the past. Towards the end of the Sixth Plan some steps were taken to promote enrolment of girls and for providing non-formal education to them wherever necessary. In the Seventh Plan, the focus of effort will be on promotion of girls' education through appointment of women teachers, attachment of pre-school centres, provision of free uniforms and other incentives.

Special emphasis will be given to the enhancement of quality and efficiency of elementary education. The Seventh Plan will seek to provide specific funds for those programmes which will enhance the efficiency of the system. There is need to have a fresh look at the design and construction of school buildings as well as the text-books in use. Various projects like population education, environment and wild life education and curriculum renewal have helped in the preparation of suitable teaching-learning material and this material will be utilised. Due to the difficult resource position and the magnitude of the task involved in the implementation of the programme of universalization of elementary education, optimal use should be made of the available infrastructure and funds. The Plan and non-Plan budget provision for elementary education and the existing teacher resources should be reviewed and redeployed on the basis of actual requirements and attendance in classes.

Part-time teachers or helper-teachers on fixed salary, selected from among locally available educated men and women will be utilised to augment teaching resources and also improve relevance and cost-effectiveness of elementary education. Community support and financial contributions will be mobilised especially for clearing the backlog of physical facilities and school buildings. The construction of school buildings will be taken up also under the National Rural Employment Programme (NREP) and similar programmes.

Early childhood education is important both from the point of view of the personality development of the child and for inculcating in the children a healthy attitude to school-going to help increase their retention rate in schools. These programmes will be dovetailed with nutrition, health care and social welfare as a package within the broad framework of the programme of Integrated Child Development Service (ICDS). Voluntary efforts to undertake innovative experiments in respect of early childhood education will be supported.

The National Policy Resolution on Education recommends the placement of disabled children in regular schools. The scheme of integrated education of disabled children was started by the Ministry of Social Welfare as a Centrally-sponsored scheme where handicapped children were sought to be integrated in the normal school system with a view to promoting their psychological acceptance. The scheme is now being implemented by the Ministry of Education. One of the difficulties facing this scheme is the lack of trained teachers in special education. As such, during the Seventh Plan, greater emphasis will be laid on teacher training.

Adult Education: Eradication of adult illiteracy and the development of a programme of continuing adult education is a major thrust area in the Seventh Plan. The task of covering all the illiterates in the age-group 15-35 years by 1990 is a formidable one. As motivation of the learner is crucial for success and as the number to be covered is about 90 million, the strategy to achieve the goal can only be through a mass movement involving social institutions, voluntary organisations, students, teachers, employers and the community. This programme will also have to be linked effectively with various development programmes especially the Integrated Rural Development Programme (IRDP). Active participation of village panchayats, mahila mandals, community centres, etc. is essential. Employers will be required to impart necessary functional education to all their illiterate employees.

The programmes of Nehru Yuvak Kendras (NYK) and the National Service Scheme (NSS) will also focus on eradication of illiteracy. Programmes for motivating the learners by holding community meetings and through publicity, through posters, films, broadcasting, etc., will be implemented on an adequate scale and with sufficient intensity to create a conducive climate.

A network of libraries and the development of literature for neo-literates will also be initiated as a follow-up programme to avoid lapse into illiteracy. Community participation in all literacy programmes will be an essential feature from village level upwards to give proper direction and orientation and lend effective support to this national programme.

Another aspect of education of adults relates to training in functional skills relevant to their respective economic activities. Programmes for this purpose will be strengthed and adequate resource support provided for organising technical and vocational skill-based courses for the benefit of adult learners through Shramik Vidyapiths and other similar institutions. As a part of the post-literacy and follow-up services, short-duration condensed training courses will be organised for upgrading the skills of the neo-literates and for increasing their awareness of various social events. The existing programmes on rural functional literacy and State adult education programmes and various training programmes for adult learners will be consolidated and dovetailed in the new mass movement programmes on adult education. Citizenship education including adult education, will be a necessary part of the entire education system, and will be specially promoted.

Secondary Education: The demand for secondary education has been growing. The expansion and effectiveness of elementary education will provide a further impetus to this growth. The projected demand for additional facilities will, to some extent, be met by better utilisation of resources in the existing schools. Provision has been made for this purpose and for promoting distance learning techniques and open school systems. Unplanned growth of high/ higher secondary schools will be checked. Norms for the establishment of secondary school will be evolved and strictly observed in order to avoid proliferation of economically nonviable and educationally inefficient institutions. In expanding the facilities, special attention will be given to the needs of backward areas of under-privileged sections of the population and of girls. Girls education will be free upto the higher secondary stage.

The teaching of science and mathematics at high/higher secondary stage of education will be strengthened and made universal. Efforts will be made to update and modernise science curricula, improve laboratories and libraries in schools and ensure the quality of science teachers through large-scale in-service training programmes. Environment education will form an important aspect of science education.

The socially useful productive work (work experience) programme component seeks to highlight the link between work and education and to develop positive work ethics and work habits. The programme would allow for better utilisation and integration of community expertise in the teaching-learning process and the use of facilities available with local industry and development institutions. Besides, the support system for development, training, management and supervision available for vocationalization programmes, will also be utilised for the programme of socially useful productive work at the secondary stage. Some courses/activities of pre-vocational character will also be introduced for more effective implementation of this programme.

In view of the importance of linking education with productivity, a major impetus will be given in the Seventh Plan to vocationalization of the higher secondary stage. Facilities for vocational education will be suitably diversified to cover a large number of fields in agriculture, industry, trade and commerce, and services. It will be ensured that there is no duplication of courses between technical and vocational institutions and the schools. The skills imparted, will be of adequate standard for securing gainful employment or self-employment. At the same time, opportunities for pursuing higher general and professional education would be provided.

Vocational/career courses in educational institutions will be introduced in the flexible manner linked to emerging work opportunities. The current intake will be considerably increased by introducing vocational courses in many more institutions.

Based on the evaluation of the on-going scheme of vocationalization, States are taking steps to reorganise and improve the programme. An Expert Committee has been set up to suggest ways and means of implementing an expanded programme of vocationalization fully coordinated with the education system and manpower needs of economic development. The report of this Committee will provide guidelines for further development.

The present wide reach of the media will be used for improving education, especially at the secondary stage. Facilities for production of the requisite audio-visual material including educational software for broadcasting and telecasting will be augmented substantially in the Seventh Plan. During the Sixth Plan, a small beginning was made in providing computer literacy to students in selected secondary schools. Based on this experience, steps will be taken to extend the programme to cover different aspects of computer appreciation and application.

One of the essential conditions for continuous improvement in the quality of secondary education is an effective system of in-service training of teachers. The existing facilities will be assessed, additional requirements identified and steps taken to meet them. The opportunity provided by the new communication technology will be explored for this purpose. Here again, special attention will be paid to the development of requisite software. Training of personnel required for effective use of modern communication technology and computers in education will be given very high priority. The NCERT which has already initiated programmes in this regard will help the States build a network for this purpose.

Education has a crucial contribution to make towards promoting national integration, understanding and a sense of togetherness and harmony. There is, therefore, great need for an integrated and value oriented education with a national perspective. This programme should be so designed that its various threads can be woven into the curricular and co curricular activities. Suitable revision of text books, strengthening of school libraries and training of teachers would be important from this point of view.

University Education: The main emphasis in higher education will be on consolidation, improvement in standards and reforms in the system to make higher education more relevant to national needs and to forge forward and backward linkages of higher education with employment and economic development. Expansion of general higher education facilities will be carefully planned so as to take care of the need to provide larger access to weaker sections and first generation learners from backward areas. In doing so, emphasis will be laid on providing access to existing institutions through appropriate reservation, scholarships, provision of hostel facilities, etc. A network of facilities will be provided through open universities, correspondence courses and part-time education to meet social demand and the need of continuing education.

The need and urgency for restructuring of undergraduate courses so as to bring in the necessary concern for relevance and use, application orientation, flexibility and diversification is well recognised. The guidelines for restructuring of courses of study indicated by the University Grants Commission (UGC) provide for addition of groups of courses that may be relevant and useful according to local or regional needs. Extension activities will be developed as components within each subject/discipline. Beneficial linkages will be developed between colleges and development institutions and programmes. Application oriented courses will be given due emphasis.

The Indira Gandhi National Open University, which is being established as a pace setting institution, will besides offering courses in higher education based on the principles of the open learning system, be also responsible for training of personnel, production of Programmes and development of material for utilisation through the electronic media. The National Open University will function as a nodal resource .centre for coordination of programmes and development of models for distance education, documentation and dissemination of information and organisation of appropriate support programmes. Besides this, six centres of educational technology being developed by UGC would serve as regional centres for the production of software for educational technology and training of personnel engaged in the programme of distance education and correspondence courses for higher education.

In the area of post-graduate education and research, emphasis will be placed on promoting quality programmes, inter-disciplinary studies and on new emerging frontiers. Research within the university system will get due emphasis and be coordinated with national research efforts under the

Science and Technology programme. The programme of strengthening infrastructure facilities for research in science and technology and of postgraduate education within the university system which was started on the recommendation of the Science Advisory Committee to the Cabinet will be further developed. Training of teachers in higher education is another area which needs special attention in the Seventh Plan. The faculty improvement programmes will be designed to impart knowledge of new methods and techniques of teaching, learning and evaluation, to develop a national value system, and to prepare the teachers for the task of restructuring undergraduate courses. Many of the reforms initiated earlier, such as autonomous colleges and examination reform, seem to have faced obstacles and delays in the process of implementation. The Seventh Plan will give high priority to the speedy implementation of various reforms already initiated and to the modernisation of university administration.

Besides concerted efforts to increase the enrolment of Scheduled Castes/Scheduled Tribes students, the most significant programmes for these students will consist of remedial teaching, preparatory training and special coaching. These programmes will be implemented on a large scale by institutions with sizeable student population drawn from the Scheduled Cast and Scheduled Tribes and other weaker sections. These institutions will be strengthened to impart a better quality of education. The scope of these programmes will also be enlarged to include training for employment, coaching for competitive examinations for recruitment to various services and adult and continuing education programmes.

Technical Education: In the context of the rapid modernisation of the economy envisaged in the near future and given the Seventh Plan objective of improvement in productivity, technical education has to play a leading role. The main emphasis in the field of technical education during the Seventh Plan period will be on the following:

i. Consolidation of infrastructure and facilities already created;

ii. Optimum utilisation of the existing facilities with attention to cost effectiveness;

iii. Identification of critical areas with a view to strengthening the facilities in the fields where weaknesses exist in the system at present;

iv. Creation of infrastructure in new areas of emerging technology vital for the development of the country and provision of necessary facilities for education, training and research in those fields;

v. Improvement of quality and standards of technical education;

vi. Removal of obsolescence;

vii. Modernisation of engineering laboratories and workshops in the technical education institutions;

viii. Effective management of the overall system of technical education for an optimum return on investments made;

ix. Innovative measures to improve existing facilities to provide low-cost alternatives to achieve various goals and objectives laid down in the Plan; and

(x) Institutional linkages between technical educations on the one hand, and rural development and other development sectors, on the other.

To achieve these objectives there would be a balanced development of institutions of technical education at all levels. The Indian Institutes of Technology which have been set up as pace-setting institutions would be further developed as advanced centres of excellence.

The Institutes have already initiated research work in a number of new areas. An expert committee has been set up to look into the requirements of these Institutes in the context of the challenges ahead. The regional and other engineering colleges would also be developed further, particularly with a view to their modernisation and to making their courses relevant to the emerging requirements.

The up gradation of standards and modernisation of polytechnics will also be accorded a high priority. A major task in the Seventh Plan will be the removal of obsolescence in equipment and revision of courses in all technical education institutions, many of which were drawn up more than two decades ago. The All India Council for Technical Education has recommended that it is necessary also to restructure polytechnic education with a view to:

a. Improving the standard and contents of technical courses;

b. Providing a lateral entry to the vocational stream from 10+2 stage

c. Restoring the balance in the employment pattern of engineering graduates and diploma holders; and

d. Providing multi-point entry to the various courses. Besides the improvement on these lines, polytechnic education for women will be given greater attention to meet their special requirements. Further, as a result of reorganisation of school education in the 10+2 system and with vocationalization becoming the major thrust in it, the polytechnics will play a significant role in the promotion and development of vocational education, particularly in engineering and allied trades. Besides modernising polytechnics and removing obsolescence in courses and equipment, special attention will be paid to emerging technologies and computerisation. Development of interaction between the technical institutions and industry will be taken up. Removal of regional imbalances would be another major objective in the development of technical education at all levels. The faculty in the technical institutions have to keep themselves abreast of the latest knowledge and advances taking place else where in the world and also have to be in constant touch with industry. A number of schemes have already been instituted under the quality improvement programme including M. Tech. and Ph. D. courses, short-term and mid-term courses, and industrial training for engineering college and polytechnic teachers. However, these arrangements need considerable strengthening. Special attention will be paid to the problems of staff training and retraining and to continuing education for staff, including those of the polytechnics, to facilitate academic and professional advancement.

A reliable manpower information system is a pre-requisite to planning in the field of technical education. A national manpower information system is being developed for storage, updating, retrieval and analysis of manpower information to assist in technical education planning. It has at present 17 nodal centres and is coordinated by the Technical Education Division of the Department of Education with the assistance of the lead centre located at the Institute of Applied Manpower Research. The manpower information system will be considerably strengthened and integrated with the planning of technical education.

Besides general improvements, polytechnics will be assisted to undertake extension services for the benefit of the community. The programme of community polytechnics, already initiated in the earlier Plans, will be expanded in the Seventh Plan to cover as many polytechnics as possible. Curriculum changes need to be introduced periodically in the light of emerging trends in technology. This will require more effective collaborative linkages with industry and research and development establishments and agencies. The allocations provided from budgetary funds for technical education have to be supplemented by contributions from user industries and organisations, which will be facilitated when closer collaborative arrangements are established.

Eighth Five Year Plan

It is now universally acknowledged that the goal of Plan efforts is human development, of which human resource development is a necessary pre-requisite. Education is the catalytic factor, which leads to human resource development comprising better health and nutrition, improved socio-economic opportunities and more congenial and beneficial natural environment for all. There is already enough evidence in India to show that high literacy rates, especially high female literacy rates, are associated with low rates of population growth, infant mortality and maternal mortality besides a higher rate of life expectancy. Although the country has not so far achieved the goals of universalization of elementary education (UEE) and eradication of adult illiteracy (EAT), the 1991 census results reveal a literacy rate of over 52 per cent, with a higher rate of growth for female literacy. This is highly encouraging and the country can hope to achieve the broader goal of 'Education for All' (EFA) by 2000 AD, which has incidentally received international recognition at the world conference on EFA held at Jomtien in March, 1990. The commitment of the Government to the National Policy on Education (NPE), implemented from 1986-87 onwards and reviewed in 1990, has been reaffirmed with revised for mutation in respect of a few paras, placed before the Parliament on 7.5.1992. On the eve of Eighth Plan, therefore, the country is poised to make a real breakthrough in achieving its long-cherished educational goals as well as in supporting the drive for higher rate of economic growth.

Elementary Education: Early Childhood Education (ECE) would be expanded by attaching pre-primary classes to selected primary schools. Voluntary agencies and other NGOs would be encouraged and provided financial assistance by reorganising the scheme of ECE. Integrated Child Development Scheme (ICDS) model would be supplemented by Balwadis, Creches and Vikas Wadis.

Primary schools or alternatives to primary schools like non-formal centres etc. would be provided to every child within a walking distance of one kilometre, with suitable adjustment for special cases. Voluntary agencies, factories, cooperatives etc. would be encouraged to set up part-time primary schools to serve several groups of children belonging to hilly, desert, marshy, forest areas and nomadic tribes, seasonal migrants, urban poor etc. with freedom to adjust the number of school days, instructional hours and appoint teachers on contract basis. Innovative programmes like Shiksha Karmi which have given good results in an experimental project in Rajasthan would be expanded. Besides, a range of activities that suit the requirements of specific groups of learners, who are usually left out of the ambit of large scale projects, would be taken up. Opening of night schools in urban areas, pre-primary and lower primary centres for children of 3-9 years of age, "half-time' instructors and special projects to tackle educational problems of areas with concentration of child labour would be tried out.

Open schools would involve themselves in the post-primary stage education on an experimental basis to provide wider access to children who are working or not in a position to attend regular schools due to socio- economic or any other reasons. Special efforts will be made to increase enrolment rates and improve participation rates at the upper- primary stage especially in respect of girls. Hence, while ensuring effective universal access to all children at the primary stage, the infrastructure at the upper primary stage will have to be considerably expanded.

Besides expansion of school facilities, there will be need to improve the quality of education by providing existing schools with sufficient facilities. Therefore, the "Operation Blackboard" scheme will not only be continued and completed during the Eighth Plan in relation to primary schools but also extended to upper primary schools. The eventual aim would be to move towards a situation where every class has a classroom and a teacher. In order to expedite universalization of middle stage education and increase the enrolment of girls, the ratio between primary and upper primary schools would be brought down from the existing 1:4 to at least 1:3 with the ultimate aim of 1:2.

Apart from expanding Tribal Sub-Plan (TSP) and Special Component Plan (SCP), special measures are required for promotion of education of SCs/STs. Certain sub-castes, tribes and communities need particular attention because literacy rates among them are extremely low. The existing scheme of residential ashram schools will be expanded to cover classes from I to X and scholarship schemes for talented children at the secondary level would be expanded.. This will be supplemented by the scheme of voluntary schools wherever possible. Suitable incentives will be provided to all educationally backward sections of society, particularly in rural areas. Hill and desert districts, remote and inaccessible areas and islands will be provided adequate institutional infrastructure. Greater attention will be paid to the educationally backward minorities keeping in view the recommendations of the Empowered Committee on Minority Education (1991).

Teacher Education: Statutory status will be accorded to the National Council for Teacher Education (NCTE) to lay down and maintain standards in institutions and courses. The schemes of DIETs, STEIs and IASEs would be continued and their coverage expanded with a view to strengthening the institutional infrastructure and programmes of teacher education. The scheme for strengthening of SCERTs would be sanctioned and implemented and suitable measures for selection and professional development of staff in SCERTs, DIETs and IASEs will be undertaken. A large number of teachers will be covered through in-service programmes, both institutional and distance education, and reputed professional organisations will be encouraged to conduct in-service and refresher courses for teachers. Open universities at the national and State level will be encouraged to introduce induction teacher training courses to supplement the efforts of the existing training institutions. The bulk of seats in teachers' training colleges would be reserved for rural women.

Adult Education: Literacy programmes will be launched in districts/regions which are educationally backward or have high concentration of SC/ST population or have low female literacy. By the close of the Eighth Plan, 345 districts including about two-thirds of all districts in the educationally backward States would be covered by the TL campaigns, while the centre-based approach would be gradually phased out and confined to hilly, tribal and sparsely populated regions. The strategy for backward districts would be two-fold. First, a few blocks would be selected where the literacy campaign can achieve success within a reasonable period. The demonstration effect of the blocks would influence the backward blocks which, in course of time, could develop appropriate literacy programmes. Secondly, the voluntary base in educationally backward districts being somewhat weak, ways and means of identification, strengthening and expansion of the same would be evolved in consultation with the respective State Governments. It is also necessary to develop technical competence among voluntary agencies so that the partnership between the Government and the operating agencies becomes meaningful.

The possibility of further enhancing contributions from the community especially in urban areas and industrial towns would be explored so that apart from voluntary service, at least 20 per cent of the total expenditure on the campaign may be met.

In States, where library movement is strong, rural libraries should be integrated with the JSNs which are envisaged as innovative post-literacy and continuing education centres. Reputed NGOs, educational institutions, distinguished individuals, ex-servicemen, war widows, award winning teachers etc. will be encouraged to set up and run JSNs. Particular. attention would be paid to the availability of a variety of quality materials in adequate quantity to the neo-literates. Reputed printing presses and publishers would be motivated to print grstis literacy materials, posters and charts.

The academic and technical support to Adult Education programmes would be provided by the newly set up NIAE, which would be involved to a greater extent in various aspects of training, action research and monitoring, so that the Directorate of Adult Education can be phased out by the end of the Eighth Plan. At the State level, the State Resource Centres will be strengthened.

The scheme of SVs, which provide a variety of training programme to the industrial workers and their families would be extended to cover workers in unorganised sector and would also experiment with a variety of training models including distance education.

The contents of adult education would also include inculcation of values like secularism, national integration, scientific temperament, small family norm, concern for environmental conservation, cultural appreciation and so on. Even a society with a literate population is required to provide many avenues for continuing education in the context of the march towards a learning society, in which open schools and open universities would play an important role.

Secondary Education: The expansion of secondary schools would be regulated and new schools opened on selective basis, particularly to cater to the needs of deprived sections like girls and SCs/STs and in rural areas generally. Quality improvement and the raising of the internal efficiency of the existing (10+2) system would be emphasised. While an increasing number of students may like to discontinue their formal studies either temporarily or permanently after 10+2, there would be provision for there re-entry into the education system at a later stage. For this purpose, education would be linked to the world of work by expanding the facilities and improving the quality of vocational education as also provision of subject wise examination credits. For widening the reach, an open channel of education would be provided to those who do not have access to regular institutions because of socio-economic and locational constraints and those who have already entered the world of work but are keen to improve their skills and income generating capacity. Open education programmes will be imparted with the help of multimedia packages and contact centres.

National Open School (NOS): The NOS will continue its existing programmes and revise the syllabi and textbooks for the secondary/senior secondary courses and bring out a fresh set of instructional materials for the bridge course. It will develop and introduce vocational courses, especially in the areas of health, agriculture and rural development in collaboration with the concerned departments. The coverage is expected to increase progressively with registration of more and more accredited institutions, which now number 191. It should also coordinate and standardise the work of similar State-level mechanisms. The idea of starting state level open schools in all the States as recommended by the Conference of Boards of Secondary Education should be pursued. The NOS is expected to provide programme and resource support to State-level Open Schools. The setting up of a National Consortium on Open Education to facilitate accreditation of courses and of maintenance of quality through a process of networking and evaluation should be pursued by NOS in cooperation with the Indira Gandhi National Open University (IGNOU).

Vocational Education: The courses which have already been started would be consolidated. Special attention will be given to paramedical vocational courses to meet the needs of health manpower in the Eighth Plan. In addition to vocational courses forming part of the higher secondary courses, efforts would be made to offer varied courses of suitable duration to women, rural and tribal students and deprived sections of society. These courses may be coordinated with the working of Krishi Vigyan Kendras/organisations which offer training for self-employment. Non-formal, flexible and need-based vocational programmes would be made available to neo-literate youth who have completed primary education, to the school dropouts, to persons engaged in work and to the unemployed or partially employed persons. Institutions of Open Education will be actively involved in this area. Suitable programmes would also be started for the handicapped.

Candidates who have completed vocational courses should have ample opportunities for career improvement and professional growth. For this purpose, bridge courses which would give them an opportunity to take up higher technical and professional courses should be a necessary component. It is essential that experimental projects with other vocational education models are also tried out, *e.g.* pre-vocational education at the lower secondary level, exposure to various occupations right from the primary level for attitudinal change etc. It is also proposed to involve major industrial houses and all large projects and to prevail on them to include human resource development as part of project cost. The services of commercial agencies and NGOs will also be utilised.

Other Programmes: The target for the Eighth Plan would be to cover about 200 blocks by following the composite area approach to the planning and implementation of the integrated education for the disabled. Crucial areas like health, physical and art education should be made an integral part of school curriculum and accorded parity with other subjects. It is necessary that the work of NCERT in the area of Value Education is supplemented by work at the State level by SCERTs and measures to enrich teacher education. The CSS for introduction of Yoga in schools should be implemented more effectively and comprehensively.

The activities of the National Population Education Project would be directed, in addition to the formal schools, towards the non-formal sector for which the curriculum, material development and facilitator orientation would have to be specially developed. It is proposed to continue assistance to State Institutes of Educational Technology (SIET) and to extend in a phased manner facilities for Educational TV programme production. The government is committed to the establishment of Navodaya Vidyalayas in each of the districts of the country. The construction work for the existing 275 Vidyalayas would be completed. The possibilities of reducing the cost of construction and expenditure towards infrastructure will be explored. The setting up of new NVs in all the remaining districts will be appropriately programmed keeping in view the stipulated target date. In view of the key role of computers in modernisation of Secondary Education, the CLASS Project will be continued in a modified form and would cover 15,000 higher secondary schools by 1997.

The project will be implemented with the collaboration of private agencies, with the elements of accountability and monitoring built in. The physical facilities and characteristics of the selected schools will be ascertained prior to the launching of the project. Full-time teachers will be provided for computer literacy by the private organisation and this subject will be taught during the normal school hours unlike the earlier practice of teaching it beyond school hours. The existing schemes of improvement of science education and environmental orientation to school education would be strengthened by improving teacher training inputs. A new scheme for improvement of teaching of Mathematics at school level is being started. The NCERT would undertake Sixth Education Survey and a scheme for examination reforms apart from watching implementation of National Curricular Framework and MLL.

Language Development, Scholarships and Book Promotion: For the implementation of the Three Language Formula in a uniform manner, 100 per cent financial assistance for appointment and training of modern Indian language teachers in Hindi-speaking States is envisaged. The Bureau for Promotion of Urdu would be accorded an autonomous status as per the recommendations of Jafri Committee. The long pending Sindhi Vikas Board would he established. The Education Department would collaborate with the Department of Electronics (DoE) in the project 'Technological Development in Indian Languages'. For promotion of classical languages, a national level body is proposed to be set up for maintaining, coordinating and improving teaching of Sanskrit and classical languages as also Arabic and Persian.

The potentialities of voluntary Sanskrit organisations for promoting Sanskrit learning would be fully utilised by reorganising and developing the existing ones. Vedic learning and its linkage with modern scientific development under the Rashtriya Veda Vidya Prathisthan (Vedic Endowment) will be strengthened. The scheme of scholarships to upgrade the merit of SC/ST students would 'be revised with respect to number of awards and amount in consultation with State Governments. The number of awards under other schemes would be suitably enhanced so as to increase coverage and make them attractive. To foster book mindedness in the country, a Readers' Club Movement would be introduced.

The National Book Trust intends to set up a National Centre for Children's Literature with the aim of producing 3,000 titles every year. Under its Adan Pradan Scheme, translations of a large number of significant books from various Indian languages would be brought out. Besides developing manuscripts for neo-literates and school dropouts by organising workshops in various States, the NBT would provide assistance to publishers and voluntary agencies for production of books. The school Library Programme under OB would continue. A National Society of Authors is envisaged to oversee the interests and needs of authors.

Planning & Management and Information & Monitoring: The Eighth Plan would focus on decentralisation of planning and management activities; providing autonomy to educational institutions; building capabilities for the involvement and participation of the stake-holders in the educational process and building up of capabilities and professional competence among the administrators and voluntary associations and NGOs. The State Advisory Board of Education (SABE) would provide strong advisory support for training, research and dissemination of information on methodologies of planning and management strategies appropriate to the State level and to the district-level bodies, namely the. DBEs referred to earlier.

The existing bodies like Central Advisory Board of Education (CABE), UGC, NCERT and NIEPA would be strengthened. The CABE needs to be reorganised and should have a number of sub-committees to continuously review and monitor the progress in specific areas of education. A standing Committee of CABE on Open Education is proposed to be set up. For streamlining the flow of information and developing the planning capacity at the district level, an Educational Management Information System (EMIS) covering all the districts in the country needs to be operationalized by the end of the Eighth Plan. The National Informatic Centre (NIC) has already developed a comprehensive computer network linking all the districts with computers. There is need to coordinate the working of educational management information system with NIC network. Following steps are also necessary to improve the system of educational statistics: (1) Compulsory registration of non-recognised educational institutions; (2) More extensive use of sample surveys to monitor the progress in respect of some critical indicators of educational development; (3) Continuation of educational surveys conducted by NCERT by clearly defining their frequency and objectives vis-a-vis other sources of data; (4) Construction of composite indicators of educational development of various States/districts and periodical monitoring of their behaviour; (5) Coordination between various sub-sectoral agencies for sharing of information; (6) Development of a comprehensive methodology and a sound data base on private costs of education to rationalise and to improve the efficiency in the use of financial resources.

Resources and Financial Allocations: The NPE statement that from the Eighth Plan onwards, the outlay on Education would uniformly exceed 6 per cent of the national income would be treated as a guideline for allocation of resources during the Eighth Plan. The present public sector allocation is much lower and requires to be appropriately stepped up. A conscious effort to tap various avenues for raising resources for education needs to be made. In view of the paucity of domestic resources, vigorous efforts to attract external assistance for financing educational programmes, especially priority programmes without compromising country's basic educational policies is necessary. While the external funding would be an additionality to the resources for education, the externally-aided projects would be in total conformity with the national policies, strategies and programmes and drawn up on innovative lines emphasising people's participation, improvement of quality, equality of education and substantial up gradation of facilities.

The project formulation would be the responsibility of implementation agencies. At present, India is availing of bilateral assistance for Shiksha Karmi Project in Rajasthan and Mahila Samakhya Project in Uttar Pradesh, Gujarat and Karnataka. Within the broad objectives of the Eighth Plan, it is proposed to take up externally-aided projects, both bilateral and multi-lateral in various educationally backward States for promotion of basic education which includes: primary schooling, non-formal education, adult literacy, women's education and development and post-literacy and continuing education. Such projects are at various stages of development in respect of Bihar, Rajasthan, U.P. and South Orissa.

Ninth Five Year Plan

In view of its significance for human resource development and economic and social transformation, education needs to be given a high priority in the allocation of resources. Considering that the present share of education in GDP is around 3.9 per cent, raising it to any substantially higher level would require a substantial enhancement of expenditures on education. The system's capacity to absorb financial resources of a large magnitude and use them productively and efficiently would also require careful consideration. As regards the convergence of Basic Minimum Services for contributing to educational development, emphasis will be laid on providing all primary schools with clean drinking water, sanitary facilities, better nutrition for the pupils through mid-day meals, health check-up and primary health-care facilities and a network of roads for making the schools easily accessible.

Early Childhood Education: Early Childhood Education (ECE) in the Ninth Plan requires attention for the following issues:

i. Strengthening the educational component of ICDS.

ii. Its linkage, as pre-school education, with universalization of primary education and consequential steps in that connection.

iii. The promotion and management of ECE under the decentralised system of Panchayati Raj institutions and Urban Local Bodies.

iv. The role of the private sector and NGOs in ECE.

v. Convergence of health education and other services at the local level in the interest of ECE.

vi. Social mobilisation for ECE, through mass media and other activities.

The issues that will be addressed in the Ninth Plan are as follows;

a. Combining pre-school and primary level methodologies, along with health and nutritional concerns, in teacher-training programmes, pre-service as well as in-service.

b. Encouraging the adaptation of ECE to the environment and home-conditions of the children through innovative alternatives.

c. Orienting PRIs and ULBs to provision of community-supported creches and day-care centres attached to Anganwadis/Primary schools.

d. Mobilisation of local women's groups to set up and manage ECE centres.

e. Production of inexpensive play materials for children by using local materials and talents of local artisans and school children engaged in socially useful productive work and social service activities according to their curriculum.

f. Strengthening resource groups for ECE at the NCERT and SCERTs as also research institutes, NGOs and other such organisations to conduct research, training, materials production and extension activities for ECE.

Primary/Elementary Education: The Indian Constitution attaches high priority to education. Article 45 declares "The State shall endeavour to provide, within a period of 10 years from the commencement of the Constitution, for free and compulsory education of all children until they complete the age of 14 years." The Constitution also guarantees educational rights for minorities and calls for the educational development of weaker sections of society. Through the 42nd Amendment of the Constitution, the subject of education has been brought to the Concurrent List in the Constitution for fulfilment of nationally accepted goals. The 73rd and 74th Constitutional Amendments further empowered the Panchayati Raj

Institutions (PRIs) to render their contribution to the development of education at the grass-root level. The Judgement of the Supreme Court in Unnikrishnan J.P. Vs. Andhra Pradesh (1993) states : "The citizens of the country have a fundamental right to education. The said right flows from Article 21 of the Constitution. This right is, however, not an absolute right. Its contents and parameters have to be determined in the light of Articles 45 and 41. In other words, every child/citizen of this country has a right to free education until he completes the age of 14 years. Thereafter his right to education is subject to the limits of economic capacity and development of the State."

Critical Issues at Primary/Elementary Stage

(i) *Backlog of Unenroled Children :* In order to achieve Universalization of Primary Education (UPE), it had been estimated for the year 1993-94 that approximately 142 million children in the age-group 6-11 years would have to be provided primary schooling, out of which 69 million would be girls.

(ii) *Drop-outs:* The problem is further accentuated by high drop-out rates. Among those who are enrolled, it is estimated that large number of children in Classes I-V drop out in between, before completing their class V. The latest available data on drop-out rates for Classes I-V for the year 1996-97 reveal that the drop- out rate for the country as a whole was 38.95 per cent. It was 39.37 per cent among boys and 38.35 per cent among girls. Further, there were wide inter-State disparities. The major problem of drop- outs as well as access to schooling is in the educationally backward States of Andhra Pradesh, Arunachal Pradesh, Assam, Bihar, J&K, Madhya Pradesh, Orissa, Rajasthan, U.P. and West Bengal.

(iii) *Unserved Habitations with Primary/Upper Primary Schools/Sections:* According to the Sixth All India Educational Survey out of 10.60 lakh rural habitations, 8.84 lakh (83.4%) were served within the national norm of one-km distance. Thus about 16.6 per cent of habitations were not served by primary schools within a distance of 1 km. The survey results also revealed that about 41,198 primary schools were being run in thatched huts, tents and open space. In case of upper primary schools, about 23.85 % habitations were not served within the official distance norm of 3 km. 5,638 upper primary schools were being run in thatched huts, tents and open space.

(iv) *Lack of other Physical Infrastructure:* Apart from availability of access to primary school within a walking distance of habitations there are other problems which have to be addressed on an urgent basis. These relate to lack of physical infrastructure like toilet facilities for girls, drinking water facilities in schools, teaching-learning equipment etc.

(v) *Availability of Teachers:* With regard to availability of teachers, the Survey further pointed out that about 4000 schools were without teachers and 1.15 lakh primary schools were being run by single teachers. However, the position has improved since then, as additional teachers have been provided under Operation Blackboard (OB).

(vi) *Low Levels of Achievement:* It is not only physical infrastructure that is inadequate to achieve UPE, there is the equally important dimension of quality which needs attention. For instance, evaluation studies on children's achievement show low levels in language and mathematics.

(vii) *Equity and Regional Disparities:* Then, there are regional disparities. Some States (like Kerala, Maharashtra, Gujarat, Tamil Nadu) have done well in providing physical access to schooling facilities as well as in improving quality of education.

- Primary education will be a major thrust area during the 9th Plan. There will be an additional enrolment of 2.5 crore children at the lower primary stage and 1.6 crore children at the upper primary level. 75000 additional rooms /buildings will be constructed at the elementary stage. 2,36,000 teachers will be appointed additionally at the lower primary level and 1,75,000 teachers at the upper primary level.

Some others (like Uttar Pradesh, Bihar, Madhya Pradesh, Orissa & Rajasthan) have still a long way to go. There are equity concerns like low enrolment of girls, educational requirements of special need groups, like SCs/STs, OBCs, minorities, disabled children, working children, children from disadvantaged locations like deserts, hilly, coastal and deep forest areas, children from migratory families etc.

Action Plan

(i) *Broad Approach:* The action plan needed to address the critical issues and achieve the desired objectives will be based upon ground realities. It will resort to a multi-pronged strategy which is both imaginative and innovative and also carries with it the attributes of flexibility, decentralisation, and improvement of quality, cost-effectiveness, result-oriented and time-bound commitment. This can be achieved through micro-planning with a focus on 'area approach' and 'target population' It will also mean community involvement, monitoring, supervision and academic support at all levels. The existing schemes will be examined with respect to these parameters and those found suitable will be promoted.

(ii) *Phasing:* Under the Constitutional obligation, Government is to provide free and compulsory education upto Class VIII. Greater emphasis will naturally have to be laid on achieving UPE at the lower primary stage, in the first phase.

(iii) Mobilisation of Community Support for School Improvement Programme

- Panchayati Raj Institutions will be empowered to serve as the nucleus in programme implementation. Non-governmental organisations will be encouraged to supplement the governmental efforts, while the private sector will also be facilitated to grow particularly in higher and technical education.

The 73rd and 74th Constitutional amendments have further empowered the Panchayati Raj Institutions (PRIs) to make a positive contribution for development of education at the grass-root level. Village Education Committees (VECs) will be actively involved in School Improvement Programme (SIP).

Training will be imparted to VEC members wherever such committees have been constituted. Arrangements for this will be made through District Institutes of Education and Training (DIETs), Block and Cluster Resource Centres and through the Distance Mode. Areas of concern of VECs in the development of SIP will be:

a. door-to-door survey of children of school-going age and help in enrolment, particularly of girls;
b. planning and execution of civil works of school buildings;
c. mobilisation of physical and financial resources;
d. provision of free accommodation to teachers, wherever possible;
e. improvement in children's attendance;
f. institutional capacity building for sustainability of schools;
g. Community ownership of the School Improvement Programme;
h. to help in implementation of the Scheme of National Nutritional Support to Primary School Children.
i. Other functions delegated by the State Governments.

(iv) Strengthening Teacher Education Programme

(a) *Curriculum Development:* The draft curriculum framework developed by the National Council for Teacher Education (NCTE) will be finalised and made the basis for curriculum change in institutions for teacher education. This will help to improve the quality of Teacher Education Programme.

(b) *Initiative for North-Eastern States:* The North-Eastern States, which have a larger percentage of untrained teachers in elementary schools will launch programmes to cover this gap by adopting the following measures:

- A Diploma Programme for Primary Education developed by Indira Gandhi National Open University (IGNOU) will be launched in collaboration with the State Governments.

- NCTE will establish a Regional Committee for North- Eastern States to provide the necessary fillip to the teacher training institutions.
- Induction programmes of 4 to 6 weeks' duration by DIETs will enrich the capabilities of freshly appointed teachers.

(c) *Upgradation of Infrastructure:* The process of strengthening Teacher Education Programme will be given a further impetus by upgrading the physical and academic infrastructure of:

- State Councils of Educational Research & Training (SCERTs)
- Colleges of Teacher Education (CTEs)
- Institutes of Advanced Studies in Education (IASEs)
- District Institutes of Education and Training (DIETs)
- Block Resource Centres/Cluster Resource Centres (on a pilot basis).
- National Council for Teacher Education (NCTE)
- Departments of Education in Universities

(d) *Reaching out to Primary School Teachers in Remote Areas:* To supplement the efforts to improve school effectiveness, an institutional mechanism will be put in place to provide on-the-spot counselling and guidance to teachers located in remote areas. This will be in the form of Mobile Teams of Resource Persons (MTRPs). Logistic arrangements will be location-specific, based upon felt needs and environment.

(v) *Alternative Education:* In order to provide access to drop-outs, working children, girls, migratory population and other similar categories, alternative education will be provided through institutional arrangements.

Non-formal Education centres for such categories of children as are unable to avail themselves of the formal system of schooling in hilly, desert and forest areas, or due to the migratory nature of the population will be expanded. The expansion will be based upon a 'cluster approach', so as to make the scheme cost-effective.

It has been found by experience that NFE centres achieve more meaningful results when these are run by NGOs. Accordingly, the number of centres run by NGOs will be enhanced significantly. Where NGO participation is not forthcoming, State-run NFE centres will be established. The scope of the National and State Open Schools will be expanded by bringing elementary education within their fold for the purpose of providing a lateral entry to NFE children as well as to neo-literates for certification.

Private initiative will be tapped in industrial project sites to run "project schools". Incentives like allotment of land on a subsidised basis and other concessions under the Companies Act or the Income Tax Act will be provided.

(vi) *Education of Working Children:* According to the 1991 census, there were 11.28 million working children in the country. More than 90 per cent of them were engaged in agricultural labour, rearing of livestock, forestry and fisheries.

Ministry of Labour has a direct responsibility at the Centre for the following:

i. to lay down policies and programmes for elimination of child labour, particularly in hazardous trades,

ii. to monitor the progress of implementation of programmes, projects and schemes for elimination of child labour; and

iii. to coordinate implementation of child labour-related projects of the various sister Ministries of the Government of India in order to ensure convergence of services for the benefit of the families which have child labour. Ministry of HRD will extend all support to the Ministry of Labour in the setting up of 'education-related projects'. These will be 'area-specific' and focused particularly in States of Andhra Pradesh, Madhya Pradesh, Maharashtra and Uttar Pradesh, where there is a large concentration of child labour.

Adult Education: Literacy, the key to most of India's development programmes, is the catalyst to accelerate initiatives in health care, agriculture, primary education and in all critical areas of development.

In the light of the 73rd and 74th constitutional amendments, literacy has assumed even greater significance. If power for local self-governance is to devolve to the panchayats and nagar palikas, literacy is an essential prerequisite for these institutions to be effective.

Critical issues in Adult Education: Despite this key role, much still needs to be done. India has the largest number of non-literate people in the world-about a third of the world's total of around 900 million. Although literacy levels have increased from 16.67 per cent to 52.21 per cent since independence, unrestrained population growth has proved to be a serious impediment.

The literacy levels of women are low-39.29 per cent as compared to 64.13 per cent for men. The fact that female literacy is acknowledged as being one of the most significant indicators of development makes this all the more alarming. With one third of the seats in panchayats and nagar palikas reserved for women, the need for them to become literate is vital. There are large regional disparities in literacy rates-between urban and rural areas, as well as between states. While about three quarters of the urban population is literate, the literacy rate in rural areas is less than 45 per cent. The literacy rate of women in rural areas is even lower at 31 per cent.

Seven states-Uttar Pradesh, Bihar, Madhya Pradesh, Rajasthan, Andhra Pradesh, West Bengal and Maharashtra-account for around 70% of India's non-literate population. The first four of these states alone, are home to around half of India's non- literate people.

In its endeavour to achieve the goals it has set for itself in adult education, India faces several challenges. Studies by expert groups and the constant evaluation of the programme, indicate several principal challenges. The four Hindi speaking states-Uttar Pradesh, Bihar, Madhya Pradesh and Rajasthan-account for half of India's non- literate population. The large number of non-literate people, and therefore the relatively small number of educated people from whom volunteers can be drawn, as well as the overall socio- economic backwardness of these states, combine to make the achievement of literacy particularly difficult in these areas.

There are large regional disparities-between states, between districts in a state, between males and females and between tribal and non-tribal areas. Campaigns have sometimes been launched without adequate planning, and quality has suffered in certain places in the preoccupation with total literacy. This preoccupation has also sometimes led to overestimation of achievements, with some districts being prematurely declared totally literate.

The vital importance of post-literacy efforts to prevent a relapse into illiteracy has already been mentioned. Post Literacy Campaigns have often not been implemented adequately or in time, even in districts where TLCs have been successful. There have often been unnecessarily long time gaps between the completion of a TLC and the beginning of a PLC in a district. To ensure that the gains of TLCs are realized, post literacy needs far greater attention and emphasis, to sustain the interest of the neo-literates, and to make them 'functionally literate' in the true sense. Greater community involvement is required to convert literacy into a people's movement.

Action Plan

1. Literacy campaigns have already covered 447 districts, of which 215 are in Total Literacy Campaigns, 173 are in Post Literacy Campaigns and 59 are in Continuing Education Phase.
    - Eradication of illiteracy is a top priority in the National Agenda for Governance. A major dent would be made by making 10 crore adults literate in the 9th and 10th plan periods.
2. In addition, 38 districts have been covered under Rural Functional Literacy Projects. Hence the total coverage comes to 485 districts. Efforts would be made to bring the remaining 40 odd districts under the coverage of literacy.

3. Gradually, all districts will be brought under the Continuing Education programme which will be further strengthened as well as linked to other socio-economic programmes such as health and hygiene, nutrition and sanitation, skill upgradation and capacity building, culture, sports, etc.
4. For such neo-literates who wish to pursue further education, an equivalency programme is being developed to enable neo-literates to enrol in courses at the national/ state open schools.
5. Efforts have been set in motion to decentralise and devolve administrative and financial powers to State Literacy Mission Authorities. The sanctioning of projects will largely be done by these authorities.
6. Sensitisation and orientation workshops are proposed to be conducted for functionaries of panchayati raj institutions so as to involve local government bodies in the literacy programme.
7. It is proposed to further strengthen and revitalise State Resource Centres and Shramik Vidyapiths (proposed to be renamed as Jana Shiksha Sansthans). This will provide additional fillip in the areas of training, skill upgradation, capacity building and preparation of materials.
8. The stress on awareness generation among women and their empowerment is proposed to be continued as one of the major planks of the programme.

Secondary Education: Conceptually, secondary education is meant to prepare young persons both for the world of work and entry into higher education. But traditionally, it has come to be looked upon as a bridge between the elementary and higher education stages. This process has to be reversed

Critical Issues in Secondary Education

(i) *Revision of Curricula:* After the formulation of the New Policy on Education in 1986 (revised in 1992) the need for change of curriculum has arisen. The change will take into account the areas of scientific development, environmental education, computer education and social issues in the context of economic liberalisation.

(ii) *Vocationalization of Education:* The scheme of Vocationalization of Education at 10+2 stage was introduced to regulate admissions at College level. The purpose was to divert at least 25% students of 10+2 stage to self-employment or wage-employment, while providing them with vocational competence in a field of their choice. However, the scheme has not taken off due to logistic and academic constraints which require streamlining and strong industry-institution linkages. At present, only 4.8% students are opting for vocational stream, against a target of 25%.

(iii) *Distance Education:* Distance Education is an alternative approach for providing secondary education. With the tremendous expansion of elementary education in the country, the demand for secondary education is likely to grow enormously in the next decade. This challenge has to be met by providing distance mode of education through the Open Learning System (OLS) in the country.

(iv) *Quality Improvement of Teaching in Mathematics, Science and Computer Education:* The quality of teaching in Science and Mathematics has deteriorated so much that it has started having adverse effects at under-graduate and post-graduate levels. Further, with the fast development of Information Technology, the need for quality education in computers at school stage has become imperative.

(v) *Hostel Facilities for Girls:* In remote and tribal areas, secondary schools do not have adequate hostel facilities for girls, and this results in failure to attract girls to them.

(vi) *Minority Education:* In spite of adequate facilities at secondary stage, children from minority groups are not taking full advantage of these.

(vii) *Integrated Education for the Disabled:* After the enactment of the Disabled Act 1995, the education of the disabled upto age 18 has become a legal obligation. Though efforts have been made to provide educational facilities to this special group, these are not commensurate with the tremendous needs.

Action Plan

(i) *Revision of Curricula:*

(a) National Council of Educational Research & Training (NCERT) in collaboration with State Councils of Educational Research & Training (SCERTs) will revise curricula and a National Draft will be prepared for discussion and adoption. New areas of concern will be included in the curriculum. After the draft is adopted, the same organisations will upgrade the text-books so as to keep pace with international standards.

(b) Simultaneously, NCERT and SCERTs will review the training needs of in-service teachers and take steps to meet the new challenges.

(c) National Council for Teacher Education will prepare a framework for pre-service teacher education, so that the standards are upgraded.

(ii) *Vocationalization of Education (VE):* The Scheme of Vocationalization of Education at 10+2 stage will be restructured so as to provide employability to the target group. An Empowered Committee representing the Government, industry and trade will be constituted to promote a meaningful partnership and better inter-departmental coordination. Vocational courses with strong linkages with industrial units will be encouraged.

(iii) *Distance Education:* Distance Education will be broad-based by providing wider responsibilities to National Open School (NOS) and the State Open Schools (SOSs). These will be in the areas of elementary education, vocationalization of education for neo- literates, drop-outs, secondary students and adult population, including working women. Special initiatives will be taken to derive full advantage from the state-of-art Information Technology (IT).

(iv) Teaching of Mathematics, Science and Computer Education

a. Special measures will be taken to promote teaching of Mathematics and Science at the secondary stage by devising new popular source-books. A Science Talent Research Scheme will be promoted.

b. Science & Mathematics will be linked to the immediate environment of the child. Efforts will be made to avoid the unnecessary load of a crowded curriculum.

c. The recommendations made by the Task Force on Computer Education will be implemented in a time-bound manner.

(v) *Hostel Facilities for Girls:* Additional hostel facilities for girls will be provided, particularly in tribal and remote areas, so that the attendance rate of girls improves. MHRD will coordinate its programmes with those of the Ministry of Welfare.

(vi) *Minority Education:*

a. The Scheme of Modernisation of Madarasas will receive all possible attention, so as to cover more Madarasas and improve the access of Muslim children to education.

b. Area Intensive Programme for Educationally Backward Minorities will be strengthened by allocating a higher outlay. A vigorous publicity drive will be undertaken to generate necessary awareness among the minority communities so that they come forward to take full advantage of the scheme. The cooperation of the leaders of the minority communities will be elicited for the fulfilment of the same objective.

(vii) *Integrated Education for the Disabled:* A composite area approach will be adopted and additional blocks covered under the programme. Training of teachers for these special groups will be organised in universities.

Technical Education: Despite efforts in the past, only a few technical institutions have managed to achieve high academic standards. Major qualitative reforms are necessary to upgrade the Regional Engineering Colleges (RECs). While the Indian Institutes of Technology (IITs) have enjoyed autonomy, flexibility and responsive governance, there is an urgent need to enhance their output and quality.

Critical Issues in Technical Education

(i) *Quality Improvement:* The areas which need specific attention are adequacy & quality of faculty, modernisation of institutional resources, upgradation of educational technology, relevance and flexibility of curricula, interaction with industry etc.

(ii) *Infrastructure Development and Innovations:* Over the years, regional imbalances have emerged in respect of infrastructure development. Further, paradigm shifts are needed across the board from knowledge-based education to skill and competence development and from classroom learning to workplace learning.

(iii) *Flexibility, Mobility, and Curricula:* Economic liberalisation and industrial expansion have brought in new institutions and programmes. Hi-tech programmes, curriculum development, flexibility and mobility assume special significance in this rapidly changing scenario.

(iv) *Governance of Institutions:* Governing and management structures at the Central and State levels need to be strengthened, so as to manage the manifold changes described above.

(v) *Excellence in Polytechnic Education:* Technical staff produced through polytechnics form the backbone of middle level management and technical manpower and demand for them is steadily growing. There is need for greater flexibility and autonomy to these institutions, which have also to forge close linkages with technical institutions of higher level on the one hand and industry on the other.

University & Higher Education: The country is going through major economic and technological changes. The system of higher education has to prepare its products for participation in the emerging social, economic and cultural environment. Universities are witnessing a sea change in their outlook and perspective. Information technology is leading to fundamental changes in the structure, management and mode of delivery of the entire educational system.

Action Plan

(i) *Relevance & Quality*

a. *Vocational Education:* At the under-graduate level, vocational education will be expanded in disciplines which have strong linkages with industry and improve employability. UGC, in collaboration with the universities, will restructure the under-graduate courses and actively involve industrial houses in the development of curriculum, on-the- job training etc.

b. *Higher Education:* Teaching in post-graduate and doctoral programmes and research will be oriented towards applied fields so as to establish relevance, need-based specialisation and market-driven skill generation.

c. *Faculty Improvement:* Faculty improvement scheme will be strengthened through incentives, self-development, sponsored research, in-service training through distance mode etc. Academic staff colleges will be restructured accordingly.

d. *Faculty Exchange:* Faculty exchange between industrial houses and universities will be promoted in technical disciplines so as to enrich the content of education.

(ii) *Use of Media and Educational Technology:* A purposeful action plan will be formulated in consultation with the field agencies in order to impart a multi- media approach to teaching. Quality will be ensured through Internal Quality Assessment Cells and accreditation through the National Assessment and Accreditation Council.

(iii) *Structural Arrangement of Curriculum:* Universities will be asked to develop a system of credit and credit transfers. This will help in shifting from rigid, structured, unidisciplinary programmes to the credit-based cafeteria system with core, optional and extra-developmental courses at under-graduate and post-graduate levels.

(iv) *Access and Equity*

a. *Unserved Areas:* Unserved areas will be brought into the fold by providing additional educational facilities. College mapping will be done on an area-based approach so that there is optimal utilisation of existing resources and regional imbalances are removed.

b. *Distance Education:* Since resources for expanding physical facilities are limited, Distance Education in conventional as well as open universities will be strengthened and promoted.

(v) *Linkage Changes:* Necessary changes will be made in the legislation pertaining to the UGC and the Universities so as to cope with newly emerging requirements and challenges.

(vi) *Resource Utilisation*

a. *Fiscal Discipline:* Fiscal discipline will be strongly enforced in institutions of higher education.

b. *Resource-Sharing:* Adoption of a cluster approach to sharing of resources by neighbouring institutions and setting up of inter-university centres will help in achieving economies of scale.

(vii) *Resource Mobilisation:* Additional Resources will be mobilised by :

a. *Fee Restructuring:* Restructuring of fees based upon the criteria of Unit Cost and the socio-economic background of the student.

b. *Public Funding:* Widening the public funding resource-base by attracting contributions from various departments of the Government and the community, in order to support basic infrastructure such as laboratories, libraries and new courses.

c. *Industrial Funding:* Encouraging contributions from industrial establishments for sponsored research projects.

(viii) *Performance and Accountability:* UGC will work out a concrete programme of action for ensuring better accountability. This will be done by:

a. *Leveraging UGC Funds:* Using UGC's plan and non-plan financial assistance as a leverage to encourage better performance.

b. *Evaluation:* Utilising the UGC's evaluation machinery much more vigorously to rank universities and publicising evaluation reports as widely as possible.

c. *Model Code:* Developing a model code of governance which would minimise political interference and improve standards.

(ix) *Extension Education*

a. *Continuing Education:* Adult and continuing education programmes will be targeted for those who have had the benefit of university education but need to return, for updating or acquiring knowledge or skills.

b. *Skill-based Courses:* Extension education programmes will be aimed at the needs of specific groups who would not otherwise be entrants to the university system. Such courses could be based on skills for income generation, entrepreneurship, para-legal work, etc.

c. *Community Education:* Community education programmes will be focused on transfer of skills which require upgradation due to technological progress.

Women's Empowerment: The National Agenda for Governance also states: "We will institute plans for providing free education for girls up to college level, *i.e.* under-graduate level including professional courses would be made free". An adequate provision will be made for the scheme for this purpose during the 9th Five Year Plan. On a long-term basis and in close collaboration with State and local governments, the financial implications of making education free for girls upto the graduation level will be worked out, in so far as these relate to the Department of Education.

Action Plan

Free Education for Girls: Education will be free for girls upto college level. The contours of the scheme are being worked out. A new scheme will be launched shortly.

(a) *Financial Requirements:* The financial requirements for implementation of the concept of free education to girls upto college level will be worked out by Ministry of Human Development (MHRD).

(b) *New Scheme:* A new scheme called "Free Education for Girls" will be devised and implemented in a time-bound manner.

Management Education

Critical Issues: In view of the emerging needs of Indian economy, the new dimensions of management education and research have necessitated technology upgradation to achieve quality control, use of information technology for overall improvement in output and performance as well as competitiveness. There is an imperative need for networking and linkages between leading management institutes, university departments of management and centres of management education, especially in private sector on the one hand and industrial establishments and user organisations on the other.

Action Plan: In view of the acute shortage of teachers in management education, particularly in areas like marketing and finance, programmes will be restructured to meet the demands for managerial cadres for the growing infrastructural and service sectors and in areas like International Business, Environment, Technology Management, Entrepreneurship, Material Management, etc. Institutes-industry linkages will be strengthened through consultancy, faculty/professional exchange programmes.

Language Development and Book Promotion: Language is a potent instrument of artistic expression and literary creativity. India has inherited a multiplicity of languages, which are at various stages of development. During the successive Plans, the endeavour had been to help the different languages develop to their optimum level. Emphasis was also laid on the promotion of literature in various languages.

Since Independence various programmes have been formulated and implemented for the promotion of Hindi, as a link language, and modern Indian Languages, as provided in the National Policy on Education besides giving equal stress to Sanskrit, Arabic, Persian, Sindhi, Urdu, English and other languages, both spoken as well as written.

Tenth Five Years Plan

The 2001 Census indicate that the literacy rate has gone up to 65.37 per cent -75.85 per cent for males and 54.16 per cent for females. For the first time, the number of illiterates has, in absolute terms, decreased by 31.9 million. The number of literates, on the other hand, has increased by 203.6 million between 1991 and 2001. During the period, the female literacy rate increased by 14.87 per cent as against 11.72 per cent in the case of males, thus reducing the male-female literacy gap to 21.7 per cent from 24.84 per cent in 1991. All states have, without exception, registered an increase in literacy rates of both males and females during the last decade.

Enrolment Ratios: The Gross Enrolment Ratio (GER) at the primary and upper primary levels improved significantly between 1950-51 and 1999-2000, from 42.6 to 94.9 in the case of primary levels and from 12.7 to 58.79 for upper primary levels. The gap between boys and girls in GER at the primary and upper primary levels has declined significantly from 28.5 and 29.6 percentage points respectively in 1990-91 to 19 and 18 in 1999-2000.

The Net Enrolment Ratios (NER), obtained by subtracting the number of underage and overage children enrolled in grades I-V and VI-VIII, were significantly lower than GER in the case of both boys and girls. The NER for boys and girls was 78 per cent and 64 per cent respectively at the primary level in 1997-98. The overall NER at the primary level was 71 per cent, which suggests that at least 29 per cent of children in the 6-10 age group continued to remain out of school in 1997-98. Educationally backward states, and, within them, backward districts, have lower NER than the all-India average.

Educational Facilities: The availability of schooling facilities is measured by a set of indicators concerning access. Existing norms stipulate that a habitation (cluster of households) is entitled to have a primary school, if it has a population of 300 and more and has no school within a distance of one km. Upper primary schools are to be located at a distance of three km from habitations with a population of 500 and more. These norms are often relaxed in case of hilly and tribal areas, difficult terrains and border districts.

During the period 1950-51 to 1999-2000, the number of primary schools has increased by more than three times from 2,10,000 in 1950-51 to 6,42,000 in 1999-2000 whereas the number of upper primary schools increased by about 15 times from 13,600 in 1950-51 to 1,98,000 in 1999-2000. The ratio of upper primary school to primary schools came down from 1:15 in 1950-51 to 1:3.2 in 1999-2000.

Enrolment Trends: Enrolment at the primary level (grades I to V) increased from 19.16 million in 1950-51 to 113.61 million in 1999-2000. In comparison, the growth in enrolment at the upper primary level (grades VI to VIII) has been much more impressive, although it is still not adequate to attain the Constitutional goal of universal enrolment of children up to the age of 14. From 3.12 million in 1950-51, enrolment at the upper primary level increased to 42.06 million in 1999-2000, indicating a 13.5 times increase as against six times at the primary level.

The percentage share of girls in total enrolment, both at the primary and upper primary levels, has increased consistently between 1950-51 (28.1 per cent) and 1999-2000 (43.6 per cent). However, girls' share in total enrolment at the upper primary level (40.4 per cent) continues to be lower than their share at the primary level in 1999-2000. The total number of teachers increased from 6,24,000 in 1950-51 to 3.2 million in 1999-2000, an increase of more than five times.

The number of female teachers increased from 95,000 in 1950-51 to 11,52,000 in 1999-2000, an increase of more than 12 times. The percentage of female teachers to total teachers, which was 15.2 per cent at the primary level and 15.1 per cent at upper primary level in 1950-51 has increased to 35.6 and 36.1 per cent respectively in 1999-2000. However, the teacher-pupil ratio (TPR) has worsened over the years. During 1950-51, the TPR in primary schools was 1:24, and 1:20 in middle schools. In 1999-2000, this ratio has increased to 1:43 in primary schools and 1:38 in upper primary schools.

Despite an increase in the number of habitations and population, the coverage of both primary and upper primary schools, in line with the norms, has increased significantly. Of the one million rural habitations in the country, 5,28,000 had a primary school within the habitation itself in 1993-94. About 83.4 per cent habitations had a primary school/section within a one km distance.

Presently, about 1,00,000 habitations remain unserved as per prescribed norms. The alternative and innovative programme envisages opening of non-formal education (NFE) centres in habitations where opening of a full-fledged school is not economically feasible or academically viable. Over a period of time, infrastructure and other facilities in schools have also improved significantly although a large number of primary and upper primary schools continue to suffer from deficiencies, making it difficult for them to function smoothly and preventing them from providing optimal conditions for teaching and learning.

Sarva Shiksha Abhiyan: The Sarva Shiksha Abhiyan was launched towards the end of the Ninth Plan to achieve the goal of UEE through a time-bound integrated approach, in partnership with states. The programme, which aims to provide elementary education to all children in the 6-14 age groups by 2010, is an effort to improve the performance of the school system and provide community-owned quality elementary education in the mission mode. It also envisages bridging of gender and social disparities at the elementary level. The Sarva Shiksha Abhiyan has a special focus on the educational needs of girls, SCs and STs and other children in difficult circumstances.

Under the programme, habitation plans, prepared after micro-planning, household surveys, school mapping and diagnostic studies, form the basis for the District Elementary Education Plans (DEEP).

Funds released to states would be channelised to registered societies at the state level. The Sarva Shiksha Abhiyan is expected to accord the highest priority to community monitoring, transparency in programme planning and implementation of capacity building at all levels as also to the adoption of a mission approach by the mainstream Education Department functionaries. A National Mission for Sarva Shiksha Abhiyan was constituted in November 2000 with the Prime Minister as the Chairman and the Minister for Human Resource Development as Vice-Chairman.

The scheme is expected to absorb most of the existing programmes, including externally aided programmes, within its overall framework with the district as the unit of programme implementation. To make the approach totally holistic and convergent, efforts would be made to dovetail programme implementation at the district level with all other departments. This would include programmes for children in the 0-6 age group under the Department of Women and Child Development, sports-related interventions of the Ministry of Sports and Youth Affairs, establishment of public libraries under the Department of Culture and nutrition and health programmes of the Ministry of Health. Objectives of Sarva Shiksha Abhiyan:

- All children to be in schools, Education Guarantee Scheme centres, alternate schools, back-to-school camps by 2003;
- All children to complete five years of primary schooling by 2007;
- All children to complete eight years of schooling by 2010;
- Focus on elementary education of satisfactory quality with emphasis on education for life;
- Bridge all gender and social disparities at the primary stage by 2007 and at the upper primary level by 2010; and
- Universal retention by 2010.

Goals, Targets and Strategies for the Tenth Plan

Goals and Targets: In the elementary education sector, the Sarva Shiksha Abhiyan is in place with clear focus and medium-term goals as specified. The Tenth Plan targets in respect to elementary education are:

Universal Access

- All children in the 6-14 age group should have access to primary schools, upper primary schools or their alternatives within a walking distance of one km and three km respectively.

- All children in the 3-6 age group must have universal access to early childhood care and education centres.
- Need-based expansion of upper primary education facilities, particularly for the disadvantaged sections. There should be one upper primary school for every two primary schools.
- All schools should have buildings, toilets, drinking water, electricity, playgrounds, blackboards and other basic facilities. There must be provision of one classroom for every teacher at the elementary stage.

Universal Enrolment

- Enrolment of all children in schools or alternative arrangements by 2003.
- All children to complete five years of primary schooling by 2007.

Universal Retention

- Universal retention in the primary stage by 2007.
- Dropout rate to be reduced to less than 10 per cent for grades VI-VIII by 2007.

Universal Achievement

- Improve the quality of education in all respects (content and process) to ensure reasonable learning outcomes at the elementary level, especially in literacy, numerics and in life skills.

Equity

- Bridge all gender and social gaps in enrolment, retention and learning achievement in the primary stage by 2007 and reduce the gap to 5 per cent in the upper primary stage by 2007.
- Special interventions and strategies to include girls, SC/ST children, working children, children with special needs, urban deprived children, children from minority groups, children below the poverty line, migratory children and children in the hardest-to-reach groups.

Strategies for Universalization of Elementary Education

The strategies and interventions during the Tenth Plan will mainly be guided by three major considerations: (a) magnitude of the task; (b) present challenges; and (c) the existing administrative and policy framework and the one that will be in place during the Plan period.

Magnitude of the Task: The Working Group on Elementary and Adult Education for the Tenth Five-Year Plan has estimated that in order to achieve the goal of UEE by 2010, enrolment at the primary level needs to grow at an average annual growth rate of 1.12 per cent for boys and 4.16 per cent for girls during the Plan period. At the upper primary level, the growth rate must be 4.62 per cent for boys and 8.03 per cent for girls. The average growth rate for boys and girls taken together should be 2.51 per cent at the primary and 6.08 per cent at the upper primary levels. The year-wise estimated additional enrolment during the Plan period.

Present Challenges: Achieving the goal of UEE poses three main challenges: (i) access to basic education for the unreached segments and social groups; (ii) qualitative improvement in content and processes so as to raise learning achievements; and (iii) tackling high drop-out and low retention rates in primary and upper primary schools.

Administrative and Policy Framework: The administrative and policy framework needs to be guided by the following concerns.

- The national resolve to provide free and compulsory education of satisfactory quality to all children up to the age of 14 years, as stipulated in the National Policy on Education;
- The 93rd Constitutional amendment making the right to elementary education a fundamental right and enforcing it through necessary statutory measures; and
- The spirit of the 73rd and 74th Constitutional amendments setting the stage for greater decentralisation of power and a significantly enhanced role for local bodies, community organisations as well as voluntary agencies in the efforts towards UEE.

Given this backdrop, the Tenth Plan strategy for achieving UEE must have the following salient features:

Holistic and Convergent Approach : As the existing policies and programmes are either for specific target groups/ regions, there is need for an all-comprehensive programme covering the entire country. The Sarva Shiksha Abhiyan is such a programme and will be the main vehicle for achieving the goals of UEE.

Community Participation in UEE Programmes : The involvement of the community will be made more systematic by involving the panchayati raj institutions (PRIs) and urban local bodies. Further down the hierarchy, VECs, Mother-Teacher Associations (MTA) and Parent-Teacher Associations (PTA) would have a formal role in the management of schools in the village.

Target-Groups Oriented Strategy: The Tenth Plan will lay emphasis on identifying the problem areas and formulating a separate strategy for each area, under the overall umbrella of the Ṣarva Shiksha Abhiyan. There will be special focus on children who have never enrolled or those who have dropped out without completing eight years of elementary schooling. Specific strategies would be devised for the difficult-to-reach groups in order to ascertain the reasons for their staying away from school system and to take steps to provide them quality elementary education.

Programmes for Achieving UEE: The following schemes would be the instruments by which these strategies would be translated into action during the Tenth Plan.

Secondary Education: While, in terms of absolute numbers, state financing of secondary education continued to grow (though it is still inadequate), financing of secondary and higher education has shown a declining trend in terms of percentage spending on education from the Sixth Plan onwards. The share of elementary education in total spending has been increasing, reflecting the priority to implement free and compulsory elementary education. Participation of the private sector (including non-governmental organisations or NGOs) in the management of secondary schools with official recognition and, in many cases, with financial assistance, has also increased.

Private organisations currently manage around 51 per cent of secondary schools and 58 per of higher secondary schools.

In order to meet the educational needs of those who have not been able to enrol themselves in the formal system, opportunities have been provided through the National and State Open Schools, utilising contact centres and multimedia packages. Distance education in the school sector also got a fillip with the National Open School was started in 1989, identifying new vocational areas and providing on-demand examination.

Improvements in the content, process and quality of education, particularly environment education, science, mathematics and computer literacy have been emphasised with central financial support available for schemes related to this. New initiatives taken after the National Policy on Education was revised in 1992 include the revision of the curriculum, setting up of resource centres for value education and a National Centre for Computer-aided Education etc. Several measures taken to enrich the school curriculum are being continued with added thrust.

However, the scheme of vocationalization of education has not appealed to the stakeholders because lack of industry-institute linkages, manpower demand surveys and various academic constraints. At present, only 10 per cent of the students are opting for the vocational stream, against a target of 25 per cent by 2000.

Educational development of children with special needs received an impetus with the enactment of the Persons with Disabilities (Equal Opportunities, Protection of Rights and Full Participation) Act, 1995.

The Act entrusts the appropriate governments and the local authorities to provide children with disabilities access to education, employment, preferential allotment of land for certain purposes, non-discrimination in transport, financial incentives to Universities to enable them to undertake research etc. Programmes for attitudinal changes, capacity building among teachers and training institutions to educate children with special needs have been taken up. Along with providing opportunities for equal access and ensuring a minimum level of learning achievement for all, it is equally important to nurture talented children especially those from the rural areas and those belonging to lower income group.

There are several programmes for the development of talent. Residential Jawahar Navodaya Vidyalayas from Class VI to XII are established in the Seventh Plan as model schools and to provide quality education to talented children from rural areas selected on the basis of a common admission test. Each district is supposed to have one such school. Currently, there are 462 Jawahar Navodaya Vidyalayas with about 1,25,000 students on their rolls. The National Council of Educational Research & Training (NCERT), New Delhi, conducts a National Talent Search Examination to identify talent. International Chemistry, Mathematics and Physics Olympiads are held every year to identify talent in these subjects. India has been participating regularly in these Olympiads.

Talented students from rural areas are provided scholarships at the secondary stage in order to develop their potential by providing them access to good schools. A total of 38,000 scholarships have been awarded to students. Internal compulsions and international commitments are forcing the secondary education system to gear up to meet the ever-increasing demand for education. Initiatives such as the externally-aided District Primary Education Programme (DPEP), the Sarva Shiksha Abhiyan, increasing number of schools in the private sector and the drive for elimination of the gender gap in line with the Dakar Declaration on Education for All in 2000. Concerted efforts, backed by national consensus, are called for to meet these daunting challenges.

The major thrust in the Tenth Plan, thus, is to meet the increased demand for secondary education. The Government has to play a greater role to the encourage opening of new secondary schools, expansion of capacity of the existing schools including double shifts, upgrading of upper primary schools in backward, unserved and underserved areas, as also expansion and diversification of open schooling and distance education system. One of the many options being considered during the Tenth Plan is for the Kendriya Vidyalaya Sangathan to establish schools in partnership with voluntary agencies. It is proposed to set up 150 Kendriya Vidyalayas (fully funded by the Government) in addition to the present network of 854 schools. Another option is to provide a one-time grant/ seed money to societies, trusts and not for profit organisations like the R.K. Mission, the Jesuits, the DAV Trust, which already run reputed schools to encourage them to set up more schools. It is proposed to establish more Navodaya Vidyalayas to cover the districts which do not have one right now and also to strengthen these existing schools by providing them facilities for cultural activities, computers and sports facilities. It is also proposed to help the Central Tibetan School

Vocational Education: The Centre provides 75 per cent of the expenditure on vocational school staff while the state governments fund the remaining 25 per cent. The states have to completely finance the expenditure on conducting examinations and providing vocational guidance. The Pandit Sundarlal Sharma Central Institute of Vocational Education (PSSCIVE), Bhopal, under the NCERT, provides research and development support and training to key stakeholders from states/Union Territories. The Institute draws up the curriculum in the major areas of agriculture, business and commerce, engineering and technology, health and para-medical services, home science etc. for courses of one to two years' duration for adoption by the SCERTs.

Issues of Concern in Vocational Education: The vocationalization of education at the secondary stage of schooling has achieved only partial success. The students prefer general courses – like science, arts or commerce at the +2 level and later in tertiary sector of education. They constitute the bulk of the 60 million educated unemployed youth in the country. On the other hand, the country requires technical and skilled manpower particularly in view of the liberalisation of the economy in recent years.

There are immense opportunities for trained manpower in a developing economy like India's, especially in the agriculture, manufacturing and social services sector. A properly planned and effectively implemented vocational education system will enable the unemployed youth to take up some useful employment. The scheme was evaluated by Operation Research Group (ORG) in 1996 and also by the NCERT in 1998. Some of the important findings of the ORG evaluation are:

(a) States are according low priority to vocational education;

(b) The Directorate of School Education, by and large, are found to be working in isolation with little interaction with other relevant departments;

(c) State governments are reluctant to appoint full-time teachers because they are worried about taking on a long-term committed liability, in case the scheme is discontinued.

Some of the important recommendations of the NCERT Evaluation of 1998 are:

(a) The vocational courses should be provided in general schools in active partnership with industry and in close collaboration with the block level vocational institutions (BLVI) that may be established in rural areas.

(b) The vocational stream should be treated like the arts, science and commerce streams and students passing out from this stream at the +2 stage should have direct access to the tertiary stage in a related discipline.

(c) The National Curriculum Framework of the NCERT should be restructured to give due emphasis to work experience, pre-vocational and generic vocational competencies at various levels of school education.

(d) Full time teachers must be appointed on a regular and permanent basis as in the case of the academic stream.

(e) All vocational courses at the +2 level must be covered under the Apprenticeship Act, 1961.

(f) The large infrastructure in polytechnics and the +2 vocational wings in the higher secondary schools, besides those of various departments and NGOs should be reviewed for optimal utilisation of facilities in the existing vocational education programme.

Keeping in view the growing problem of unemployment, the Planning Commission constituted a separate Working Group on Vocational Education for the Tenth Plan in 2000. In line with the recommendations of the working group, the centrally sponsored scheme is proposed to be recast in the Tenth Plan with the following features.

- The vocational courses in schools should be competency-based and in modular form with a credit transfer system and provisions for multi-point entry/exit.
* There is a need to establish linkage between vocational courses at the +2 level and courses at the university level. The present admission criteria for entry into vocational courses at the graduation level also needs to be changed.
* The existing scheme should be strengthened by involving industries through memorandums of understanding, in designing of the course, development of the curriculum, training of faculty/students and certification of the courses.
- In order to sustain the scheme, schools may consider charging fees and the courses may be designed on a self-financing basis.
- The apprenticeship training facility needs to be utilised fully and made compulsory. To achieve this, the placement of those who have completed vocational studies for apprenticeship and training should be decided by the Board of Apprenticeship Training immediately after the results of the +2 examinations are declared.
- Before vocational courses are started in schools, local business and industry should be closely involved in studying the need and for conducting district vocational surveys.
- Facilities for running vocational courses should become mandatory for the Kendriya Vidyalaya and Navodaya Vidayalaya school systems.
- Persons with disabilities should be given special treatment while designing vocational courses and their needs and integration into courses should receive appropriate attention.
- Financial assistance may be provided under the scheme for creating testing and certification systems in states

in cooperation with user bodies and professional associations.

- The All India Council for Technical Education's (AICTE) vocational education board needs to be reactivated for providing technical support to the school system and for establishing linkages with other technical institutions.

The Steering Committee on Secondary, Higher and Technical Education set up for the Tenth Five-Year Plan recommended that the vocational education at the secondary school level, polytechnic education and Industrial Training Institutes (ITIs) should come under one department of the state government for better networking, linkages, focused targeting and optimal utilisation of resources. An outlay of Rs. 350 crore has been allocated for the Centrally-sponsored scheme of Vocationalisation of Secondary Education in the Tenth Plan.

Industrial Training Institutes: At the national level, the Directorate General of Employment & Training (DGE&T) in the Ministry of Labour is the nodal department for formulating policies, laying down standards, conducting trade testing and certification, etc. in the field of vocational training. Vocational training being a concurrent subject, the responsibility is shared by the central and state governments. At the state level, the concerned State Government departments are responsible for vocational training programmes. Starting from 54 ITIs in 1953, the number of functioning ITIs institutes has gone up to 4,274 (1,654 in the government sector and the remaining 2,620 in the private sector). The seating capacity has progressively risen from 10,000 to 6,28,000 at present. The Apprentice Act, 1961, was amended from time to time to regulate the programme of training of apprentices. The Central Apprenticeship Council advises the Government on policies, norms and standards in respect of the apprenticeship training scheme.

The Apprentices Act serves a dual purpose – firstly, to regulate the programme of training apprentices in industry to ensure that it conforms to the syllabi, period of training etc. prescribed by the Central Apprenticeship Council; and secondly, to utilise fully the facilities available in industry for workers. As on 31 March 2001, over 17,800 public/ private sector establishments were covered under the Apprenticeship Act and the number of seats allocated were 2.20 lakh, out of which about 1.58 lakh seats were utilised. The Craftsmen Training programme relates to theoretical training on any area of craftsmanship with little exposure to practical training. This training is being imparted in 43 engineering and 24 non-engineering trades in order to reduce unemployment among the educated youth by equipping them with suitable skills for industrial employment.

Skill development and employment services, as in the past, continue to be provided to vulnerable sections with special needs like women, SCs/STs, and persons with disabilities, including disabled ex-servicemen. To provide training facilities to women so as to enhance their participation in industry as skilled workers and/or to help them in acquiring skills for taking up self-employment, income-generating activities, training programmes, exclusively for women, are being provided through the National Vocational Training Institute (NVTI) and 10 Regional Vocational Training Institutes for Women (RVTI). The present training capacity of these Institutes is 2,068 seats. In the state sector, there is a network of 231 ITIs. exclusively for women, besides 534 Special Wings for Women in general ITIs with 46,750 seats, offering craftsmen training in various engineering and non-engineering trades.

In spite of the available infrastructure and facilities, skill development and training in the country is highly inadequate. Every year 5.5 million students pass out of Class X, of which 3.3 million go to Class XI, leaving 2.2 million out of the education stream. There are, besides, those who drop out after Class VIII, who number 19 million. These are the people who look for vocational training and self-employment avenues. Therefore, attention has to be paid to this 21 million-target group. As against this, available formal training capacity of the country is only 2.3 million students, which leaves a gap of 18.7 million. The ITI system needs to be revamped to fill up this gap. Further, there is an urgent need to look into training of trainers as only 40 per cent of the 55,000 instructors have undergone a full instructor-training course.

Besides these initiatives of the Ministries of Labour and Human Resource Development, there are several other programmes and activities under the purview of different Departments/ Ministries. These include Ministry of Rural Development, Department of Women and Child Development, Ministry of Industries, Khadi & Village Industry Commission, etc. All these programmes largely cater to the needs of the informal sector in a limited manner and need to be expanded to meet the emerging needs.

Higher Education: The importance of education, especially higher education, has been constantly growing and knowledge-based industries are now occupying the centre stage in development. Though the modern higher education system in India is almost 135 years old, its growth has been much faster after India became independent.

Over the past 50 years, there has been a significant growth in the number of new universities and institutions of higher learning in specialised areas. There are now 273 universities/ deemed to be universities (including 18 medical universities and 40 agricultural universities) and 12,300 colleges (of which 4,683 are in the rural areas. The Ninth Plan reiterates the objectives/ policy directions of the National Policy for Education, 1986, and its Programme of Action, 1992. Broadly, the Ninth Plan emphasises on the following strategies to improve the higher education system: a) Consolidation and expansion of institutions.

Higher and Technical Education: During the Ninth Plan, an outlay of Rs. 2,520.06 crore was allocated for the university and higher education sub-sector against which an expenditure of Rs. 2,270.92 crore was incurred.

The Ninth Plan period saw the emergence of separate universities for science and technology and health sciences, autonomous colleges with the freedom to design curricula, evolve new methods of teaching and research, frame admission rules and conduct examinations as well as Centres of Excellence and the National Assessment & Accreditation Council (NAAC). There are also institutions of higher learning recognised as deemed to be universities with their own sources of funding in addition to Government grants. The major emphasis in strategies relating to higher education during this period has been on an integrated approach, with an emphasis on excellence and equity, relevance, promotion of value education, and strengthening the management systems. Autonomous centres have been set up within the university system to provide common facilities, services and programmes to universities and for the promotion of quality.

It is increasingly recognised that in the context of major economic and technological changes, the system of higher education should equip students with adequate skills to enable their full participation in the emerging social, economic and cultural environment. Universities are thus witnessing a sea change in their outlook and perspective. Also, information and communication technologies are leading to fundamental changes in the structure, management and mode of delivery of the entire educational system. Many universities have already recognised the strategic significance of open and distance learning and offer correspondence courses. At the beginning of the decade, there were 64 universities offering courses through correspondence. The developments in the field of information communication technology and expansion of infrastructure for communication all over the country have created an unprecedented opportunity to serve the needs of continuing education and also to meet the demands for equal opportunity for higher education.

The Indira Gandhi National Open University (IGNOU) established in 1985, has 1.2 million students on its rolls and offers 72 programmes. The University has created a countrywide network of student support structures, with 46 regional centres and 765 study centres. It has also created a media network and teleconferencing system to electronically link all distance-teaching institutions in the country. Many departments of correspondence courses in various universities were converted into independent open universities during the Ninth Plan period. There are, at present, nine open universities in the country, all started by different states during the nineties. The issues of access and equity are central to the university/higher education system. Only about six per cent of the estimated population in the 18-23 age group is currently in the university system. Measures to increase enrolment, including that of the disadvantaged sections, will thus be given attention during the Plan.

7

The Non-formal Education System

Education was the privilege of a few, belonging to the—upper classes, in early days. Only Brahmans had the right to-be 'Gurus' and no 'Sudra' or 'Vaishya' was allowed to learn the alphabets. The 'Kshatriyas' who were the rulers of those days had to be in the 'Gurukula' for their education under reputed 'Gurus'. 'Gurudakshina' was a must in those days.

The story of Ekalavya who had to cut off his finger to please his Guru, in the guise of 'Gurudakshina' to indirectly safeguard 'Arjuna' who learnt lessons at the Guru's feet while Ekalavya, belonging to a lower caste learnt it hiding in the bushes. The Gurukula system of education of the past is nothing but a system of non-formal education prevalent in those days.

There was no fixed curricula, duration, etc. but only the Guru-was to declare that his disciple has mastered everything needed for life. At the Gurukula one had to live with the Guru's family and do all sorts of jobs (good and bad) for them for the sake of learning the alphabets and many other arts. Vedas and Upanishadas were also taught at this level. Lord Krishna was no exception to the Gurukula system. He learnt with 'Kuchela' just because he was a Brahman (Poverty was not a problem, as Kuchela belonged to the uppermost caste). The Guru used to identify the hereditary interests and innate abilities and then offer the disciple whatever suits him.

The education was life oriented as well as client centred. The system was not loaded with teaching learning materials, as we find now-a-days. Examinations were not thrust upon them. The Guru was the only examiner certify the mastery of a disciple. The aim of all education was to promote better life.

SYSTEM OF MONITORING

In the absence of the Guru, 'monitors' were authorised to control the class. He is usually next in rank to the 'Guru', his confidant and deputy. He is also called 'Chattampi' (or a villain) who has physical stamina and will power to control the batchmates. This monitor system is even now prevalent in the formal system in some form. Maintaining discipline in the class in the absence of the teacher, listing late comers and mischief makers, collecting and distributing materials, serving the teacher as a messenger or representative are among the current duties of monitors. In the early schools (Pre-primary, Nursery, Creche, Balawadi or Kudippallikkoodam as we call them) alphabets are to be drilled very often. This duty also is given to the monitor or the leader. Class and school leaders are 'elected' now-a-days and not nominated. This is due to the democratisation of such procedures and systems. Thus monitorial system came to the formal schools from the early non-formal system.

Formal Vs. Informal

Even upto the middle of the twentieth century we had only two types of education-formal and informal. All that is institutionalised, having so many rigidities by way of age of admission, syllabus, time table, text-books, duration, examination, teaching techniques, teachers qualification, school plant, etc. come under the heading 'formal' and all other types of education were designated as 'informal'. Actually informal is that which is not formal, that which is accidental, that which is not purposive, that which is flexible etc. This could be the early lessons that a child gets at home to the tricks and trends that an old man acquires towards the fag end of his life. It could be short term courses of an academic or vocational nature. It could be a course in a foreign or Indian language, on human relations, tourism, banking etc. or for updating ones' own knowledge and abilities in a specialised field or in an allied one. Thus the facets are many in informal education.

EMERGENCE OF NON-FORMAL EDUCATION

However, in the sixties of the 20th century people witnessed the emergence of a new concept 'non-formal education' to represent any educational activity carried on outside the four walls of the institution in an organised way and with specific purposes. Whatever is not included in this category and previously belonged to the informal sector remain in the same name. So confusion has arisen in the minds of people as to what is non-formal education and what remain still as informal education. Watertight compartmentalisation, however, is not possible even between formal and non-formal system of education, not to speak of the distinction between informal and non-formal education.

Flexibility is the main attribute of non-formal education. People of different age levels, varying abilities, having different occupations or without any occupation, from different geographical having different areas, values of life and aspirations assemble at a place for short periods to achieve some common aims and objectives. This gathering is non-formal in many ways. No one will insist on regular attendance. The learner or participant is well motivated and experienced and hence problems are very few unlike in the cases of children in formal schools.

Non-formal Education is not only Adult Literacy Work

The major aim of all non-formal education is to improve the living conditions of people, especially of the downtrodden and depressed sections of the society. Hence a major part of non-formal education in India is geared to the provision of literacy and numeracy. In India even after 38 years of independence, the number of illiterates is on the increase. As against 28.5 crores of illiterates in 1951, in 1981 their number has risen to 44 crores, though there is marginal increase in terms of percentage of literacy. That too is not much consoling. The percentage of literacy rose of 16 in 1951 to 36, in 1981, keeping the average annual increase to the tune of 0.66%. It has been estimated that by the year 2000 A.D. India will have more than 50% of the world illiterate population in the age group 15-35. It is also estimated that India will be the only country having illiterates, in the 21st century. The number of illiterates in the age group 15-35 was estimated at 11.0 crores in 1981. The statistics available from the Government of India, Ministry of Human Resources Development shows that only 2.3 crores could be approached during the period 1981-86; leaving 8.7 crores to be tackled in the coming. 4 years if the declared target of ensuring 100% literacy at the 15-35 age level before 31st March 1990 could be achieved. This gigantic task has attracted the attention of almost all concerned and hence the main thrust of non-formal education is on eradication of illiteracy and consequent conscientisation.

The NAEP and After

On October 2, 1978, a massive time bound ambitious programme for the eradication of illiteracy was put-forth by the Government of India. It aimed at helping 5 crores of illiterates in a time span of 5 years. The programme called NAEP (National Adult Education Programme) had literacy, functionality and conscientisation as its major objectives. The attempts could not bear fruit due to relapses on many sides. An interim evaluation committee headed by Dr. Kothari suggested changes in the modalities of NAEP. Consequent on this and the changes in regime at the centre, the programme had an untimely death. However, there came an alternative in item 16 of the new 20 pt. economic policy of the Government of India. According to a three pronged approach was suggested. (i) ensuring 100% enrolment in schools at the specified age 5+. (2) prevention of dropping out from the primary classes through appropriate measures (3) provision of non-formal education for the adults and aged. If there three are simultaneously attempted and ensured the literacy rate can be considerably increased. Adult Education Centres have been started with this aims in view. But the centre based approach has its own advantages but limitations outweigh them. Hence the current thinking is on a mass programme for functional literacy (MPFL). This is again a non-formal approach.

College and University students and teachers have been requested to identify one to five adult learners from their' locality or their neighbourhood and help them becomes literacy in about 6 months. The reduction in duration and multiplication in the number of volunteers are expected to solve the problems earlier than envisaged. Here identification of learners, implementation of the programme, their certification after the duration etc. are all non-formal. Hence at the moment *i.e.* from

May 1, 1986, the MPFL is the most important non-formal education programme in India.

NFE for 6-14

Dropping out of the formal schools, especially at the primary level is a strange phenomenon in all Indian states. These dropped outs, in due course, relapse into illiteracy even if they were semi-literates at the time of their discontinuing studies. They add to the number of illiterates in India. Reasons are many for this dropping out. Socio-economic, cultural and health reasons are generally attributed. Suggestions have put forth for preventing this wastage. An alternative suggested is the provision of non-formal education for dropped outs *i.e.* of the age range 6 to 14. This is mostly done in the schools, after school hours, with the cooperation of school teachers and voluntary workers. The main intention of this kind of non-formal education is to bring them back to the main stream at appropriate levels. At least relapsing into illiteracy can be prevented through this approach.

Children are allowed to pursue their studies at their pace and convenience and then enter the formal system at relevant stages. They are permitted to sit for class IV, VII and X examinations as private candidates along with the normal stream of regular students. This preparation whether done in schools or in non-formal education institutions or in small groups of tuition classes, can be formed 'non-formal'. A system of parallel colleges have come to stay in Kerala to cater to the needs of all SSLC holders who could not get admission in the regular colleges. Further private registration is also allowed by most universities through their correspondence courses or direct. This kind of study also come under the title 'non-formal education', `out of school education', 'own time education', 'continuing education', 'further education' etc.

THE OPEN UNIVERSITY SYSTEM

At the top of the educational pyramid is the University system. Indira Gandhi National Open University has been established at the Centre. In many states open universities have been established or are being established. This multimedia approach education system is partly non-formal and partly formal. But non-formality is more and hence is listed under non-formal sector, at its climax. Irrespective of age and even without any previous entry qualification, one can register for Universities Degrees and work at his/her pace and obtain Degrees as and when they feel confident to take the test. This study can go along with one's occupation search for a job 'learn while you earn' can be practised here. In the formal system the slogan is just the reverse *i.e.* earn while you learn and children are persuaded to take up some socially useful productive activity (SUPVV).

Extension as Third Function

During 1981-86, non-formal education gained more acceptance and respectability in India consequent on the UGC's accepting extension as a third and equally important responsibility of the institutions of higher learning, along with teaching and research. By now 98 universities in India have established Departments/Centres for Adult, Continuing Education and Extension. There are really non-formal education centres catering to the diverse needs of the community starting with literacy, going upto para professional and specialisation courses. Population education, Continuing education, Planning Forum, 'Legal literacy, Environmental education, Science for the Masses, National Integration and Peace Education are certain: allied programmes coming under the big umbrella of adult and continuing education. These are nothing but non-formal education, especially for the masses. In the teacher preparation programmes, especially at B. Ed. level, working with the Community has become one of the practical activities. Thus non-formal education has come to stay even in the formal sector.

Non Academic Non-formal Sector

This does not mean that non-formal education is only for; academic subjects and as a substitute for formal education. It can be preparation for life through apprenticeship or practice in any vocation of one's choice. It can be training in occupation through one can improve his/her economic status. Extension lectures on various topics of contemporary relevance on science, literature, democracy etc. also can form part of non-formal education. The rural library service extended to the masses, helping them to ensurer 'life long education' are also non-formal institutions. The 'community centres' envisaged in the 'new education policy' also are likely to cater to the Non-formal education needs of people.

NEW POLICY OF EDUCATION

The significance of non-formal sector in Indian education—has been well established in the policy document 'challenges to Education'. As parallel and complementary to the formal system, non-formal education programmes are essential and without pursuing education through such measures one cannot boast of being 'educated'. The traditions and culture of India can only be transcended to the coming generations through non-formal approaches. The freedom struggle in its correct perspective can be communicated to the emerging citizens through a multimedia non-formal approach. Directorates of Non-formal education have been established in many states.

Role of Voluntary Agencies

Voluntary agencies have a great role to play in non-formal education as they are working with the community knowing fully the needs and aspirations of the people. Only with such agencies can flexibility flourish. Proper coordination has to be ensured between formal educational institutions and voluntary agencies engaged in non-formal education of some kind or other. Non-formal education has to be linked with developmental activities and programmes. Non-formal education is not an alternative to formal education. It is not a panacea for all the evils in the formal sector. Even the proponents of non-formal education will agree to have these cautions. In order to ensure all round development of the individual, non-formal education is also needed along with the time boring formal system of education. "Education is not the amount of information that is put into the brain and runs riot there, undigested all your life. We must have life-building, man-making, characters-making, assimilation of ideas". These words of Swami Vivekananda are emphasising nothing but a mixture of formal and non-formal education. In India what we trying to do through the new education policy is in consonance with this legitimate task. Let us strive to achieve this goal.

Jana Shikshan Nikayas

In the New Education Policy adopted by the Indian Parliament in 1986 there are certain novel features which could bring in prosperity to the country. One such is the starting of Jana Shikshan Nilayas (JSNs) all over the country. It has been suggested that for every 5000 population, one JSN may be established to cater to the allround development of each and every citizen in that area, irrespective of age, sex, caste, occupation etc. It is hoped that JSN's will be started on an experimental basis during 1987-88 itself.

Location: It is hoped that the JSN's could be established in local Primary schools thereby ensuring the linkage between formal and non-formal education. The educational institutions are lying unused for nearly two-thirds of the day. Through proper planning and execution these could be utilised for about double the time it is used now. In addition to the buildings, playground, auditorium etc. facilities like library, laboratory, audiovisual aids etc. could also be used for the local community. If schools are not available, other public buildings like library, sports club, youth club, Mahilamandals etc. may be thought of. Even sheds or outhouses of temples, churches and mosques are convenient places for imparting non-formal education to the masses. If no such facility is available, a semi-permanent or temporary building or shed may be thought of. Anyway an ideal location is inevitable for ensuring participation of local people.

Content and Organisation

The JSN may work from early morning-say 6 a.m. onwards upto 10 p.m. catering to diverse groups. Early morning can be devoted to youngsters while adults and all interested can make use of the evenings. Formal and non-formal programmes can be launched in the same building. Like the Adult Education Institutes of the west, the JSN's can offer any number of courses/programmes simultaneously to attract all sections of the community. There should be library facilities, gymnastics,, sports and games cultural programmes, etc. attached to the JSN. In addition to recreational facilities, refreshments should also be made available to the needy. Thus each JSN will be a self contained institution of the locality. It can be the nucleus of the community. Providing a community hall, marketing facility etc. are also worth thinking of. Counselling facilities,, coaching centres, reference section, Information centre etc. should be built into the JSN's. These may provide literacy, post-literacy as well as continuing education of all types according to the needs and interests of the local people. 'Lifelong education' in its real sense will be available in these centres.

Selection and Training of Personnel

Properly trained social workers should man the JSN's. Three to five persons will be required to run each JSN. Depending on the type and extent of programmes guest artists may be engaged. At least one person should be a graduate trained in social work, human relations and having a commitment to the community and the nation at large. Others may be professionals or trained community workers capable of discharging diverse responsibilities like an ayah or matron to a library worker/counsellor/teacher. If possible JSN workers should be Jack of all trades. Adequate orientation or training will have to be given to all selected workers. Those with field work experience may be preferred. Regular salary for leading at least an average life should be given to the JSN workers. Adequate incentives also should be provided in the scheme so that effectiveness could be ensured.

Facilities Needed

In addition to providing newspapers, periodicals, reference materials like gazettes, bullettins etc., a radio/transistor, TV, audio-cassettes, video-cassette players etc. should also be supplied to each JSN. Necessary finances will have to be found out by the Government or community participation even in this regard may be thought of. Some of the existing Adult Education Centres/Post Literacy Centres may be converted into JSN's with necessary infrastructure and inputs of all kinds. The JSN's will the course of time develop into community Education Centres of rather Rural Extension Centres which might parallel the folk schools or Community Colleges in Denmark. Before the take off stage, necessary planning and preparation are needed for JSN's. Otherwise this will also be another failure.

BIBLIOGRAPHY

Allen, G. : *New Education: American Opinion*, May issue, 1971.

Elliott, J. : *Action Research for Educational Change*, Milton Keynes, Open University, 1991.

Furth, H.G. : *The World of Grown-ups: Children's Conceptions of Society*, New York, Elsevier North Holland, 1980.

Galbraith, M.W.: *Education Through Community Organizations*, San Francisco, Jossey-Bass, 1990.

Giroux, H. : *Critical Theory and Educational Practice*, Geelong, Australia, Deakin University, 1983.

Gordon, A. : *Cultivating Leadership in Schools*, New York, College Press, 2001.

Grace, G. : *School Leadership: Beyond Educational Management*, London, Falmer, 1995.

Hilbert, D.R. : *Color and Color Perception: A Study in Anthropocentric Realism*, Stanford, CSLI, 1987.

Holland, D. and Millican, J. : *Adult Literacy, A Handbook for Development Workers*, Oxford, Oxfam, 1995.

Kemmis, S. : *Becoming Critical: Education, Knowledge and Action Research*, London, Falmer, 1986.

Kirkwood, C. : *Living Adult Education, Freire in Scotland*, Milton Keynes, Open University Press, 1989.

Kruger, A. : *Community Education in the Western World*, London, Routledge, 1990.

Lakomski, G. : *Knowing Educational Administration*, Oxford, Pergamon, 1991.

Lee, Jeong-kyu : *Historic Factors Influencing Korean Higher Education*, Seoul, Jimoondang, 2000.

Michael, J. : *Education Fever: Society, Politics, and the Pursuit of Schooling in South Korea*, Honolulu, University of Hawai Press, 2002.

Miller, N. : *Working with Experience: Animating Learning*, London, Routledge, 1997.

Nias, J. : *Seeing anew: Teachers' Theories of Action*, Australia, Deakin University, 1987.

Nuna, S.C. : *Education and Development*, NIEPA, New Delhi, 1987.

Premi, M.K. : *Educational Planning in India*, New Delhi, Sterling, 1972.

Reimer, E. : *School is Dead, An Essay on Alternatives in Education*, Harmondsworth, Penguin, 1971.

Roderick, R. : *Habermas and the Foundations of Critical Theory*, Basingstoke, Macmillan, 1986.

Rogers, A. : *Adults Learning for Development*, London, Cassell, 1992.

Santosh, A. : *Three Language Formula: An Educational Problem*, New Delhi, Sian, 1991.

Scott, C. : *Social Education*, Boston, Ginn and Co., 1908.

Shourie, Arun : *Indian Controversies: Essays on Religion in Politics*, New Delhi, Manohar, 1993.

Simkins, T. : *Non-formal Education and Development*, Manchester, Manchester University, 1977.

Smith, M. : *Using Informal Education*, Milton Keynes, Open University Press, 1990.

Stephens, S. : *Children and the Politics of Culture*, Princeton, Princeton University Press, 1995.

Stewart, J. : *Management for the Public Domain*, New York, St, Martin's Press, 1994.

Thomas, A. : *Educating Children at Home*, London, Cassell, 1998.

Wa tkins, K.E. : *Informal and Incidental Learning in the Workplace*, London, Routledge, 1991.

William, C. : *A Tradition of Teachers: Sankara and the Jagadgurus Today*, Delhi, Motilal Banarsidass, 1983.

William, C. : *Working Toward Sustainable Development: The Narmada Dam Project*, Armonk, New York, 1994.

Zvelebil, Kamil V. : *Companion Studies to the History of Tamil Literature*, Leiden, Brill, 1992.

INDEX

A

B

C

D

E

□□□